Sieben Moki-Pueblos von Arizona.

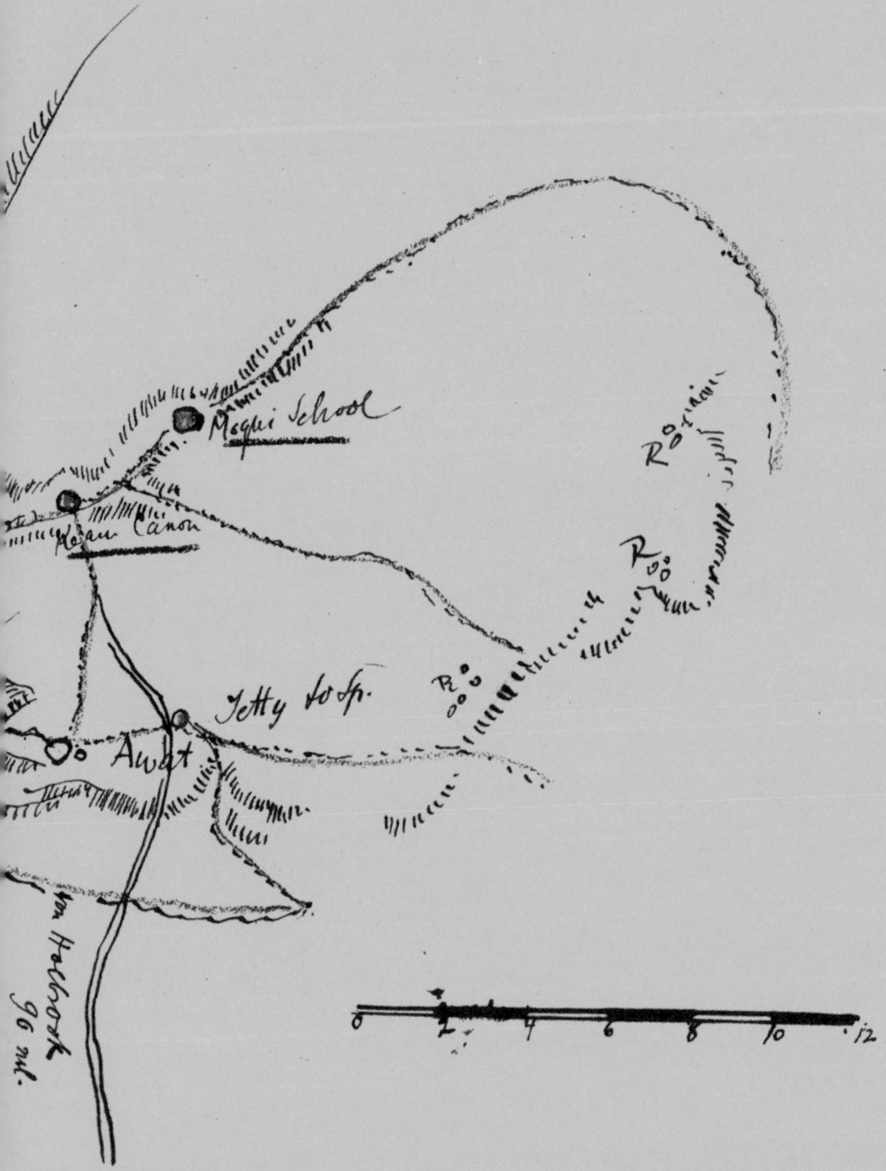

Moqui School

Keam Cañon

Awat

von Holbrook 96 ml.

0 2 4 6 8 10 12

The Snake and the Lightning
Aby Warburg's American Journey

Uwe Fleckner

The Snake and the Lightning
Aby Warburg's American Journey
Uwe Fleckner

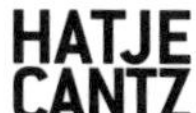

Contents

About this Book

When Aby Warburg set off for the United States of America in September 1895, he had no idea that his pursuit of the symbolic fundamentals of art would become one of the most fascinating events in the scientific history of his field of study. The most famous elements were not so much his stay in the Pueblo territory of the American Southwest or his early travel reports written after he returned, but the lecture on the so-called Snake Dance that he gave in 1923, a quarter century after his journey, as a recovering patient at the Bellevue Sanatorium in Kreuzlingen. And, decades later, the lecture would help to justify, and internationally enhance, Warburg's reputation as a pioneer of cultural history and indeed cultural psychology.

While editing the various versions of both the early and the later texts of the lecture, which were published together with Warburg's photographs and the reconstruction of his locally acquired collection of Indigenous artworks in a volume of his *Collected Writings* (2018), it was impossible to ignore how many misunderstandings, errors, and legends continue to influence our ideas about this journey to America. This was confirmed by the international conferences devoted to Warburg at the Universidad Nacional Autónoma de México in 2017 and the Biblioteca Nacional Mariano Moreno in Buenos Aires in 2019, and finally by the preparation of an exhibition of his as far as possible complete collections of Pueblo art and other artifacts at Hamburg's Museum am Rothenbaum in 2022. With the publication of *Bilder aus dem Gebiet der Pueblo-Indianer in Nord-Amerika* (Images from the Region of the Pueblo Indians of North America) the art historian's texts are now available in a reliable, fully illustrated and annotated edition; and the often difficult detective work of identifying the motifs in the photographs he took in the United States has allowed the necessary progress to be made in analyzing the material. Yet much has remained unclear or even unknown to the publisher of Warburg's texts and photographs, and to art historians in general—from the most superficial details of the journey and his both touristic and scientific endeavors to the numerous art-, cultural- and religious-historical references that can serve to provide a comprehensive picture of Warburg's research.

The purpose of this book is to fill such gaps in the available knowledge. Although not all the possible questions could be asked of the available archive material, it may be assumed that some essential documents have been successfully analyzed and hence that future research has been substantially facilitated. Attention is paid to selected photographs by Warburg and ethnological drawings made by him and others during the journey, as well as maps, notes, and many other sources. However, this documentation has not been treated only as testimony to his activities in the lands of the Cochiti and the Zuni, the Tewa and the Hopi, but above all as evidence of a shift in Warburg's scientific thinking that would eventually lead to the pioneering cultural-comparative methodology for which he is today—quite rightly—renowned throughout the world.

I have opted here for a form that is not self-evident in writings on art history: the picture book or album, although—of course—with accompanying commentary. There is no need to emphasize that this genre is best suited to the work of Warburg, the originator of the *Bilderatlas Mnemosyne (Mnemosyne Atlas)* and numerous other plate works. The publication thus stands or falls by its illustrations, or rather—at least let us hope—the interplay between image and text. It may also be hoped that this album, in accordance with the original intention of such pictorial collections, will encourage a (virtual) voyage of discovery. It crosses an extensive continent of research in which we will also meet some of the Indigenous and other people Warburg spoke to, including a trader and a missionary, a Hopi chief, a flamboyant fraudster from Cochiti, and a Zuni who was accused of being a sorcerer; and it crosses a by no means arid terrain full of settlements and villages, of ritual objects and artworks, and of symbolic representations of lightning and snakes that Warburg studied and collected. We can visit the religious ceremonies that the explorer saw or did not see (such as the famous Snake Ritual). And the album even teaches us a great deal of value regarding Warburg's much later involvement with the photographs, drawings, and notes about the journey during his stay in the Kreuzlingen sanatorium.

The fact that such religious features which are today deemed culturally sensitive are occasionally also documented in Warburg's photographs and in the drawings that he made or received as gifts from the Indigenous people he spoke to is something of a problem. Admittedly—at least as far as we know—Warburg always obtained permission to photograph the rituals that interested him, and the drawings and commentaries entrusted to him still retain the authentic voices of his Indigenous informants. However, such features were—and are—seen in the Pueblo communities as the secret knowledge of the initiated (male) members of the various religious societies. Photographs in which the traveler is shown violating taboos he was fully aware of (see the chapters "The Grasping Man" and "The Mask") are particularly delicate here. One of the purposes of this book is to shed a critical light on such intrusive behavior, which was also observed in other situations, and on Warburg's resulting photographic practice. However, this confronts the author with a not inconsiderable scientific dilemma, for the young Warburg's at times ethnocentric approach can only be elucidated—as is nowadays crucial—if the reader can actually see the questionable illustrations.

The original photographs and other archival materials related to Warburg's visit to the Pueblo villages are preserved at the Warburg Institute in London. In preparing for the 2022 exhibition *Lightning Symbol and Snake Dance. Aby Warburg and Pueblo Art* (at Hamburg's Museum am Rothenbaum), the cultural preservation officers of the three communities in question reviewed all of the images and requested that a number should not be shown. The Warburg Institute not only complied but has now embarked on a collaborative process to ensure that the Pueblo materials in its care are described, handled, and shared in an appropriate manner. While this process is undertaken, it will not be providing reproductions or permissions for the culturally sensitive documents: An explanation of the policy and suggestions for further reading can be found at www.warburg.sas.ac.uk/archive. In consultation with the Warburg Institute, the author has therefore taken them from other sources for this publication.

Aby Warburg reached New York on September 13, 1895, and on May 28, 1896, he set sail once more for Hamburg. His journey to America thus took only a few months, and his stay in the Pueblo territory lasted only a few weeks. But my journey through the continent of his research has already taken several years, some of them strenuous but others exhilarating; and yet at times it seems to have only just begun.

In Pursuit of a Symbolic Art
Aby Warburg in Pueblo Territory

Aby Warburg's American journey, which took the Hamburg art historian from the East Coast of the United States to the Pueblo villages in the southwest of the country, is one of those events in scientific history that would have a long afterlife (fig. I).[1] To this day the lecture Warburg gave at the Kreuzlinger sanatorium in April 1923 about his stay in Colorado, New Mexico, and Arizona is undoubtedly one of his most important and most widely discussed contributions to an art history that had been developing ever since the late nineteenth century; the lecture, which he modestly described as "images with accompanying words," has had an almost inestimable impact on art and cultural history research throughout the world.[2] Yet the supposed text of the lecture was only published long after his death in an English version compiled by his former colleagues. This problematic version was to be followed decades later by further editions and translations.[3] Under the suggestive title "Serpent Ritual," which Warburg had never intended, this text promised to be an authentic testimony to his later retrospective theoretical involvement with his travel impressions.

However, until quite recently–and in some cases to this day–many details of the journey were largely unknown. With published exceptions, the photographs Warburg took in the United States were for decades only available in the archive of the Warburg Institute in London; and

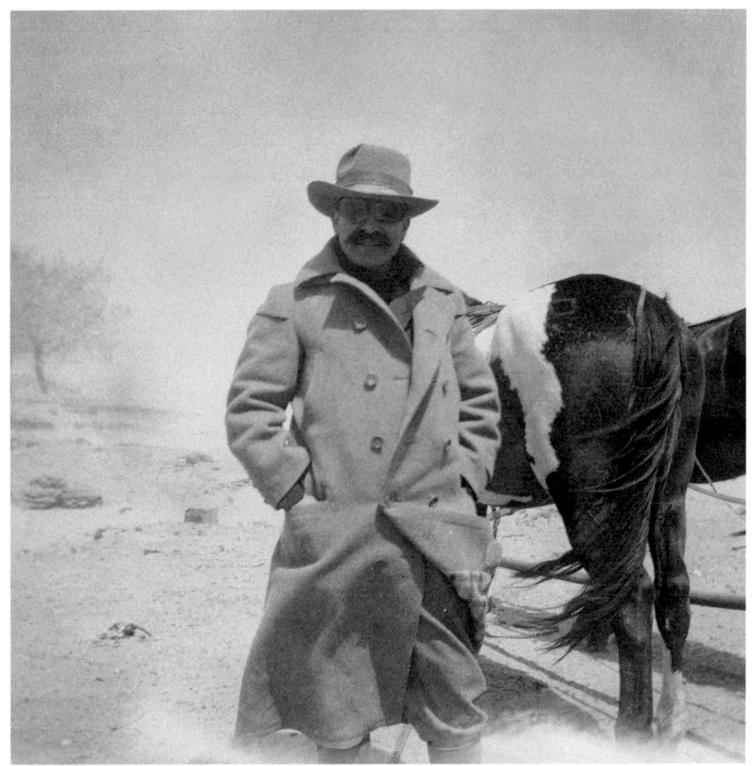

I Unknown photographer (probably Frank Allen, taken with Aby Warburg's camera): *Aby Warburg in front of his coach horses in a sandstorm between Bitahochee and Keams Canyon*, 1896

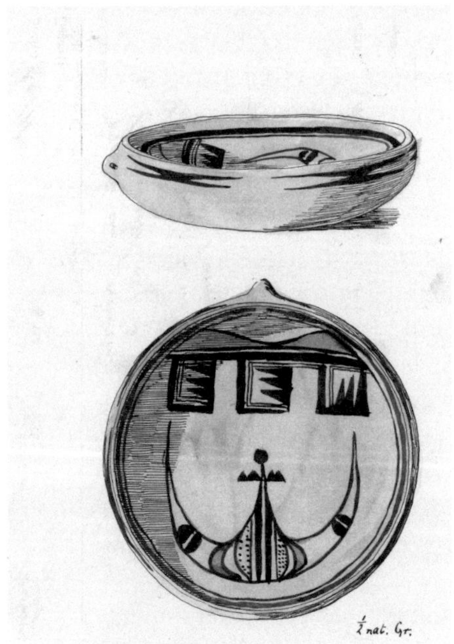

II Unknown woman artist: *Clay dish (ascribed to Nampeyo)*, ca. 1890–1895, index-card drawing, after 1907

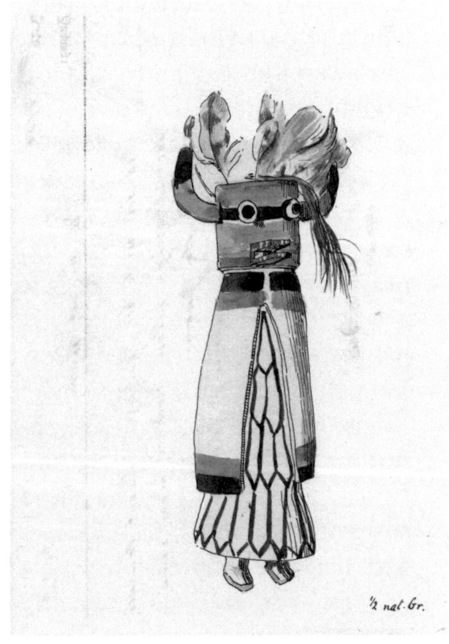

III Unknown woman artist: *Katsina figure (Si'osa'lako tihu)*, ca. 1890–1896 (purchased by Aby Warburg from Thomas Varker Keam), index-card drawing, after 1907

what was shown in them was barely, or wrongly, identified.[4] Likewise only sporadically published, and to this day at best only barely appreciated by researchers, are the numerous drawings that Warburg made or was given during his stay. Not even his lecture, much less the texts of earlier travel reports, appeared in reliable editions and were only solidly published a few years ago.[5] Although it was known that Warburg had also assembled a fair number of ceramic objects, dance paraphernalia, Katsina figures, and other things that he donated to Hamburg's Museum of Ethnology after his return, the nature, number and provenance, iconography, and exact dating of the objects he acquired remained as uncertain as the great majority of the artifacts that lay unnoticed in the museum storerooms. Only current research has managed to reconstruct the full extent of the collection that found its way to the Hamburg museum, and publish it in inventories of all its exhibits (figs. II–III).[6]

Yet the significance in the history of science that was attached to the journey seemed evident: The art historian's encounter with the art and culture of the Cochiti and the Zuni, the Tewa and the Hopi supposedly enabled him to depart from the canon of his own research interests and methods, and his previous focus on Italian Renaissance art and his ideas about the afterlife of antiquity in Western European art were crucially expanded in the American Southwest; the ethnocentricity of art-historical research was accordingly overcome by Warburg's pioneering work in the pueblos, and its methods replaced by a comparative cultural-anthropological approach. This assessment will be critically examined below in a brief outline of his travel activities and the question of the art historian's intentions during his stay in the United States. Above all, however, the attempt in this publication to analyze a selection of documents–photographs, drawings, maps, notes, and other sources–and Warburg's related research will contribute to a firmer foundation.

From Hamburg to Oraibi

In September 1895 Aby Warburg boarded the German steamer *SS Fürst Bismarck* on the first leg of his journey to the United States, where he first of all attended the wedding of his brother Paul and the banker Solomon Loeb's daughter Nina in New Jersey. But he combined this private reason for his journey, which took him into the highest echelons of the Jewish-American moneyed aristocracy, with scientific interests, visiting museums and libraries on the East Coast, above all the Smithsonian Institution in Washington DC, which in 1879 had founded the Bureau of Ethnology (to be renamed the Bureau of American Ethnology in 1897) and established extensive archives on the languages and cultures of North America's Indigenous peoples.[7] He came into contact with leading scholars, with anthropologists, archeologists, ethnologists, and linguistic and religious historians; and his exchanges with Cyrus Adler, Franz Boas, Frank Hamilton Cushing, Jesse Walter Fewkes, Frederick Webb Hodge, James Mooney, and John Wesley Powell, and his conversations on pre-Columbian America, on the artifacts, ornaments, and rituals of the Pueblo communities confirmed his decision, which he had taken by the time he reached Washington out of "honest disgust" at an "aestheticizing art history," to set off for the Southwest in order, as he wrote retrospectively in 1923, "to visit Western America both as a modern creation and in its lower Hispano-Indian strata."[8]

Starting in Chicago, where Albert A. Robinson, the former vice-president of the Atchison, Topeka and Santa Fe Railway Company, provided him with important letters of recommendation and a free ticket for the whole rail network, Warburg arrived in Colorado by train in late November 1895.[9] In early December he spent a few days in Mancos Canyon on the Alamo Ranch, owned by the family of Richard Wetherill, one of the discoverers of the pre-Columbian cliff dwellings at Mesa Verde. After hours on horseback Warburg reached the dwellings, which had first developed in the twelfth century, and whose ruins he had already studied in publications and now marveled at as an "American Pompeii."[10] Warburg traveled on to Santa Fe, where he again met the town's leading personalities, as well as the alleged kiva guard (and forger of religious artifacts) Cleto Yurina from Pueblo de Cochiti and his son Anastacio who, with reference to some drawings, explained to him their local dance rituals, their cosmological worldview, and the furnishing of their cultural spaces (figs. IV–V). From Santa Fe he made extensive excursions into the surrounding area, and before the end of December he visited his first Pueblo village: San Juan, now known as Ohkay Owingeh. Near the ruins of San Cristóbal, together with the German-American theologist and poet Gotthold August Neef, he studied early rock paintings and carved drawings, explored some other Pueblo community settlements, such as the cliff village of Acoma, where he saw his first dance ritual, and also attended a Catholic mass, on January 1, 1896. More dances were to follow in Cochiti and Laguna in the course of the month, particularly in San Ildefonso Pueblo, where he recorded the local Buffalo Deer Dance in a series of photographs (figs. VI–VII).

In February, Warburg recovered from the arduous horse rides and no less uncomfortable stagecoach trips in Pasadena, California; then, after a stay in Los Angeles, at Coronado Beach in San Diego, always residing at the best hotels, he took excursions to the areas around the cities he visited, learned to ride a bicycle, and was invited to dinner parties and a hunting trip. At the end of the month Warburg traveled on to San Francisco, where he again took part in the city's vibrant social life and visited Chinatown, which was near his hotel. From there he went to the universities at Berkeley and Stanford, and he planned to travel on to Japan, even taking a few hours of Japanese language lessons in preparation. But he eventually abandoned his long-distance travel plans in favor of further visits to the Southwest: In early April, after a trip to the Grand Canyon, his route took him via Albuquerque and Fort Wingate to Zuni Pueblo, and finally from Holbrook to Keams Canyon in Arizona. There he met Thomas Varker Keam, who had been trading since 1874 in Pueblo ceramics under a license from the Bureau of Indian Affairs and had built up a large collection of artifacts, some of them pre-Columbian, that would later end up in American and European museums. Warburg also purchased from Keam a series of objects that he donated to Hamburg's Museum of Ethnology, together with artifacts acquired from other traders, after his return.

In late April 1896 Aby Warburg finally arrived in Oraibi on the Third Mesa (a flat-topped mountain), his real destination: "... there, because it was the farthest from the railroad (and seventy kilometers from Keams Canyon), I hoped to find the original situation."[11] However, this "original situation" was wishful thinking on the part of not only the Hamburg art historian, for the Hopi had already been living for some time under the influence of Christian missions and modern schooling, which many of them perceived as an oppressive yoke, and for this and other reasons were embroiled in fierce political conflicts which Warburg evidently failed to observe.[12] Despite its remoteness, by the mid-nineteenth century Oraibi, as the center of the Hopi's threatened culture, was visited by countless explorers and tourists, who were all drawn by the same object of interest that fascinated Warburg, the Hopi dance rituals: "For I had come to Oraibi to be able to see such a dance, which is ethnologically of supreme interest."[13] Together with the Mennonite missionary Henry R. Voth, who studied Hopi religion, culture, and language, and also traded in native artifacts, Warburg experienced the preparations for the spring dance in Oraibi, gained access to a kiva (a ceremonial space used for the preparation and performance of sacred rituals), and inquired there about the meaning of the symbols that decorated the dance masks.[14] On May 1, 1896, he was able to see the Hemiskatsina ritual, which he documented in an impressive series of photographs. However, Warburg did not watch the performances all the way through; the two men left the dances early, for they considered the gestures of the scantily clad dancers of the Tohskuti fraternity, the

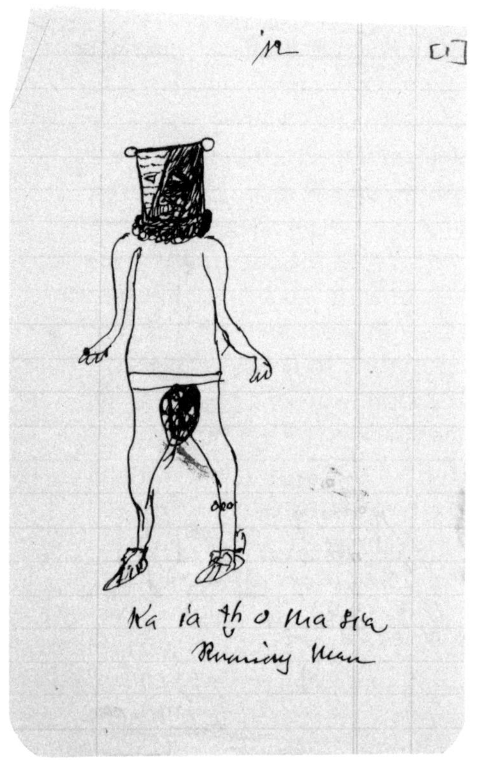

IV Anastacio Yurina (with comments by Aby Warburg): *Katsina dancer ("Running Man"),* 1896, ink on paper, 14.2 × 8.9 cm

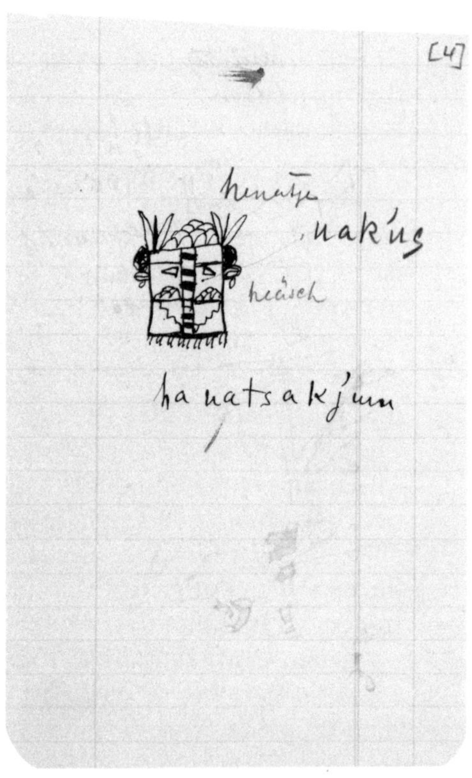

V Anastacio Yurina (with comments by Aby Warburg): *Dance mask with cloud symbols*, 1896, ink and pencil on paper, 14.2 × 8.9 cm

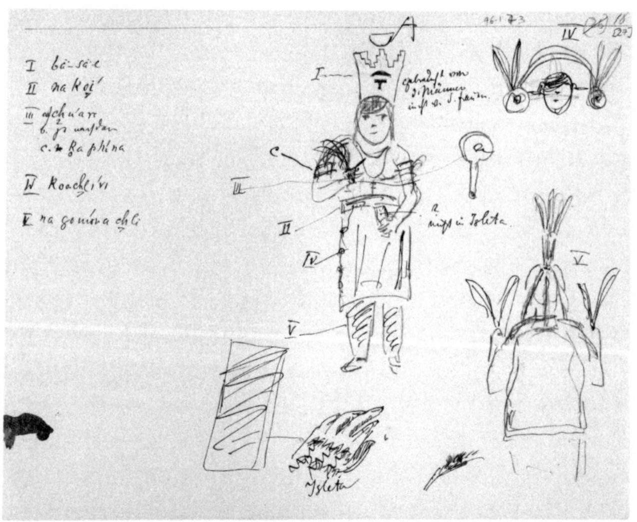

VI Aby Warburg: *Woman dancer from Pueblo de Cochiti and costume features*, 1896, pencil and ink on paper, 9.6 × 15.6 cm

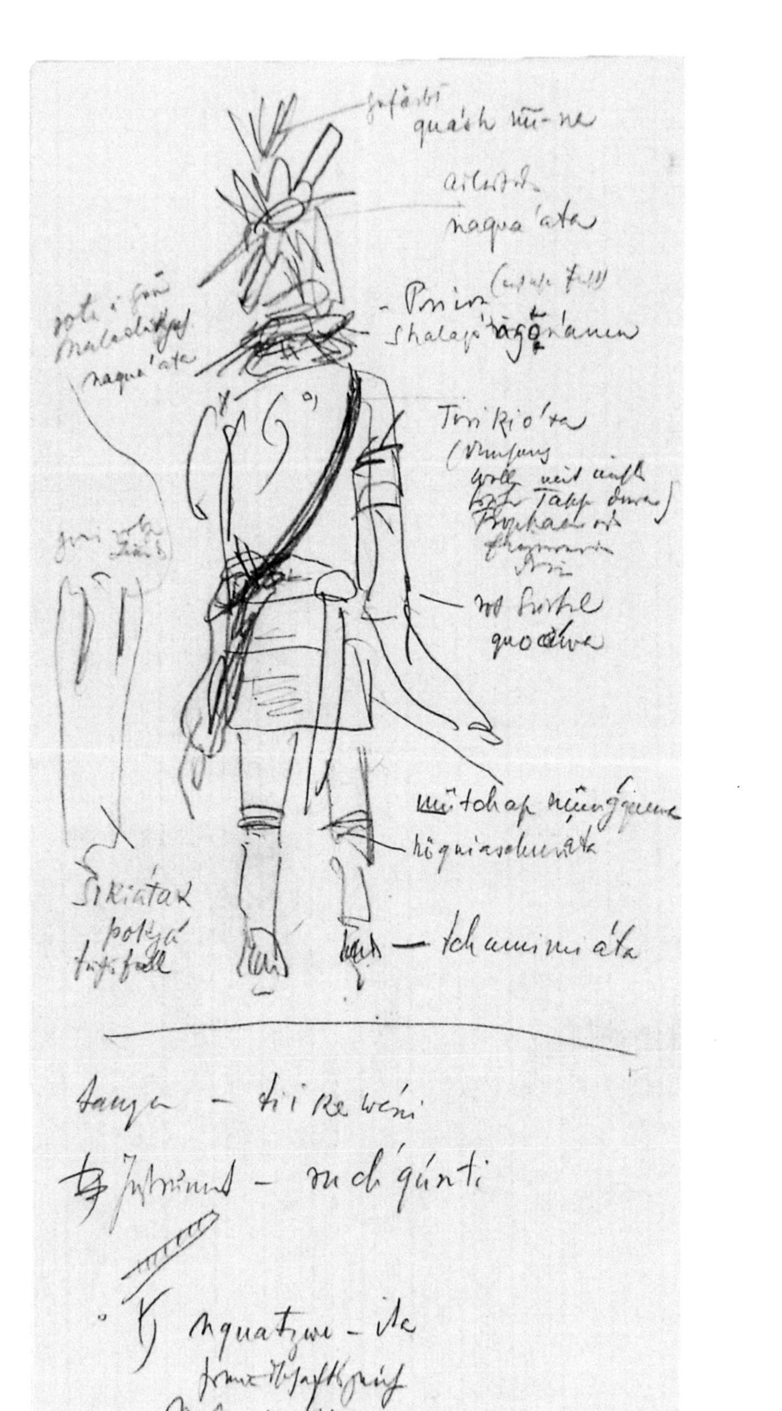

VII Aby Warburg: *Dancer from Isleta or Laguna*, 1896, pencil and ink on paper, 26 × 12.3 cm

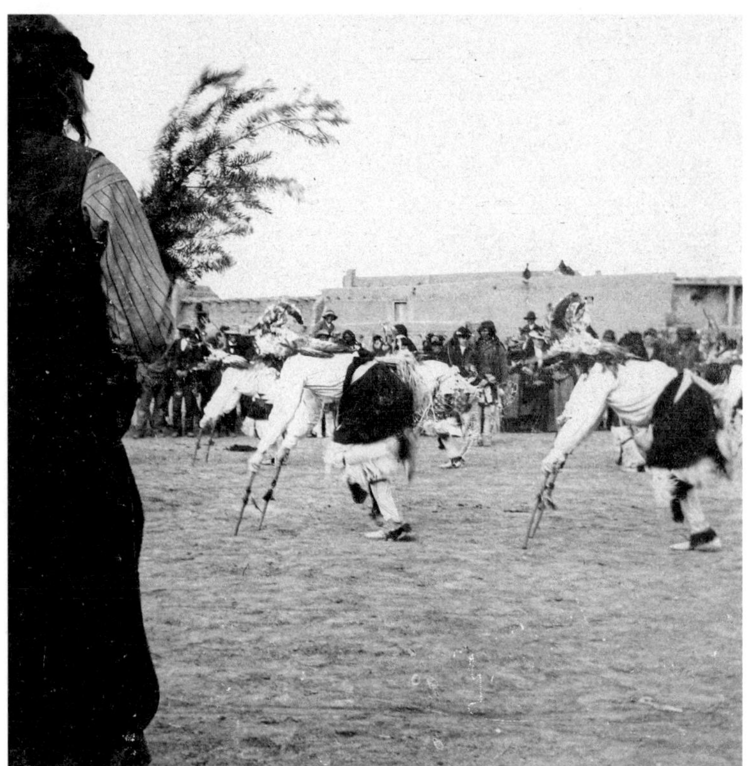

VIII Aby Warburg: *The Buffalo Deer Dance in San Ildefonso Pueblo*, 1896, photograph

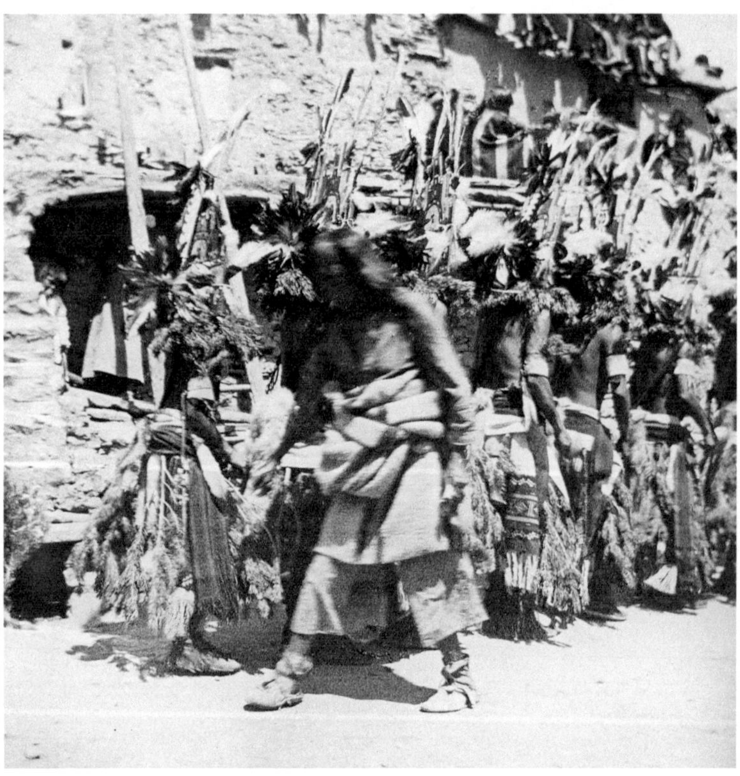

IX Aby Warburg: *Hemiskatsinam during the spring dance in Oraibi*, 1896, photograph

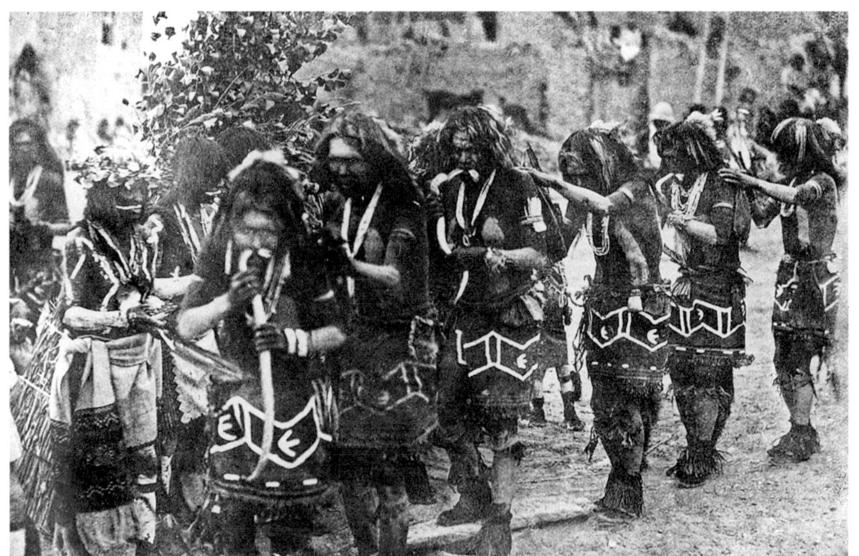

X George Wharton James: *Hóveima and other priests of the Snake fraternity during the dance ritual in Oraibi*, 1898, photograph

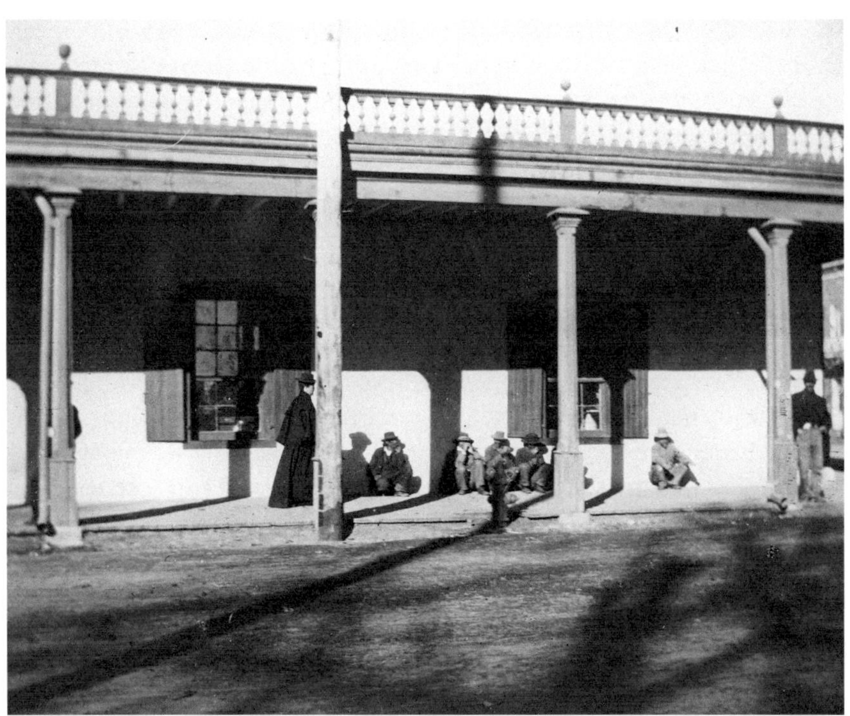

XI Aby Warburg: *Waiting Mexicans and a woman passerby in the arcades of the Palace of the Governors, Palace Avenue, Santa Fe*, 1895–1896, photograph

sacred clowns, "highly obscene."[15] Warburg would never see with his own eyes the actual "snake ritual," a several-day ceremony culminating in dances with live snakes and an appeal for rain.[16]

"Between physically grasping men and intellectually grasping men ..."

As we have seen, Aby Warburg's journey to America gave him an opportunity to settle scores with "aestheticizing art history," with "barren word-mongering" that focused entirely on a "formal approach" to the image, whereas this should rather be understood in terms "of its biological necessity as a product between religion and art."[17] Inspired by an image of Native Americans that was widespread in Germany and was certainly also influenced by his childhood reading of James Fenimore Cooper's *Leatherstocking Tales*, Warburg had initially hoped to achieve such an understanding by studying the art of nomadic tribal communities, "the truly 'warlike' wandering Indians" who appeared to correspond to these romanticizing notions.[18] Yet his work in the library of the Smithsonian and his conversations with leading researchers into the Pueblo cultures rapidly led him to assume that in the Southwest of the country he would come across sedentary communities whose art and culture were settled in, as it were, a surviving antiquity between primitive magical ideas and progressive, already distancing/reflective symbolization: "Deliberately distancing oneself from the outside world may surely be considered a fundamental act of human civilization" was Warburg's summary at the end of his life of the insights into this civilization process that he had also gained in studying the Pueblo communities, of which in his view symbolic art forms were a key component.[19]

As a historian of the afterlife of ancient pictorial formulas in Renaissance art, Warburg believed that in the United States he had an opportunity to experience at first hand the process of such symbolization: "What specifically made me, as an art historian, visit the Pueblo Indian group in New Mexico and Arizona was that the relationship between pagan religious ideas and artistic activity was nowhere more readily recognizable than among the Pueblo Indians and that a wealth of material for the study of how symbolic art emerges can be found in their culture."[20] He therefore used the various forms of decoration above all on Pueblo ceramic works, in wall paintings, or on dance costumes and props, as well as by attending the actual dance rituals, in an attempt to understand for himself how threatening or longed-for natural phenomena were expressed in art: In the Buffalo Deer Dance in San Ildefonso Pueblo he perceived a mimetic adaptation of the animals by the dancers, in the mask dance of the Hemiskatsinam in Oraibi a symbolic appeal for the rain required for a good harvest, and in the actual Snake Dance, which he only knew from descriptions and photographs, the "most pagan of all ceremonies," for here the animal and the dancer still supposedly formed a "magical unit" (figs. VIII–X).[21]

However, the lectures the art historian gave in Berlin and Hamburg in 1897 after his return only touched on such aspects. He would only present the sum total of his findings at the Kreuzlingen sanatorium in 1923 when, amid a personal loss of distance from his menacing, fear-laden phantasms, he attempted to prove to himself and his physicians through his work on the documents assembled in America that he had overcome his own manic-depressive condition of uncontrollable magical primitivism.[22] At one point in his lecture manuscript Warburg sums up his thoughts on the symbolization of the Pueblo with a wordplay so typical of his writing: "They are midway between magic and logos, and the instrument they use for orientation is the symbol. Between physically grasping men (*Greifmenschen*) and intellectually grasping men (*Begriffsmenschen*) stands the one who is linking with the means of symbols."[23]

This chronological, perhaps even evolutionarily conceived progression from a pagan/primitive culture via a symbolic culture as embodied by the Pueblo communities to an enlightened/technologized culture–of which, however, he became increasingly critical over the years–also shows that Warburg saw the existence of the Pueblo between tactile and intellectual people as very seriously threatened. As he saw it, the very civilizing achievements that he witnessed in the American Southwest, from railroads and the telegraph to a school system perceived as colonializing, destroyed the "conceptual space," the necessary mental distance between humans and their environment, represented in Pueblo art and culture by the much-used distancing symbols.[24] As early as February 1896, when asked by the daily newspaper *The San Francisco Call* about the purpose of his journey, he expressed these concerns as follows: "In a few years the Indians will all be educated in American ways and the Indian art will be gone."[25]

From ethnocentrism to cultural-psychological self-contemplation

Yet during his stay in the United States Warburg did not always show himself to be so carefully considerate regarding the cultural peculiarities of the people he met on his journey. In his attempts to make contact with the inhabitants of the pueblos he occasionally violated the restrictions placed on such encounters and failed to display the required deference. Even though he was well aware "that nearly all Indians have a superstitious dread of being photographed," he did not always respect these restrictions.[26] His comments also included stereotypical characterizations. Thus he spoke of "indolent Mexicans" sunning themselves in the marketplace in Santa Fe (fig. XI); he sneered at the "brutish loitering" of waiting Mexicans and Pueblo, and perceived Navajo men as "spirited, devious lads"; a Zuni priest was caricatured as "a typically crafty old *cacique*"; and two Chinese workers he photographed in San Francisco not far from the city's Chinatown were described as "sons of the Celestial Empire who would not allow their repose to be disturbed."[27] It is certainly difficult to recognize in these and similarly phrased passages the same Warburg who, as the nemesis of "border surveillance," helped introduce the postcolonial globalization of cultural studies that marks a good deal of writing on art history today.[28]

However, the ethnocentric prejudices that appear in the early lecture texts should be viewed in the light of then entirely typical scientific practice which Warburg shared with other traveling ethnologists and anthropologists. Although in Colorado, Arizona, and New Mexico the young art historian acted as a tourist with an interest in cultural anthropology who had only just begun to acquire insights into the art and culture of the pueblos he visited, his fast-growing knowledge of the religious symbolism of the Hopi, in particular, was already providing the crucial impulses that would place his future research on a comparative cultural and cultural-psychological basis: "I believe I am not mistaken in seeing the acquisition of a vivid notion of the life and art of a 'primitive' people as a valuable corrective to the study of any art."[29]

But it was not until 1923, when Warburg reviewed his American study material in a highly precarious personal situation, juxtaposing and comparing the evidence from both Indigenous and European culture on an equal footing, that he was able to take full advantage of his field research: Analysis of the notes, drawings, and photographs he had accumulated in the United States taught the art historian something not only about an alien culture but also about his own culture and his own psyche; and at the end of his time in the Kreuzlingen sanatorium he recovered the reflective distance, the "conceptual space between man and the object," that mattered so much to him.[30] As a result, his investigation of the hybrid and threatened culture of the Pueblo between "physically grasping men" and "intellectually grasping men" also led Aby Warburg to produce an anamnesis of European cultural achievements between magic and logos, and eventually to reflect on his own threatened existence: And so his exploration of the art and culture of the Pueblo communities ultimately became for him a form of cultural-psychological self-contemplation.

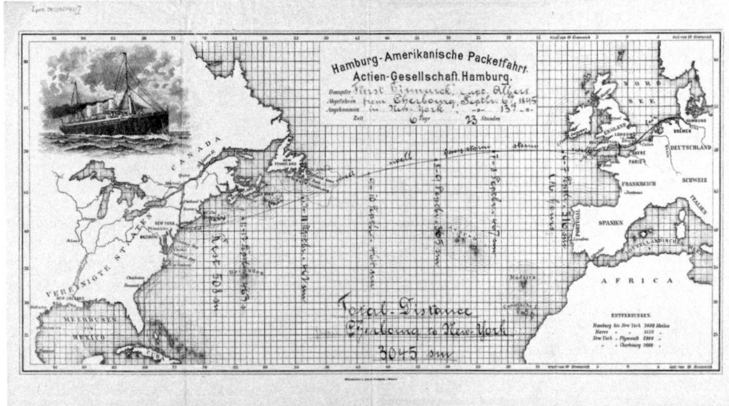

1 Hamburg-Amerikanische Packetfahrt Actien-Gesellschaft: *Nautical chart with route from Hamburg to New York*, 1895, leaflet, lithograph and letterpress on cardboard

Liste der Cajüts-Passagiere

des

„FÜRST BISMARCK"

Capitain **A. Albers,**

am Donnerstag, den 5. Septemb. 1895.

Frau Lizzie Abeln
Herr Richard H. Adams
Frau Richard Adams
Herr S. Appel
Frau S. Appel
Fräulein Dorothy Appel
Fräulein Sophia Appel
Herr Geo Aschenbach
Fräulein Marie E. Aschenbach
Laura Aschenbach
Fräulein Cora M. Anton
Herr Dr. Arnold
Frau Dr. Arnold
Fräulein Wanda Ammer
Fräulein Agnes Almess
Herr Max Auerbach
Herr B. Beinecke
Frau B. Beinecke
Alice Beinecke
Fred Beinecke
Theo Beinecke
nebst Bedienung
Herr Morris Barnett
Frau Morris Barnett
Helene Barnett
Sylvan Barnett
Herr Walther Bruck
Fräulein Kate Bough
Herr Henry Brasch
Frau Henry Brasch
Fräulein Blanche Brasch

Fräulein Agnes Blanche
Colonel Georg Boker
Mrs. Georg Boker
Herr Max Borck
Frau Edda Borck
Jessie Borck
Charley Borck
Herr M. W. Bartlett
Herr H. G. Bannon
Herr Georg C. Boldt
Herr Georg C. Boldt jr.
nebst Bedienung
Herr W. Belcher
Frau W. Belcher
Fräulein V. M. Buffum
Herr Morris Black
Herr J. R. Blumenthal
Frau J. R. Blumenthal
Fräulein J. C. Belden
Fräulein K. C. Biglow
Herr Dr. L. C. Boscher
Herr Leopold Brunhild
Frau Mathilde Boldt
Frau Jeane Bloch
Frau D. Bergesen
Herr Henry Fr. Brinckmann
Heinrich Brinckmann
Herr Dr. Lidney F. Budget
Frau Lidney Budget
Frau Helene Brick
Anna Brick

2 Hamburg-Amerikanische Packetfahrt Actien-Gesellschaft: *List of cabin passengers on the Fürst Bismarck*, September 5, 1895, leaflet, color lithograph and letterpress on paper

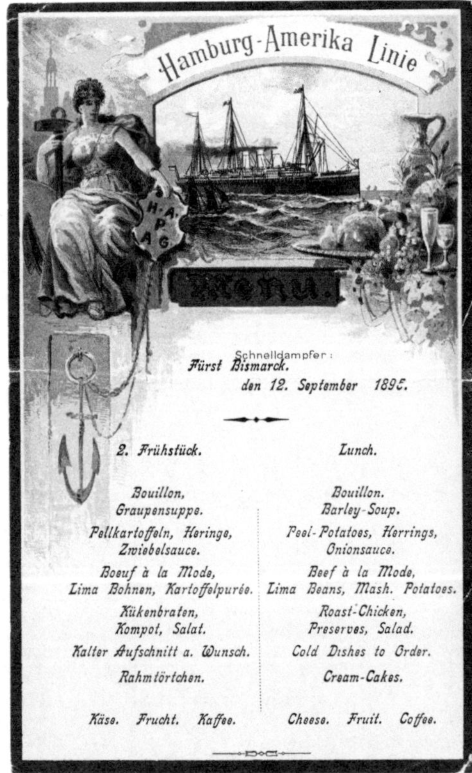
Hamburg-Amerika Linie

H.A.P.A.G.

Menu.

Schnelldampfer: Fürst Bismarck.
den 12. September 1895.

2. Frühstück.	Lunch.
Bouillon, Graupensuppe.	Bouillon. Barley-Soup.
Pellkartoffeln, Heringe, Zwiebelsauce.	Peel-Potatoes, Herrings, Onionsauce.
Boeuf à la Mode, Lima Bohnen, Kartoffelpurée.	Beef à la Mode, Lima Beans, Mash. Potatoes.
Kükenbraten, Kompot, Salat.	Roast-Chicken, Preserves, Salad.
Kalter Aufschnitt a. Wunsch.	Cold Dishes to Order.
Rahmtörtchen.	Cream-Cakes.
Käse. Frucht. Kaffee.	Cheese. Fruit. Coffee.

3 Hamburg-Amerikanische Packetfahrt Actien-Gesellschaft: *Menu on the Fürst Bismarck*, September 12, 1895, color lithograph and letterpress on cardboard

The Ship

Aby Warburg set out on his journey from Hamburg to New York on September 5, 1985, on the vessel *SS Fürst Bismarck* of the company Hamburg-Amerikanische Packetfahrt Actien-Gesellschaft (HAPAG), also known as the Hamburg-America Line. Built at the Vulcan shipyard in Stettin (now Szczecin in Poland), the steamer was at the time Germany's largest passenger ship, under the command of the highly decorated captain Adolph Albers, who had already completed more than a hundred Atlantic crossings. After stops at Southampton and Cherbourg, the *Fürst Bismarck* usually made the crossing in under six days, and was thus one of the fastest ships between Europe and the United States. On its teak-trimmed steel decks the steamer carried nearly 1,300 passengers, of which the largest group–most of them emigrants–were accommodated in the cramped tweendecks. However, the first- and second-class passengers had comfortable cabins, dining rooms and lounges with pompous historicist decor, as well as a smoking lounge for the gentlemen, and a band playing marches and dance music.[1] The menus, of which Warburg kept a few copies, bear witness to the luxury lives of the cabin passengers. Printed with an illustration of the ship out at sea, framed by a nautically attired Hammonia (the goddess personifying Hamburg), and an opulent still life with fruit, a carafe of wine, and glasses, the sequence of dishes on (for example) September 12, 1895, shows that travelers in the better classes lacked for nothing, from *bœuf à la mode* to cream cakes.

The surviving passenger lists for both arrival and departure make clear that Warburg was in the company of illustrious fellow passengers, including the businessman Bernhard Beinecke with his children Alice,

Theodora, and Frederick, the later founder of Yale University's Beinecke Rare Book & Manuscript Library, as well as George C. Boldt, the owner and manager of the Waldorf Hotel in New York. On board he also made the acquaintance of the attorney and politician John Maynard Harlan, whom he was to ask some weeks later for a letter of recommendation to his father, a Supreme Court judge. Warburg hoped to obtain John Marshall Harlan's support in gaining access to the Smithsonian Institution, where he wanted to commence his studies on the archeological sites of the cliff dwellings on Mesa Verde.[2]

On reaching New York harbor on the afternoon of September 13 –the official date of arrival was a day later–Captain Albers told a *Daily Tribune* reporter while still on board the *Fürst Bismarck* of the occasional rough weather that had prevailed during the otherwise very pleasant voyage and had at times even turned into heavy storms ("of almost cyclonic force").[3] On embarking, each passenger had been handed a blank of a map on which details of the prevailing weather and the number of nautical miles traveled since Cherbourg were entered each day. After the crossing, which this time had taken nearly a week ("six days and 23 hours") and had not been entirely comfortable, Aby Warburg set foot on American soil, with three items of baggage, on September 14, 1895.[4]

The Pioneer

Through his brother Felix, who had emigrated to the United Sates in 1894 and had married into the New York banking family Kuhn, Loeb & Co., Aby Warburg had excellent contacts with the German-Jewish moneyed aristocracy on the American East Coast.[1] Arriving in New York in September 1895 to attend his brother Paul's wedding to Nina Loeb, daughter of the bank founder Solomon Loeb, he also became acquainted with the banker and social reformer Isaac Newton ("Ike") Seligman, who had been married to Nina's elder sister Guta since 1883.[2] Since 1894 Seligman had run the banking firm J. & W. Seligman, he was a member of numerous political, economic, cultural, and charitable associations, and among other things he campaigned against municipal maladministration and child labor, and in favor of social housing, decriminalization of prostitution, and civil rights for the Black population.[3]

By the late nineteenth century, anti-Semitism had clearly increased in the United States. The Jewish families in New York also found themselves subject to extensive social exclusion by Anglo-American business dynasties. An incident in May 1877, when Isaac Newton Seligman's father Joseph Seligman was refused entrance to the Grand Union Hotel in Saratoga Springs, New York ("No Israelites shall be permitted in future to stop at this hotel"), became a national scandal.[4] The German emigrant and successful banker wanted to spend several weeks' vacation with his family in what at the time was the world's largest luxury hotel, as he had done in previous years. A press campaign, death threats against the hotel

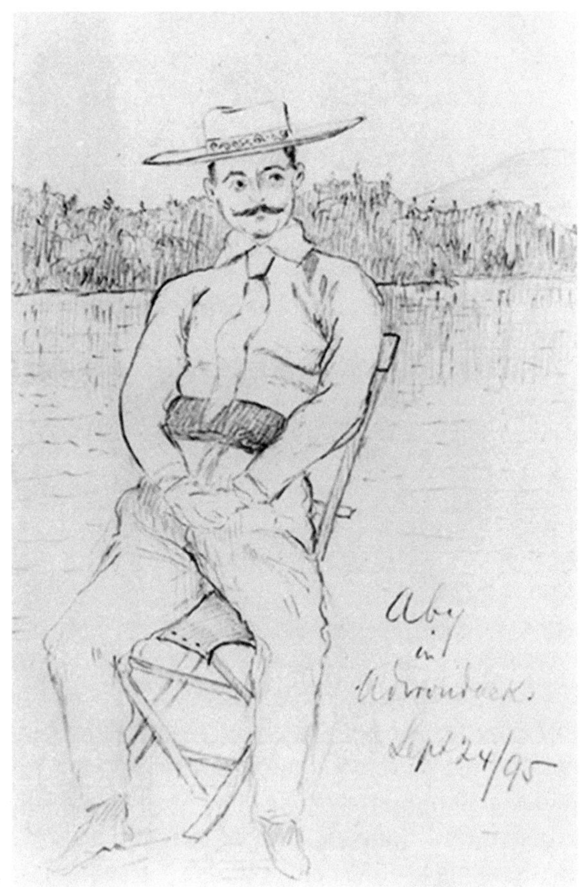

4 Isaac Newton Seligman: *Aby Warburg at Fish Rock Camp*, 1895, pencil on paper, 17.5 x 22.7 cm (sheet) / 17.5 × 11.8 cm (picture)

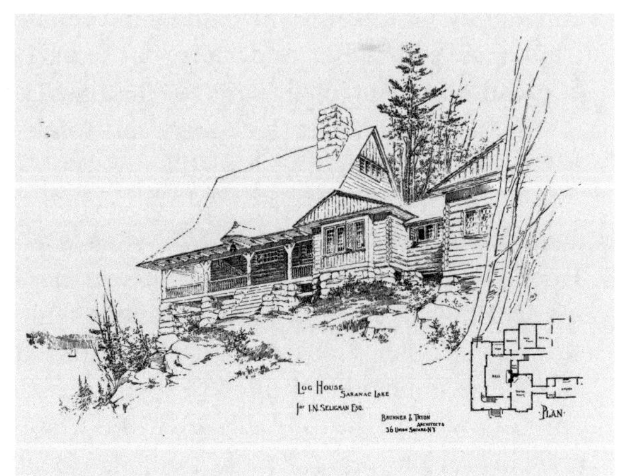

5 Arnold W. Brunner: *Design of the Fish Rock Camp log cabin*, from the *Catalogue of the Ninth Annual Exhibition of the Architectural League of New York*, American Fine Arts Building, New York 1893–1894

manager, but also against Seligman himself, and a boycott of the owner's New York department store were the result. Yet anti-Semitic posters ("No Jews or dogs admitted here") were apparently still to be seen in Saratoga Springs and other vacation resorts in the 1890s. Events such as these led Jewish families to start setting up their own vacation retreats in the hinterland of New York. In 1892, Isaac Newton Seligman purchased a piece of land on the banks of the Upper Saranac Lake in the Adirondack Mountains, where he built Fish Rock Camp (later known as Sekon Lodge), a large two-story wooden lodge in rustic style to which other buildings were gradually added, to a design by the architect Arnold W. Brunner.[5]

When Aby Warburg traveled to the Adirondacks in the fall of 1895 to spend a few days at Fish Rock Camp recovering from his long voyage and his social obligations on the East Coast, the host and amateur artist produced a drawing of him entitled "Aby in Adirondacks" and dated September 24.[6] The guest, whose characteristic features are scarcely apparent from the truly amateur portrait, although he can be recognized by his dark mustache, is sitting in a relaxed pose and with an attentive gaze in a garden chair on the terrace of the lodge, with the large expanse of the Upper Saranac Lake with the vegetation on the opposite shore and a hint of a mountain ridge visible in the background. The traveler is not dressed in a formal suit, but in the deliberately sloppy clothing of a pioneer with a wide-brimmed hat, as he can also be seen in some of Warburg's photographs from his time in America. The modest sheet of paper, which the guest received as a present, thus not only documents his personal relations with the German-Jewish families of New York's financial world, but also shows that Warburg had already equipped himself for his journey to the "wild" regions of the USA: Only a few weeks later the young scholar was to commence his train journey to Colorado, his first stop on the way to the pueblos in the American Southwest.

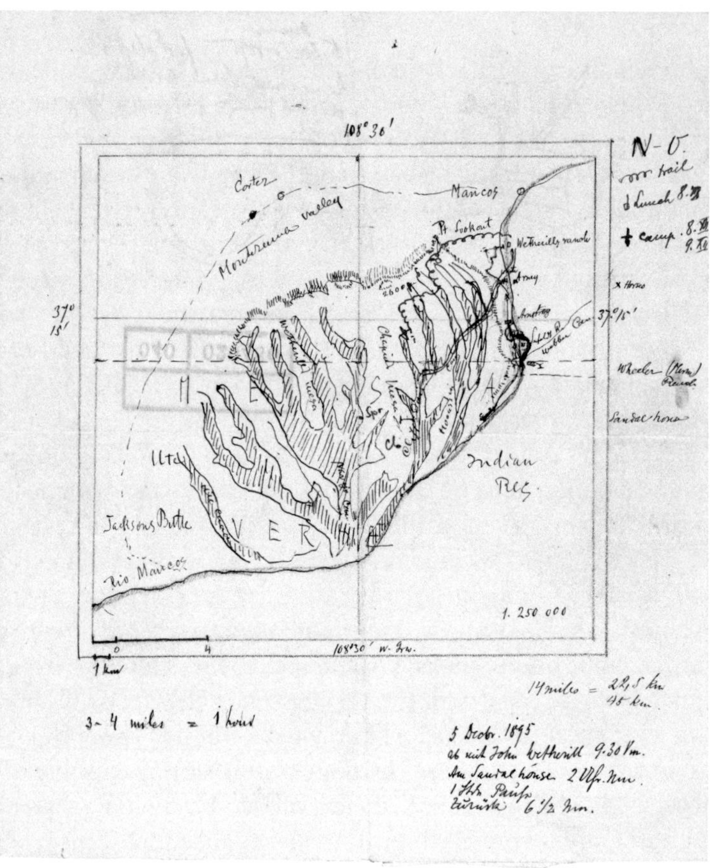

6 Aby Warburg: *Map of the Mesa Verde*, 1895, ink, crayon, and pencil on paper, 23.2 × 19.9 cm

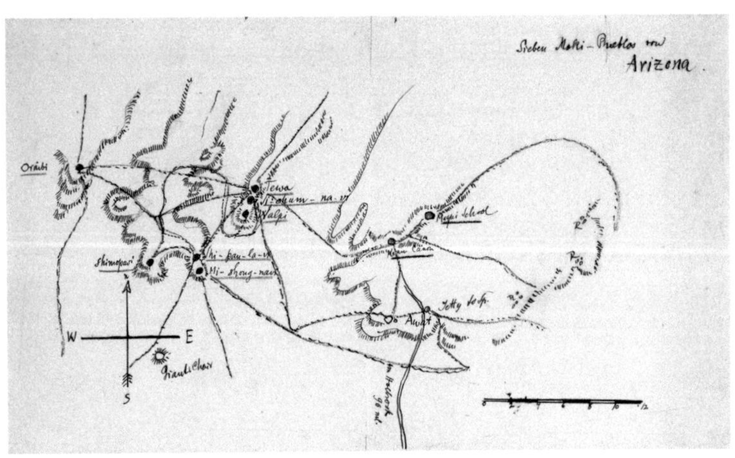

7 Aby Warburg: *Map of the Hopi Villages on the First, Second, and Third Mesas*, 1895–1896, ink, crayon, and pencil on paper, 16 × 27.4 cm

The Map

When Aby Warburg set off for the United States, his scientific curiosity was focused on the culture of the peoples that fit the romantic image of Native Americans that then prevailed in Germany: “I had first come to America with the idea that the drawings of the true ‘warlike’ wandering Indians were of art-historical interest ...”[1] Yet the comprehensive studies he embarked on after his arrival, especially at the library of the Smithsonian Institution in Washington DC, as well as his encounters with ethnologists such as Frank Hamilton Cushing and James Mooney quickly drew his gaze to the Pueblo culture in the country’s Southwest. On December 14, 1895, Warburg informed his family in Hamburg that he had therefore made it the goals of his journey “not only to get to know the American West in general, but in particular the part that is of greater importance for the history of America’s Indigenous population, and that is the area where Utah, Colorado, New Mexico, and Arizona meet; the boundaries are around 111°-106° west of Greenwich and latitude 38°-35° north.”[2] He said he wanted to devote particular attention to the cliff dwellings, the abandoned twelfth- and thirteenth-century cliff settlements in what is now Mesa Verde National Park, as well as the settlements of the Pueblo communities: “Here there are two kinds of things: in the north extensive abandoned structures that are squeezed high up into the sandstone cliffs of the Rocky Mountains, with remnants of pottery, mummies, implements, etc., most of which have already been transferred to the museums in American cities, and then in the south the ‘Pueblo’ Indians themselves, who to this day still exist in small villages around Sante Fe and in their reservations further to the west, and have to some extent maintained their old ways of life.”[3]

On the East Coast Warburg prepared his expeditions to the Southwest in meticulous detail: He consulted the already astonishingly extensive research literature that had above all been published on the archaeology and cultural history of the Pueblo and their ancestors, made initial notes on their languages, rituals, and artifacts, and probably already began to draw maps that he copied from various publications and annotated for his own guidance. On one of these sheets he recorded the road network and the geological formations in the flat-topped mountain area of Navajo County, and noted the exact position of the local settlements ("seven Moki pueblos in Arizona"), consisting of the villages of Sitsomovi ("Si-chum-na-vi"), Tewa and and Walpi on the First Mesa; Musangnuvi ("Mi-shong-navi"), Songoopavi ("Shimopavi"), and Supawlavi ("Shi-pau-la-vi") on the Second Mesa; and Oraibi on the Third Mesa; as well as Keams Canyon and the neighboring boarding school ("Moqui School"), which Warburg was to visit in the spring of 1896.[4]

At the sites Warburg also documented his travel activities with the help of drawn maps. For instance, when he explored the cliff dwellings region in Colorado from the Wetherill family's Alamo Ranch, he recorded his horseback excursions with exact details of places and dates (and in some cases even times of the day) in a sketch that he had produced from an unknown model. On it he marked the route of a one-day trip he had made on December 5 together with John Wetherill to the ruins of the "Sandal House," discovered back in 1887, in Mancos Canyon on the edge of Mesa Verde, as well as his visit to the largest of the local cliff dwellings, the famous pre-Columbian "Cliff Palace." A few days later, as the extremely accurate map makes clear, Warburg and his traveling companions bivouacked on Chapin Mesa in the vicinity for two nights.[5]

However, Aby Warburg's interest in cartography was due not only to a wish for practical geographical guidance or documentation that would trigger memories. What we are dealing with here is a fundamental, spatially oriented disposition in the cultural historian's thinking; more than once he linked up the stages of his own life in the form of drawn maps, and in addition used the same medium to provide visual portrayals of the overall object and motivic wanderings of the "image vehicles" he studied.[6]

The Railroad

On his travels within the United States Aby Warburg used the railroad for major journeys. From 1869 it had been possible to cross the entire North American continent from east to west by rail. Not only between cities such as New York and Washington, San Francisco and Los Angeles, but also between smaller places in Colorado, New Mexico, and Arizona that Warburg visited there were railroad links, some of them run by competing companies. The Atlantic and Pacific Railroad, founded in 1867, had an extensive rail network, and from 1880 it was jointly run by the St. Louis and San Francisco Railway Company and the later dominant Atchison, Topeka and Santa Fe Railway Company (AT&SF).

When Warburg reached Chicago in November 1895, he received not only several letters of recommendation from the railroad magnate Albert A. Robinson, the former vice president of the AT&SF, but also at his instigation a free rail ticket for the territories he visited, at first until the end of the year and then right up to July 1896: "Only this pass enabled me to keep making my excursions by rail from Santa Fe to the Indian villages."[1] Warburg even drew the rail connections between the localities on some meticulous maps, noting the geographical distribution of the various Pueblo communities between Albuquerque and the Grand Canyon on one of the small sheets. Constantly en route to the European immigrant settlements, which were located away from the railroad lines, and the likewise widely scattered pueblos, the traveler depended

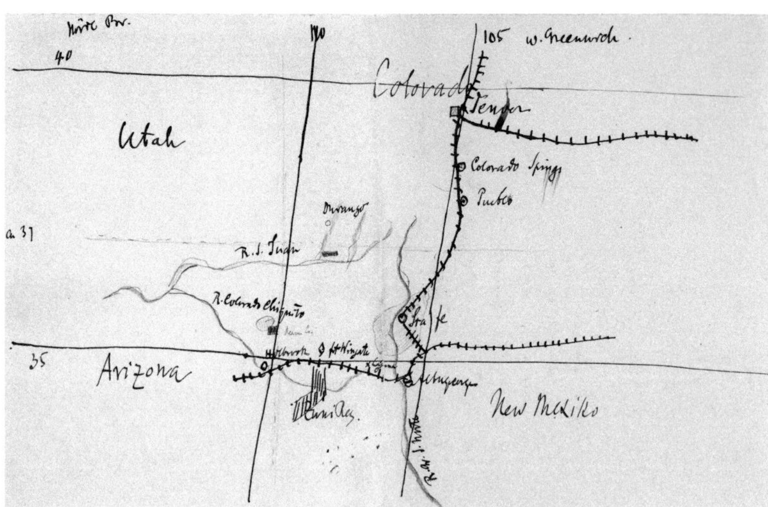

8 Aby Warburg: *Map of the rail links in the area between Utah, Colorado, Arizona, and New Mexico*, 1895, crayon, pencil, and ink on paper, 12.8 × 20.3 cm

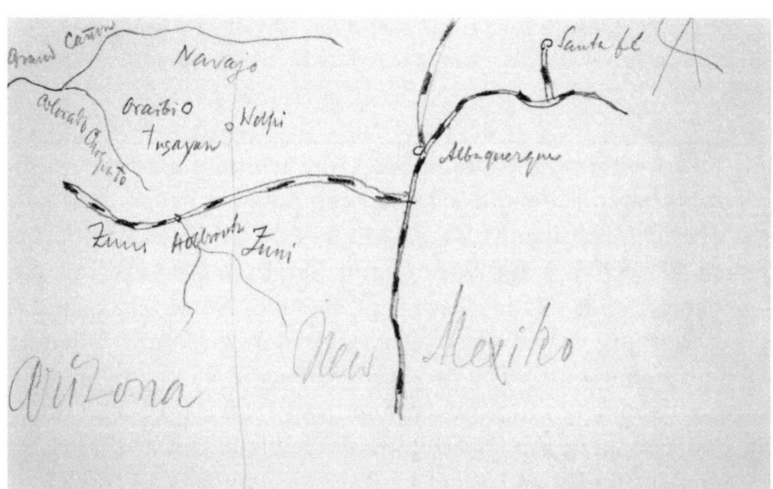

9 Aby Warburg: *Map of rail links in the area between Holbrook, Albuquerque, and Santa Fe*, 1895, pencil on paper, 9.6 × 15.6 cm

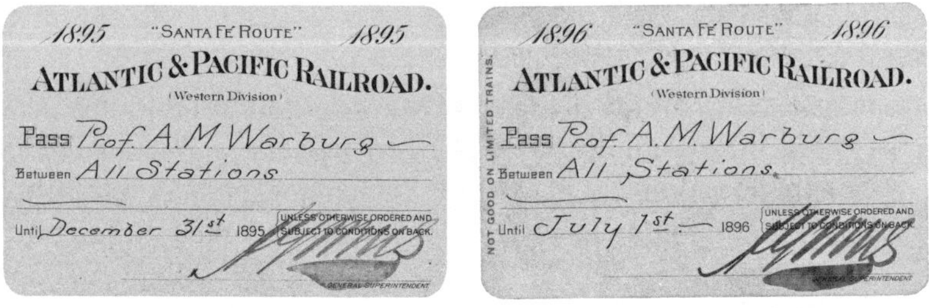

1895 "SANTA FE ROUTE" 1895

ATLANTIC & PACIFIC RAILROAD.

(Western Division)

Pass Prof. A. M. Warburg

Between All Stations

Until December 31st 1895 UNLESS OTHERWISE ORDERED AND SUBJECT TO CONDITIONS ON BACK.

GENERAL SUPERINTENDENT

1896 "SANTA FE ROUTE" 1896

NOT GOOD ON LIMITED TRAINS.

ATLANTIC & PACIFIC RAILROAD.

(Western Division)

Pass Prof. A. M. Warburg

Between All Stations.

Until July 1st 1896 UNLESS OTHERWISE ORDERED AND SUBJECT TO CONDITIONS ON BACK.

GENERAL SUPERINTENDENT

10–11 Atlantic & Pacific Railroad: *Free tickets for the whole railroad network ("Santa Fé route")*, 1895 and 1896 on horses and stagecoaches to move around. His photographs strikingly often documented both his changing means of transport and the landscapes he passed through, as if he were trying to become visually aware of the distance he covered.

Weighing up the pros and cons of the various alternatives, Warburg also kept a photographic record of the trains, routes, and structures as well as the staff of the regional railroad companies, and acknowledged the impact of the infrastructural innovation on the Pueblo: "... as long as the railroad has not yet reached the settlements, water shortages and longing for water lead to magical practices."[2] Not only was the population of the villages, who had been confronted with now even faster-growing influences on their traditions ever since the first attempts at conversion by Christian missionaries, thoroughly skeptical about the civilizing progress–so too was the art historian. In an interview with the newspaper *The San Francisco Call* on February 24, 1896, he frankly expressed his fear that the Euro-American educational system, in particular, would threaten the Pueblo culture: "In a few years the Indians will all be educated in American ways and the Indian art will be gone."[3] In retrospect, Warburg used such ideas to develop his theory of the endangered "conceptual space" in a technologized world: Like the airship, the telegraph, and the telephone, these "ominous destroyers of sense of distance," railroad traffic also threatened to destroy the necessary reflective distance that had created "mythical and symbolic thinking ... in the battle for the spiritualized link between man and environment."[4]

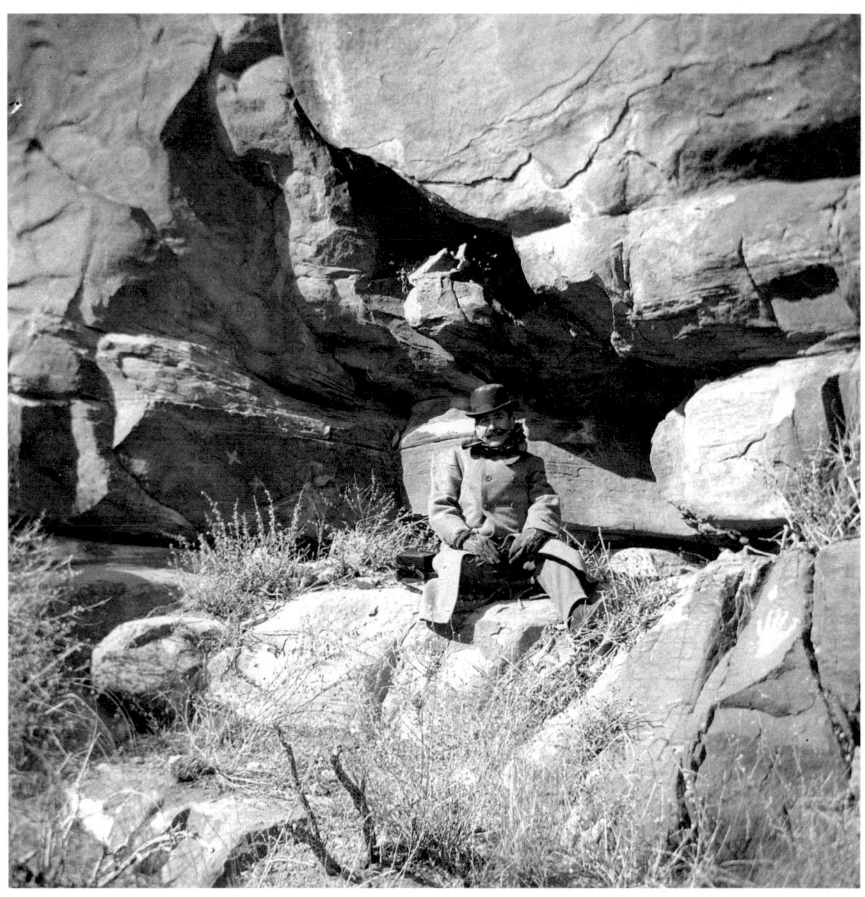

12 Unknown photographer (probably Gotthold August Neef, using Aby Warburg's camera): *Aby Warburg sitting on a rock with his "Buckeye Camera" bag*, 1896, photograph

The Rock Drawing

The area around the small village of Lamy, a few miles from Santa Fe, was one of the first places Aby Warburg traveled to after he had arrived in New Mexico in December 1895. Near the settlement, which contained only a few buildings but was nevertheless easy to reach by the Atchison, Topeka and Santa Fe Railroad, he looked at significant pre-Columbian artworks that had survived on the extensive rock formations in the arid desert landscape of the Galisteo Basin north of the ruins of Pueblo San Cristóbal. Some 30,000 drawings that were painted on or carved into the stone had so far been counted in the region, including hunting scenes as well as human and mythological figures, such as the horned or feathered snake Awanyu, a deity of the Tewa and other Pueblo communities, whose jagged body represented lightning.[1]

Warburg had visited the then still largely unresearched archeological site with the German-American theologist and poet Gotthold August Neef, whom he had most likely got to know in Santa Fe.[2] Together ("after a six-hour odyssey") the two men explored the rock drawings and documented them in photographs.[3] Whereas Neef had a large plate camera with a tripod and probably also the skills to operate it, Warburg had only a handy "Buckeye camera" which he had presumably bought just some days earlier after arriving in New Mexico.[4] Still unpracticed in its use, he photographed his traveling companion at work, as well as some of the drawings, and most of his pictures were somewhat blurred and shaky. In preparation for his field research, the art historian had decided, from a comparative perspective, to place the study of the "genesis of ornamentation on a very broad base, with use of ethnographic material," and so on

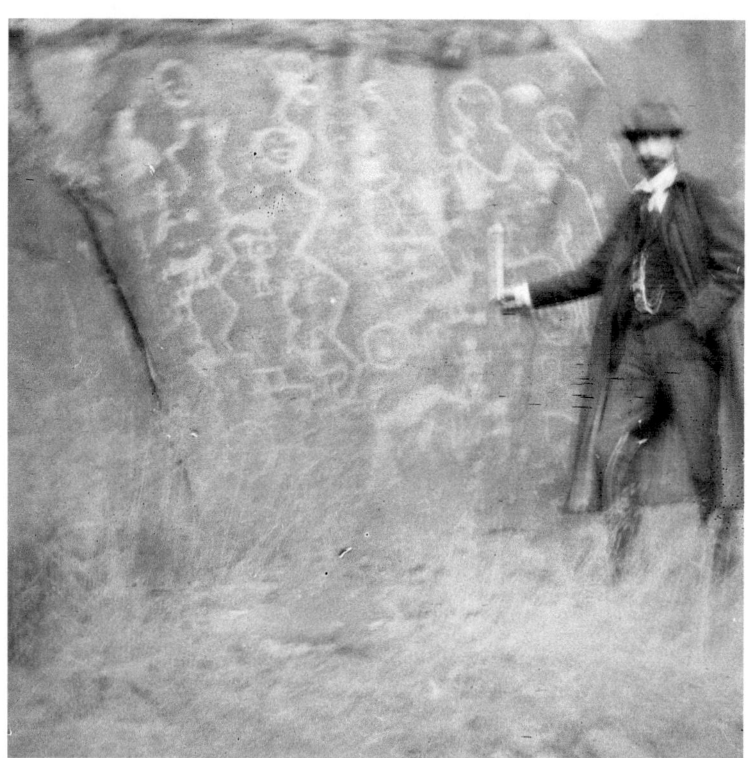

13 Aby Warburg: *Gotthold August Neeff in front of pre-Columbian rock drawings north of the ruins of Pueblo San Cristóbal*, 1896, photograph

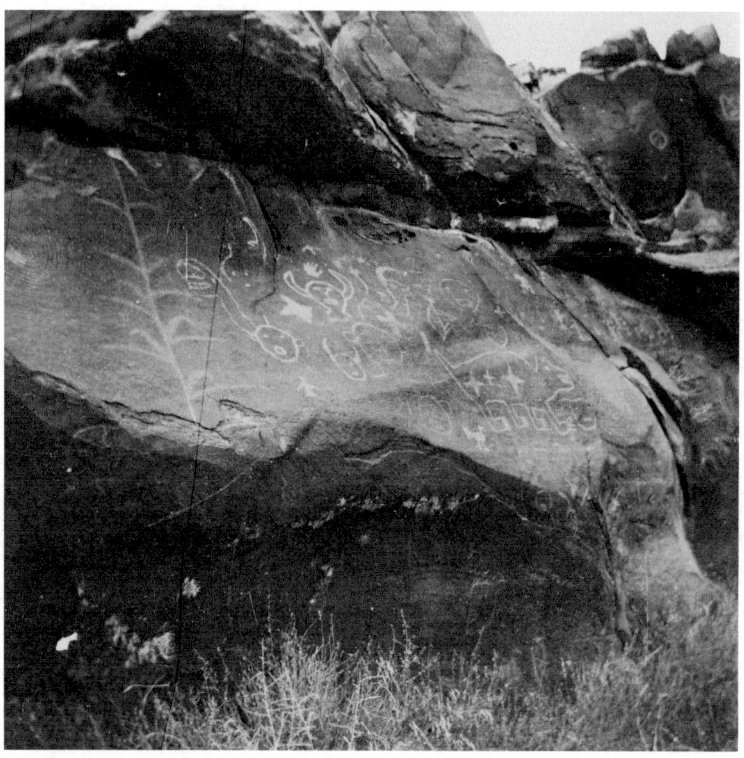

14 Aby Warburg: *Pre-Columbian rock drawings north of the ruins of Pueblo San Cristóbal*, 1896, photograph

arrival he mainly focused on the stylistic design of the drawings, which in one of his later lectures he compared with European forms, paying somewhat closer attention to one of the drawings: "Some figures of plants, masks, and animals are carved and others are painted in red; the time and purpose of the paintings are unknown. What is interesting is the ornamental treatment of the quadruped on the right (a bear?), whose carefully juxtaposed legs create a classical Greek meander pattern."[5]

Another photograph documents Warburg's scientific and not only tourist interest in these petroglyphs, for he had evidently asked Neef to hold a ruler in front of a rock with drawings so that he could later determine their exact size. In the extremely shaky picture we can also discern, approximately in the middle of the rock face, the horned snake with its zigzag body—a motif Warburg would continue to encounter during his journey. It is most probably to Gotthold August Neef that we owe the first photograph of Warburg during his stay in the United States. Dressed in a lined wool coat, with a hat, scarf, and gloves to protect him from the cold, the explorer had sat down on one of the blocks of stone; and some smaller rock drawings can be seen around him. Warburg, shown with the empty photo bag at his side, had evidently entrusted his own "Buckeye camera" to his companion and asked him to take his portrait: Clearly happy to finally be able to see in the original the works of the older Pueblo culture that so interested him, he gazes into the camera that will accompany him during his research in the months to come.

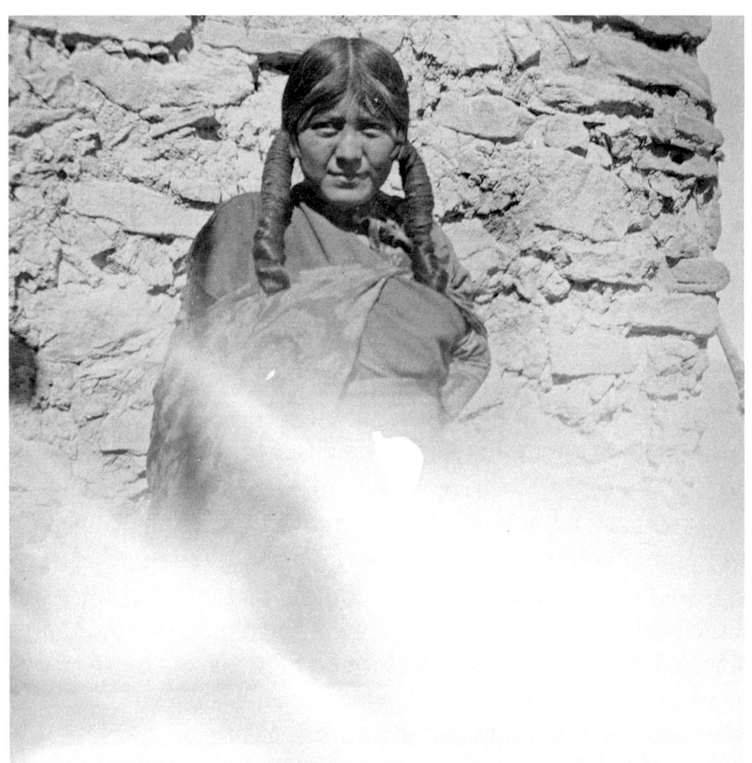

15 Aby Warburg: *Hopi girl from the audience at the spring dances in Oraibi*, 1896, photograph

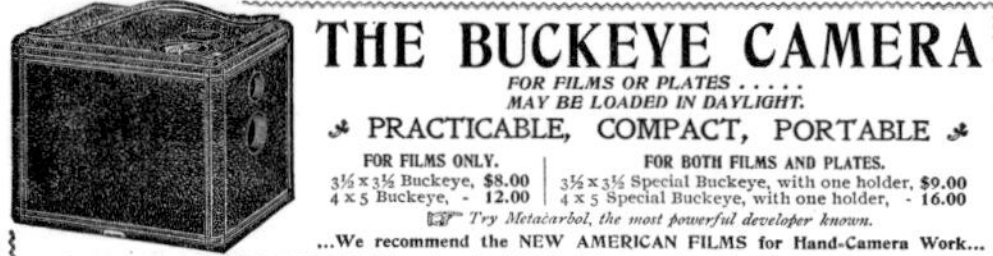

16 E. & H. T. Anthony & Company: "The Buckeye Camera," advertisement, from *The Century. Illustrated Monthly Magazine* 56-6/1898

The Photographer

Aby Warburg had probably bought a "Buckeye camera" in Santa Fe in December 1895. The easy-to-use box camera with rolls of film that could be inserted in daylight had just come onto the market.[1] Like nearly all the cameras sold by Eastman Kodak, this one was expressly intended for amateurs ("you press the button, we do the rest"[2]). Warburg could quickly make use of his camera, which was lightweight and designed for medium-sized pictures, and this came in handy not only when recording dance rituals. However, the art historian was not an accomplished photographer, and his snapshots display numerous technical shortcomings: The pictures were impaired by blurriness, injudicious cropping, superimposed shots, Warburg's own shadow in the frame, and unwanted intrusion of figures standing next to him. However, such a camera of course suited his documentary intentions, for Warburg expressly referred to his photographs as "momentary shots," emphasizing his claim to have authentically recorded the situations he captured.[3]

However, the "Buckeye camera" also to some extent dictated the way it was used, for it had only one circular, and hence unreliable, viewfinder at the top of the camera housing; this meant that Warburg had to hold it at chest or stomach level and could only have an approximate idea of what the result would be when he released the shutter.[4] Furthermore, his face was not concealed by the body of the camera, and in many of the pictures this led to eye contact between Warburg and his models, for example in the portrait of an unknown Hopi girl in Oraibi: a photograph that should really have been considered a complete failure because the lower half was heavily overexposed, but for the impression made by the clearly very self-confident young woman as she regarded the photograph without any trace of suspicion. Through this often-dialogical exchange, the art historian abandoned his distance from the people he observed and so not infrequently violated the required restrictions on such encounters. However, in the pueblos of the American Southwest he also became aware "that nearly all Indians have a superstitious dread of being photographed"; this meant that many of the pictures had had to be taken without preparation, something Warburg used to excuse the technical shortcomings of his photographs: "Hardly any picture is without its faults," he stated in 1897 to his listeners–or rather viewers–at his Berlin slide show on his journey to America, which he himself described as an "illustrated diary."[5]

All in all, Warburg thus compiled a comprehensive photographic record of the life and culture of the Indigenous population of the southwestern United States at the end of the nineteenth century. Not only at the dances in San Ildefonso and Oraibi did he produce some highly remarkable pictures that clearly displayed the people he observed and their actions, clothing, and implements. In order to fulfill the meaning and purpose of his journey, to be able to investigate the emergence of the symbolic/distancing art of the Pueblo communities as reflected above all in the dance rituals, in the movements, costumes, and paraphernalia, Warburg had to assemble an expressive collection of pictorial evidence; he sketched numerous motifs with his pencil, during his stay he purchased a substantial number of thematically relevant photographs from his fellow researchers, such as the missionary Henry R. Voth, who left countless records of the Hopi, but also from George Wharton James, Thomas Varker Keam, and Adam Clark Vroman.[6] However, as a pictorial historian he above all wanted to document his own eyewitness testimony, his immediate presence in a pictorial and symbolic culture that had not yet been entirely destroyed by civilizing influences. Aby Warburg was never to take a single scientifically motivated photograph after leaving the United States.

The Curiosity Shop

Basketwork and a striped blanket, the hide of some animal, a musket, and a plate of photographs decorate the entrance to a flat and simply plastered building made of the typical regional clay tiles known as "adobe." The building can be recognized by two signs above the door–"Old Curiosity Shop" and "Gold's"–as well as the trademark, a picturesquely decrepit wooden cart on the roof, as the trader Jake Gold's curiosity shop. Aby Warburg photographed the place, officially known as Gold's Free Museum and Old Q'rosity Shop, in December 1895 while staying in Santa Fe at the Palace Hotel, which was not far from the address where Gold ran his shop. In Colorado the traveler had begun to purchase regional handicrafts for his rapidly growing study collection, and so it made sense for him to visit the widely known business in San Francisco Street.

He had probably already rummaged through the *bric-à-brac* on display there and perhaps even bought some things, for he had evidently asked the store owner to stand outside the building with another customer or a partner, where Warburg took his portrait: With a peaked cap and cigarette, his legs spread self-confidently, his right hand deep in his pants pocket, Jake Gold is looking into the camera against the glare of the sun, fully aware of his successful business.

Gold had not in fact founded his firm in 1862, as a sign above the entrance boastfully indicates, for in that year this son of Polish Jews, born in New York in 1851, had only just arrived in Santa Fe, where his father was already a trader.[1] But the general store that he had taken over from his brother Aaron, part of it in May 1881 and the rest two years later, specialized in handicrafts and antiques, and Gold's business acumen soon

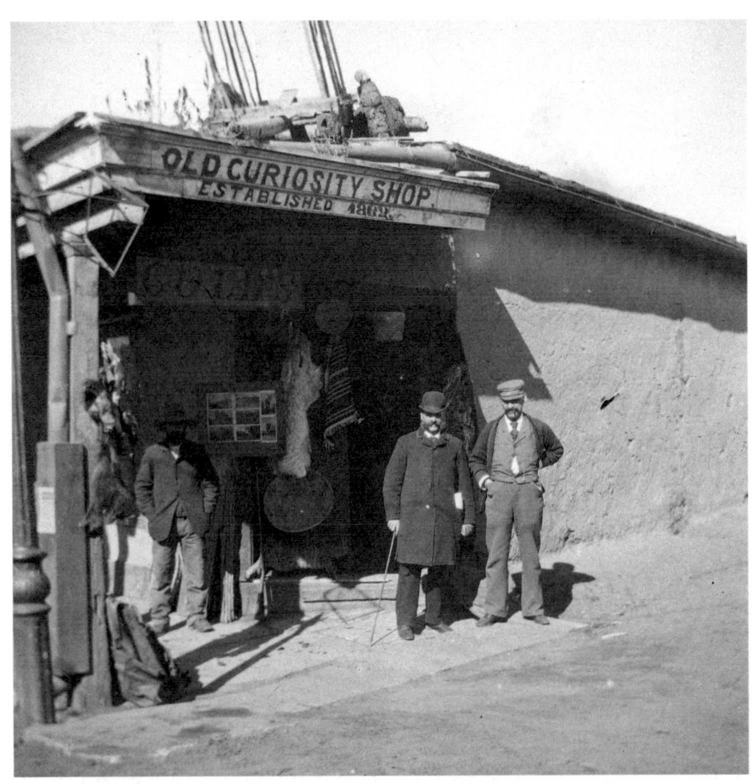

17 Aby Warburg: *Jake Gold and an unidentified man outside of Gold's Free Museum and Old Q'rosity Shop in Santa Fe*, 1895, photograph

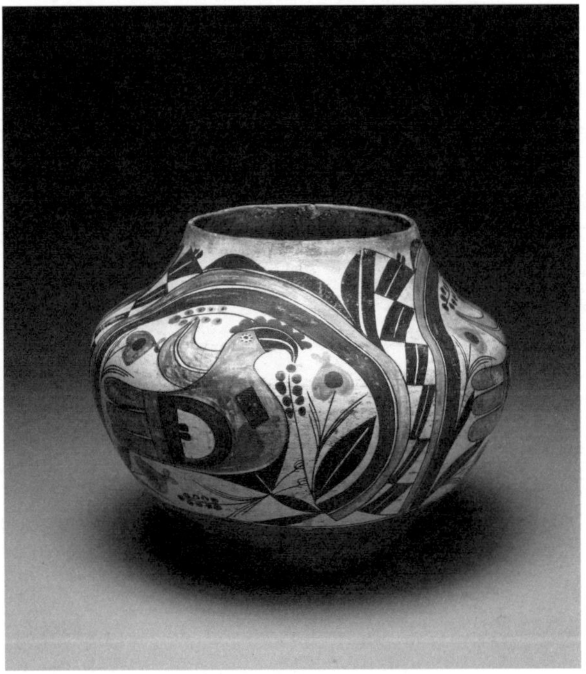

18 *Vessel ("olla")*, ca. 1890, painted clay, 28.5 × 36 cm (purchased by Aby Warburg from Jake Gold)

Established 1862.

Santa Fe, N. M., Dec. 15th 1895

M Dr Phil A. Warburg

In Account with GOLD'S FREE MUSEUM AND OLD Q'ROSITY SHOP.

Wholesale and Retail Dealer in

Indian and Mexican Pottery, Navajo Blankets,

Apache Water Baskets, Cactus Plants and Canes, Stone Vessels from the Cliff Dwellers, Furs, Robes, Rugs, Wax and Feather Work.

Terms JAKE GOLD, Propr. San Francisco Street.

4 large ollas	2.50	10 00	
1 Basket		1 00	
1 Matachino Crown		1 00	
1 Squaw Belt		1 50	
1 Navajo Blanket		10, 00	
1 Moqui Basket		25	
12 photographs		1 15	24.90

Paid Jake Gold

Established 1862.

Santa Fe, N. M., Dec 18 1895

M

In Account with Gold's Free Museum and Old Q'Rosity Shop,

Wholesale and Retail Dealer in

Indian and Mexican Pottery, Navajo Blankets,

Apache Water Baskets, Cactus Plants and Canes, Stone Vessels from the Cliff Dwellers, Furs, Robes, Rugs, Wax and Feather Work.

Terms JAKE GOLD, Prop'r. San Francisco Street.

1 War Bonnett	3 00	
1 Calf Skin	75	
2 Strings Beads	1 00	
1 Pr Moccasins	1 00	$5.75

19 *Receipts from Gold's Free Museum and Old Q'rosity Shop*, Santa Fe, December 15/18, 1895

made it a popular address with explorers. In 1889, one of his catalogues praised Jake Gold himself and his goods in the following terms: "The undersigned has known and been known by the people of New Mexico for 27 years. He is familiar with their country, their customs and their languages. His collectors are all the time gathering curios from the remotest parts of the Territory where the stranger could not penetrate. There is no archeological treasure which does not come to his hands, from relics of the Stone Age to the implements used by the aborigines of to-day. All articles are genuine, and it is well known by New Mexican travelers that each article can be bought more cheaply from him than from the Indians themselves."[2] Yet in 1899 the assiduous businessman, who in general seems to have been economical with the truth, had to relinquish his store; he broke the law several times, did time in jail, and in 1905, after vainly attempting to restart his curiosity shop, died in a mental institution without a penny to his name.

Jake Gold was one of a series of Jewish merchants who in the second half of the nineteenth century helped build up a market for regional handicrafts, especially textiles and ceramics, in the United States. They thus enhanced the romanticizing image of the "Indians," whose artifacts were not only becoming sought-after tourist souvenirs and decorative objects in middle-class homes, but also finding their way into the collections of researchers and the now emerging American museums of ethnology. With licenses from the US government, some of these "Indian" merchants established trading posts in the areas inhabited by Indigenous peoples, where they bartered food and other daily necessities for the artifacts. In Santa Fe, New Mexico's leading transport hub and trade center, there were then a large number of businessmen selling artworks and handicrafts, as well as natural history objects of all kinds, fossils, feathers, or stuffed animals; and quite a few of them were Jewish immigrants from Western and Central Europe.[3] Gold himself successfully presented himself as a connoisseur and preserver of Indigenous traditions, producing sales catalogues, setting up a mail-order business, and extending his trading network far into the Pueblo areas, as reported in the *Weekly New Mexico Review* in 1894: His flourishing business "procured items from hundreds of self-employed agents with pack animals, journeying throughout remote and isolated areas of New Mexico, Arizona, and Colorado, trading German-town tools and brightly colored prints of saints for old blankets and pottery."[4]

Drawn by Gold's reputation and his extensive range of goods, Aby Warburg visited the curiosity shop on San Francisco Street a number of times, and, as two surviving receipts from December 1895 go to show, bought among other things some ceramics by Pueblo artists, as well as baskets and textiles, beads, and a pair of moccasins, a painted calf hide, and a dance prop used in the Rio Grande pueblos in the "Matachines Dance."[5] The colorful abundance of these objects shows that Warburg did not initially proceed very systematically when making his acquisitions. But through purchases from other traders, including Abraham F. Spiegelberg, also from Santa Fe, as well as Thomas Varker Keam and Henry R. Voth, he finally managed to focus his collection on Pueblo ceramics and basketwork, dance paraphernalia, Katsina figures, and prayer sticks (*pahos*). On his return he donated the over a hundred items he had accumulated in the United States to the Hamburg Museum of Ethnology.

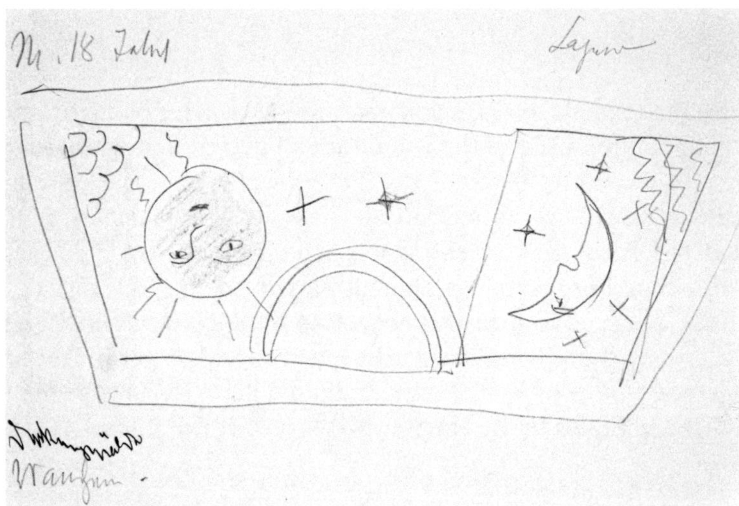

20 Aby Warburg: *Altar heaven at the San José mission church in Laguna*, 1895, pencil, crayon, and ink on paper, 9.6 × 15.6 cm

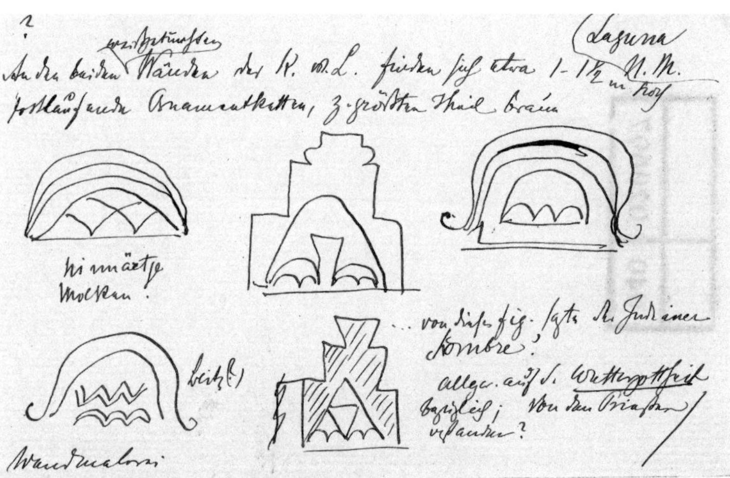

21 Aby Warburg: *Ornaments from the murals at the San José mission church in Laguna,* 1895, pencil on paper, 9.6 × 15.6 cm

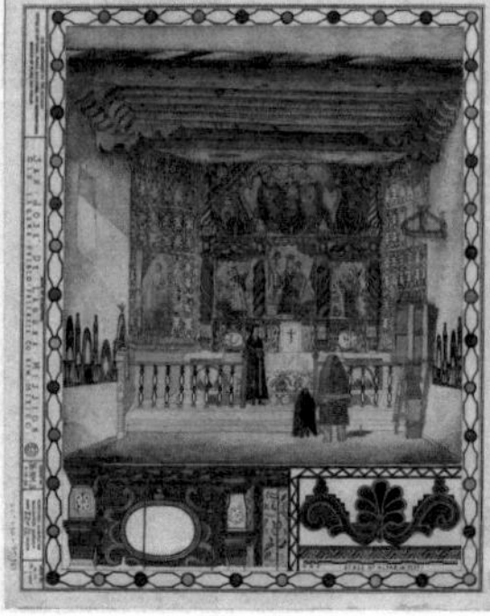

22 W. Howard Speer: *Choir of the San José mission church in Laguna*, 1934, pencil and watercolor on paper, 48.3 × 61 cm, Washington, Library of Congress

The Ornament

After Aby Warburg had arrived in New Mexico from Colorado in 1895, he rapidly began visiting the villages of the various Pueblo communities. He initially traveled to San Juan (now Ohkay Owingeh) and Laguna, some forty-five miles west of Albuquerque in Cibola County, where he viewed the San José Franciscan monastery with its mission church. Founded in 1699 under Padre Antonio Miranda, the buildings were extended several times up to the nineteenth century, and at the time when Warburg stayed in the small village some of them were seriously damaged.[1] He had been particularly impressed by the hybrid decoration of the church, which included New Spanish Baroque paintings and a corresponding high altar from the second half of the eighteenth century, with decorative elements from the local Pueblo culture.

In the church the art historian discovered, above the altar pictures of the Virgin Mary with the baby Jesus and the Holy Trinity, a compositionally related canopy with depictions of the sun, moon, stars, clouds, and rainbows, painted on buffalo hide–which would certainly have fascinated Warburg, had he been aware of it–and he copied this constellation of motifs into his sketchbook. He was evidently interested in this ceiling painting because the Christian iconography of the sun and the moon, which usually appear in the sky at the same time as aspects of the crucifixion, had been extended in the monastery church by the addition of meteorological features which Warburg captured with clumsy strokes, coloring the sun in red, as in the original. On a second sheet he drew a selection of five pictorial elements from the side walls which had struck him because they seemed to consist entirely of native decorations–arcs and zigzag lines–without any Christian content. He conscientiously noted on his sketches: "On both whitewashed walls of the Laguna church are chains of largely brown ornaments that reach to a height of some 1–1½ meters."

While he was there Warburg had the meaning of these ornaments, which had also been painted after the mid-eighteenth century, explained to him by the natives, and concluded that they were not purely decorative, but were "allegorically related to the weather deity" and hence introduced a surprisingly pagan iconography into the church.[2] The compositions he copied, symmetrical assemblies of arcs and steps, including two of the stair ornaments that Warburg was to investigate in even more detail during his journey, accordingly represented meteorological phenomena such as lightning, clouds, or rainbows, depictions of which were used by the Pueblo to summon up weather propitious to their harvests.[3] Fascinated by the simultaneous use of Christian and Indigenous symbols in a Christian building, Warburg wondered in another of his notes "if the Catholic priests did perhaps know the secret meaning of the paintings?"[4] The decorations of the Laguna church therefore provided him with one of those examples of interconnected motifs from different cultures that he would later describe as "products of encounter."[5]

The Steps

Aby Warburg encountered symmetrically stepped jagged ornaments over and over again on his journey through the southwestern United States. They could be seen on ceramics, textiles, and masks, even on the drawings that his informant Cleto Yurina in Santa Fe made for him.[1] The fascinated Hamburg art historian registered this recurring motif and attempted to decipher its iconographic meaning. When he visited the San Esteban del Rey mission church in Acoma in January 1896 he also saw such ornaments on the walls of the single-nave church, which may have been built with older remains in the late seventeenth century, and interpreted it as "a jagged ornament symbolizing steps."[2] He copied some of the ornaments onto the small sheets of a sketchbook, using a pencil to record the varied sequences of the stepped patterns, which later reminded him of rough-hewn timber ladders that he could also see in the villages and was able to photograph at the foot of the First Mesa, "though not the square brick steps, but a much more primitive form, that of steps carved from a tree, which still exists in the pueblos."[3]

In Acoma, Warburg included in one of his sketches the image of one of the small birds that were also painted on the wall there, and made notes in order to document the exact location, the evidently inadequate dating provided by the priest George J. Juillard, and the technical execution in light-colored terracotta.[4] He also mocked the fact that he had not been allowed to visit the church again during the day and was therefore unable to produce a photographic record of the design of the wall because the members of the congregation, as Warburg noted on the drawing with sarcastic quotation marks, "were 'unable to find' the key

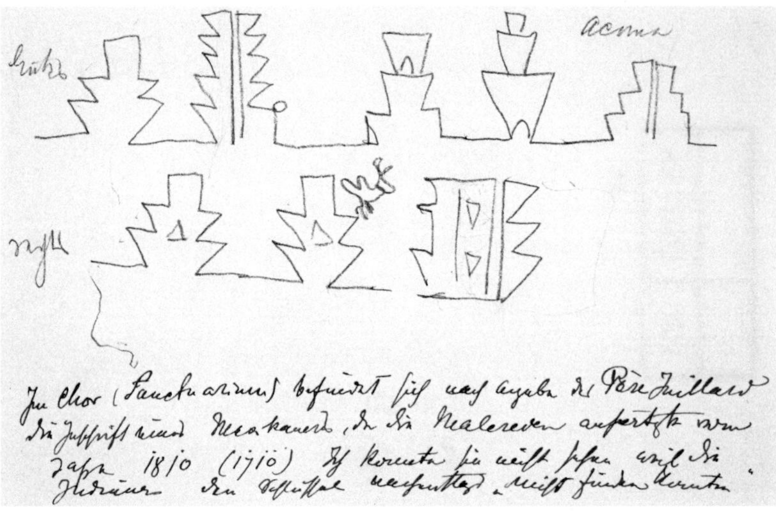

23 Aby Warburg: *Eight stepped ornaments from the murals in the San Esteban de Rey mission church in Acoma*, 1896, pencil and ink on paper, 9.6 × 15.6 cm

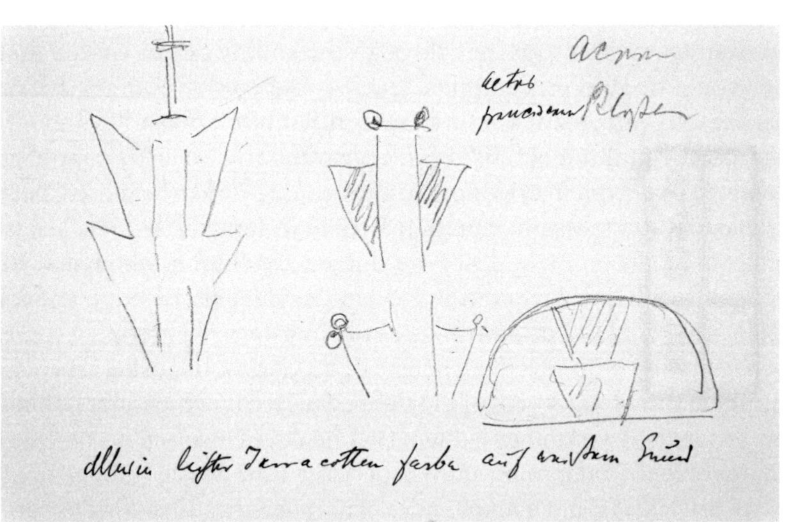

24 Aby Warburg: *Four stepped ornaments from the murals in the San Esteban de Rey mission church in Acoma*, 1896, pencil and ink on paper, 9.6 × 15.6 cm

during the afternoon." In one of his lectures he described this incident in more detail, and attributed it to the Pueblos' fear of cameras: "The photographs from which the glass images I have just presented were produced came from Prof. [George Wharton] James, who had taken them some months before we arrived; I did not know them at the time, and so I got Père Juillard to ask for the key to the church, so that we could study or photograph the ornaments at our leisure. But all of a sudden the key could not be found, and so, owing to the suddenly aroused superstitious fear of photography, we were unable to record these interesting ornaments. As a result, our stay almost ended in a virulent quarrel between Père Juillard and his congregation."[5]

Earlier, with regard to similar wall paintings in Laguna, it had been explained to Warburg that such forms of steps were cosmological/meteorological symbols used by the Pueblo "to depict the earth and heaven in their pagan manner, above all in order to produce rain and thunderstorms."[6] In the ornament he copied as the "roof of the house of the world," which he occasionally also interpreted as a symbol of longed-for rain clouds, he later saw a "pan-American, perhaps global symbol of the cosmos," and from this idea he developed a far-reaching cultural history theory of humanity's wish to transcend attachment to the earth: "For those who want to symbolize the process of becoming, of up and down in nature, the step and the ladder are the primeval experience of humanity. They are the symbol of the conquest of up and down in space, just as the circle–the curly snake–symbolizes the rhythm of time. For primitive people, happiness lay in being able to ascend. Steps are the symbol of walking humans' urge to rise aloft. This is the excelsior of man who seeks to ascend from the earth to heaven–the truly symbolic act that confers on walking humans the nobility of a raised, upward-turned head."[7] Since he had encountered this motif not only in Pueblo objects of worship but specifically in a Franciscan missionary church–and, furthermore, surmounted by a Christian cross–Warburg pondered on the hybrid nature of the symbol "between Catholic ecclesiastical doctrine and paganism."[8]

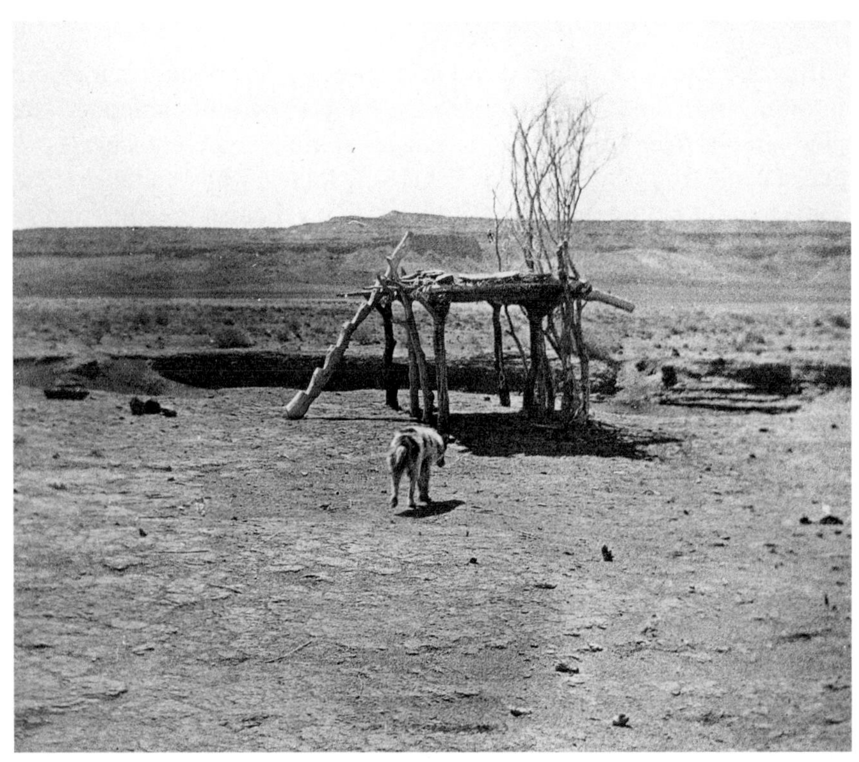

25 Aby Warburg: *Wooden structure for drying corn and other foods*, 1896, photograph

The Forger

Researchers who traveled to the southwestern United States around 1900 were interested in the customs, the art and archeology, and the myths and religions of the Pueblo communities they visited; but the personal identities of the people the ethnologists and anthropologists encountered there mattered little to most of them. In contrast, Aby Warburg's documents also identify some of his Indigenous contacts by name—men with in some cases striking histories who supported the traveler's research in one way or another. In Warburg's papers we thus come across "Nick the interpreter" from Zuni pueblo, who can been identified as the charismatic Nick Dumaka; Victoriano Sisneros from Santa Clara pueblo, who familiarized the art historian with the native nomenclature of the Buffalo Deer Dance; and Loololma, a local Hopi leader whom Warburg met in Oraibi in May 1896, and who often took pro-government positions in his people's political conflicts.[1]

However, among Warburg's indigenous informants, one man from Pueblo de Cochiti was of quite special significance, even though the art historian could probably only have had a slight inkling of his colorful and outright dubious character. Warburg had met him in Santa Fe on January 10, 1896, noting his name as "Cleo Jurino," which has been recorded thus in research on the journey to America.[2] And yet, annoyingly, no biographical details related to him could so far been detected beyond the references in the Hamburg art historian's notes. But new archive findings have now shed some light on this interesting individual, who turns out to have been Cleto Yurina (c. 1847/1848–1901) and has left remarkably clear traces in the documentation of his time.[3] Yurina, whose birth name has come down to us as Shäere'we, owes the Hispanicized form of his name to a distortion of the name of his father Jö'rena, who was known in Spanish as Huero Yurina.[4]

Warburg's encounter with the man from Cochiti, who introduced himself as a priest and guardian of one of the kivas in his native village, seems to have impressed him so much that he made a photographic portrait of Yurina during their meeting.[5] The photograph shows the half-length figure of the man in close-up, with some vehicles and low buildings somewhat further in the background; the man is wearing a shirt and waistcoat, as well as a cloth wrapped around his forehead. Cleto Yurina, who is looking at the photographer with evident sympathy, had accompanied his son Anastacio (1876-1904) to the Palace Hotel, where the researcher was staying while in Santa Fe.[6] The photograph was probably taken there, from a veranda that surrounded the building.[7] On the morning of the same day, Warburg had first met the son at the home of the former governor of New Mexico, LeBaron Bradford Prince, and had then had the meaning of some ceramic objects explained to him by the young Pueblo during their joint visit to Abraham F. Spiegelberg's antique store.[8] Anastacio Yurina must have had good contacts with passing researchers, for around this time a bust portrait of him based on casts of the model was commissioned by the anthropologist Frederick Starr, probably for anthropometric purposes.[9]

At the hotel ("in my room 59") that afternoon, Yurina senior and junior then gave the art historian "valuable explanations of Indian customs," as we can read in a draft of the 1897 lecture *A Journey Through the Region of the Pueblo Indians in New Mexico and Arizona*.[10] The two men, who were members of the Water Clan in Cochiti, spent at least two days in Warburg's presence drawing some illustrations with cosmological/religious motifs from the kiva of their religious community, the Kwe'rena society, for which Cleto Yurina, as we are told by the art historian, also worked as a painter.[11] These ceremonial spaces were—and are—wholly or partly underground, and mostly only reachable via a ladder; with their altars and murals they are used for various activities, especially the preparation or execution of sacred rituals. In the floor of many kivas is a small hole (*sípàapuni*), which according to Pueblo mythology symbolizes the path that people travel on their way from the underworld to the earthly world. Only initiated (male) members of the religious society were– and are– allowed to enter such a kiva. Yurina, who claimed to be a priest, was thus not only, as he told Warburg, the "guardian of the keys" of his kiva, but also the keeper of secret religious knowledge, which after initial hesitation he eventually passed on to the art historian.[12] These depictions gave Warburg deep insights into the Pueblo's cosmological worldview, which guided him in his further research in the American Southwest.

From his new acquaintance, who also worked as a healer, Warburg acquired for his growing collection a medicinally magical "stroking stone," and, as he proudly noted in his travel diary, "even his main fetish," a small carved stone figure which he said represented a bear.[13] This artifact, which Cleto Yurina in all probability presented to him as an archeological find, is indeed a very unusual object, but not in the way that Warburg had hoped it would be; for Yurina, described in contemporary sources as an erratic character, a liar, a drunkard, and a gambler who was constantly in financial difficulties, was notorious in Cochiti for making such objects himself and selling them to Euro-American collectors as pre-Columbian fetishes, which some Pueblo saw as "the greatest joke ever played by an Indian on the Americans."[14] Together with his wife Reyes Archibeque (c. 1850–1897), whom he had married in 1874, and possibly supported by his son, in the mountains north of his village, Yurina used simple tools to secretly carve the highly abstract figures out of gypsum, sandstone, tuff or other kinds of stone that were easy to work, painted some of them, and claimed to have excavated these alleged relics of magical practices from the ruins of the Pajarito plateau or other sites in the area around Cochiti.

It was no accident that Warburg encountered the faker's son in Governor Prince's home, for the politician was also chairman of the Santa Fe-based Historical Society of New Mexico and an honorary member of the American Numismatic and Archeological Society.[15] Driven by his interest in antiques, Prince and his wife Mary C. Beardsley, who was also a member of the Historical Society and produced some scientific studies, brought together an extensive collection of Pueblo artifacts, including an unknown but apparently vast number of "fetishes" from Yurina's workshop.[16] And such highly valued items were also acquired for the Historical Society, and published as early as 1896 together with a scientific treatise on their history, origins, design, and iconography ("No other public institution in this country or Europe possesses even one").[17] However, Prince and his wife could have suspected that these works were not (or only exceptionally) authentic religious objects, for according to a letter dated March 5, 1886, from the collector to her husband the trader Jake Gold had his doubts as to the authenticity of the items offered by Yurina ("all the things brought were new ones") and probably instigated the Cochiti village council to sentence him to fifty lashes after the faker had illicitly sold the governor a sculpture of a lion or a bear.[18]

By the late nineteenth century such trickery was also becoming notorious in scientific circles, and around 1916 Prince eventually saw no other option but to pack away his vast collection, which he had acquired piece by piece from Yurina, and sink the items owned by the Historical Society in the well at the Palace of the Governors in Santa Fe; according to a

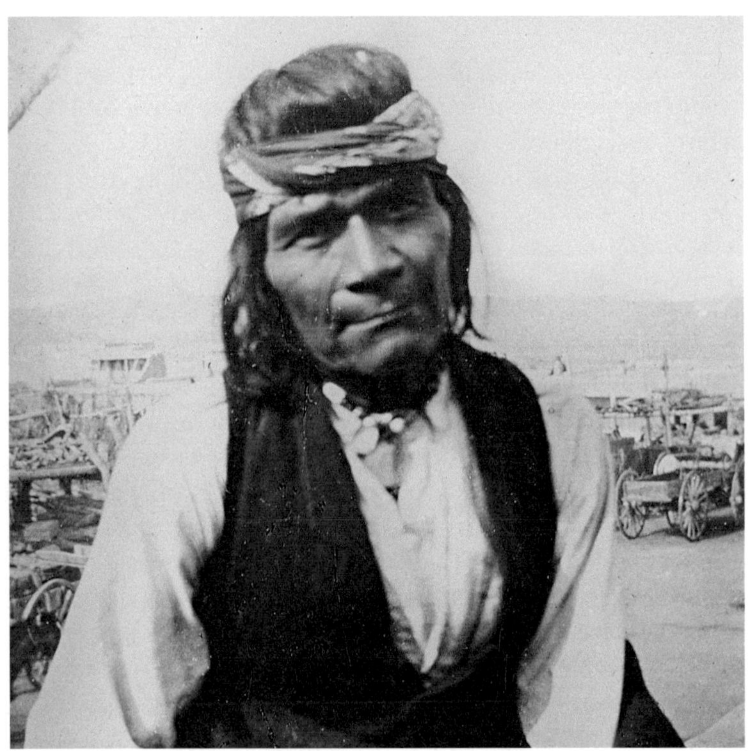

26 Aby Warburg: *Portrait of Cleto Yurina*, 1896, photograph

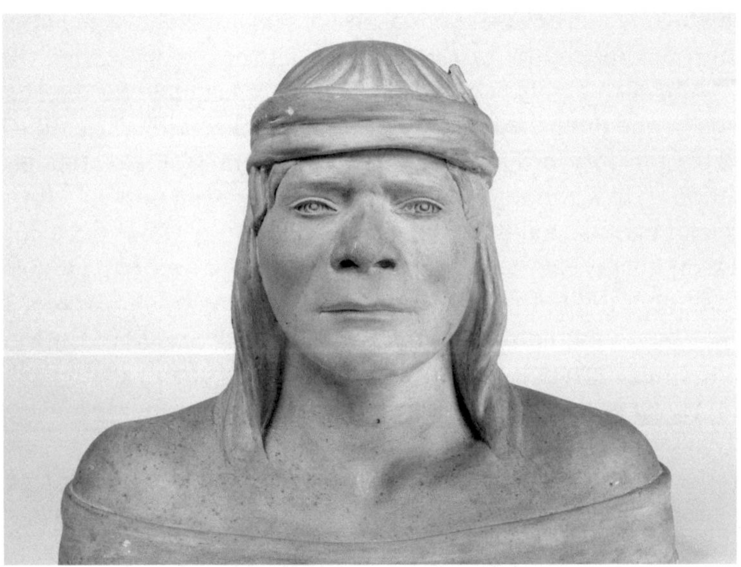

27 Unknown artist: *Bust of Anastacio Yurina*, ca. 1896, plaster, colored, 38 × 47 × 23 cm, Leiden, Nationaal Museum van Wereldculturen

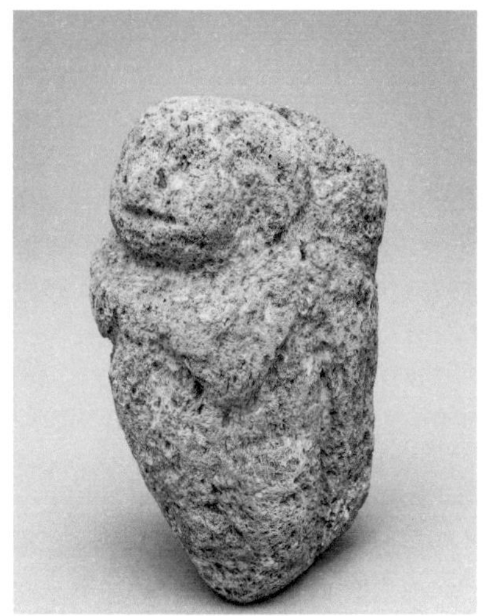

28 Cleto Yurina (attributed): *Fetish figure in the form of a bear,* ca. 1885–1895, stone, 18 × 11.5 × 9 cm

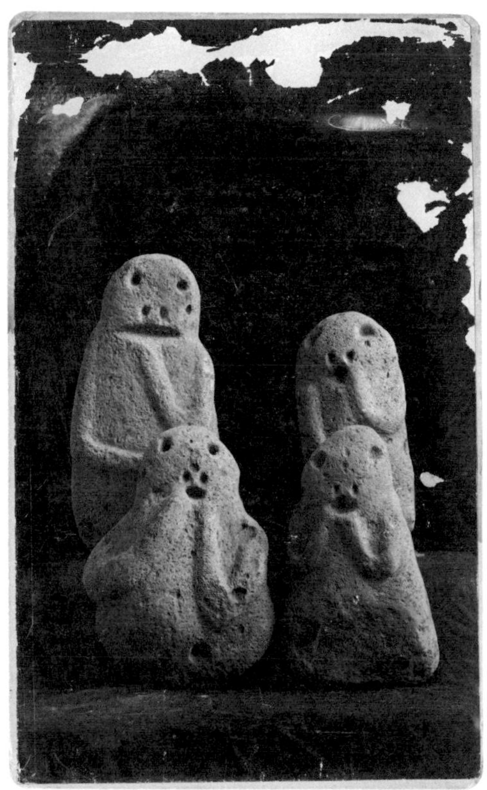

29 Unknown photographer: *Fake figures made by a Cochiti Indian for sale*, around 1900, picture card of the Atchison, Topeka and Santa Fe Railway Company, 21.6 × 14 cm, Santa Fe, New Mexico History Museum

local legend they are still there, awaiting their actual "excavation."[19] Yet not only the governor of New Mexico, but also other over-eager private collectors and even some American museums in such places as Milwaukee, Brooklyn, and Washington DC, acquired stone sculptures from the man from Cochiti that would eventually be exposed as fakes; in the 1930s the Smithsonian Institution went so far to actually destroy all but three items of these artifacts in its collection.[20]

Although the "main fetish" so gullibly acquired by Warburg, with its archaic form that only hints at the animal body, differs considerably in appearance from the published figures now proven to be fakes, the small sculpture was also judged a forgery by the Tribal Council of Pueblo de Cochiti.[21] Yurina probably had some originals as models for his free imitations, but it is most unlikely that he sold one of these works to a traveler who then had scant knowledge of pre-Columbian archeology and would only be spending a short time in the region. So it cannot be ruled out that Warburg's otherwise incomprehensible comment that the kiva guardian from Cochiti was a "false man of honor" can be explained by the art historian's suspicion that there had been something amiss about his encounter with Cleto Yurina: "Unfortunately he is a *faux bon homme*."[22]

The Worldview

When Cleto Yurina and his son Anastacio visited the traveler in his hotel room in Santa Fe in January 1896, the two men from Cochiti Pueblo were reluctant to divulge the religious knowledge of their community. And yet ("after some hesitation") they produced in Aby Warburg's presence a series of drawings and helped him capture their depictions in conceptual detail.[1] Unlike the many illustrations in the scientific literature on Pueblo art and religion that had been published ever since the late nineteenth century, these works were authentic testimony in which the voices of the Indigenous initiators can still be clearly heard to this day. As in this case, the esoteric knowledge of the Pueblo communities was often communicated outside the villages, for this allowed the informants to evade social control by their fraternities. False or at least misleading information was also occasionally provided; but the authenticity of Anastacio and Cleto Yurina's drawings and explanations has been largely verified by contemporary research.[2]

On one of the sheets the two men explained their notion of the "world house" as symbolized in the Cochiti kiva (Spanish *estufa*), which was inaccessible to non-Indigenous visitors.[3] Anastacio Yurina had commenced the colorful drawing, which was then, as noted on the sheet, completed by his father and shows the "arrangement of the Yaya fetishes before the *estufa* mural." The ceremonial access to this area of the shrine is also indicated in the caption: "The blue line is the path the priests walk to the painting in the *estufa*." This path, probably made of scattered cornflour, is also shown in a second picture that directs the viewer's gaze to the ground in front of the mural of the Yaya ("mother") figures.[4] Cleto Yurina, according to Warburg also responsible as a member of a local priestly fraternity for the painting in one of the kivas in Cochiti, here shows a system of concentric semicircles, including the sun and the moon as heavenly bodies, and in front of them four small ovals to which the long vertical line of the path leads. These, as Warburg also recorded in writing, were the footprints of Masewa and Oyoyewa, the sons of the sun (regarded as male), a mythical pair of twins referred to in numerous Pueblo legends.[5]

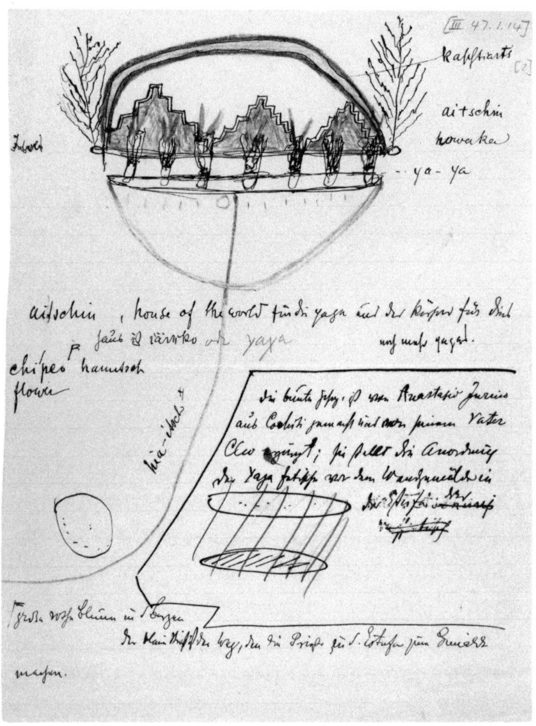

30 Anastacio Yurina and Cleto Yurina (with commentary by Aby Warburg): *The arrangement of the "Yaya fetishes" in front of the mural in a kiva in Cochiti pueblo*, 1896, crayon and ink on paper, 25.5 × 19.4 cm

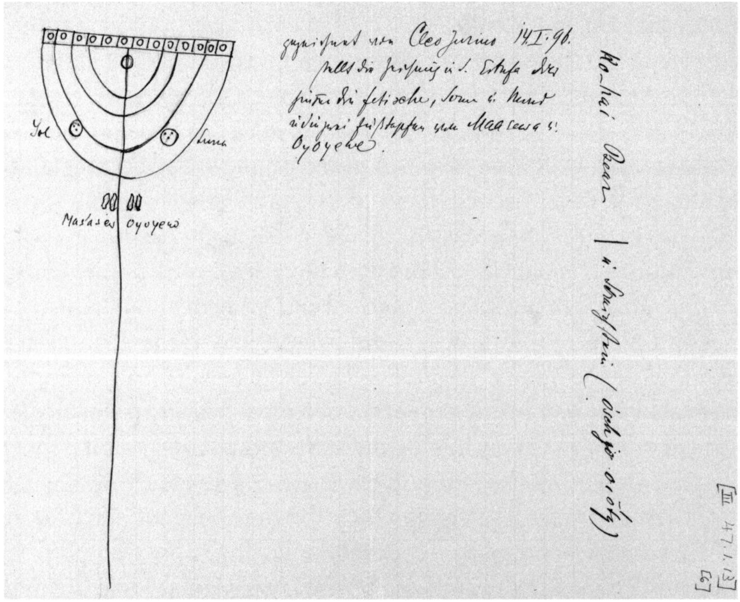

31 Cleto Yurina (with commentary by Aby Warburg): *Floor of a kiva in Cochiti pueblo*, 1896, pencil and ink on paper, 20.2 × 25.5 cm

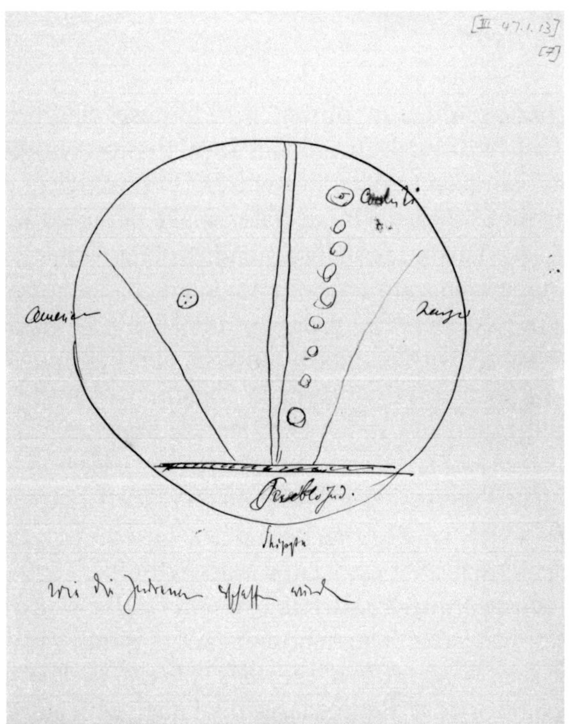

32 Aby Warburg (on the basis of information provided by Anastacio Yurina and Cleto Yurina): *Diagram of the creation myth ("How the Indians were created")*, 1896, ink on paper, 20.2 × 25.5 cm

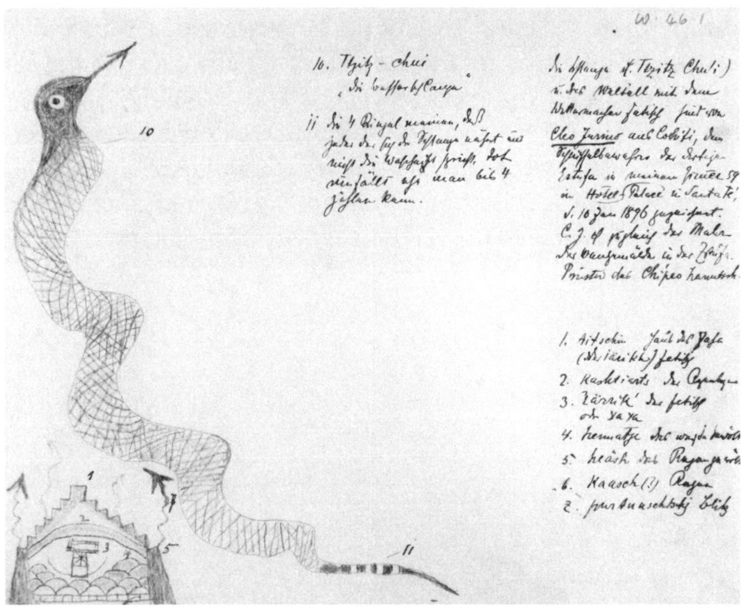

33 Cleto Yurina (with commentary by Aby Warburg): *The snake as a weather deity and the world house*, 1896, pencil, crayon, and ink on paper, 20 × 25.1 cm

The stepped architecture of the "world house" had fascinated Warburg at least since his visit to the San José mission church in Laguna, and this motif can also be seen in the third cosmological drawing that was made for him.[6] Below a large water snake depicted with an arrow-like tongue, Cleto Yurina, actually a member of the Water Clan and identified in the paper's margin notes as belonging to the unverifiable clan (*hanutsh* in the East Keres language) of the "Chi'peo," is designing the "house of the Yaya," with clouds, a rainbow, and lightning. He dictated to Warburg the terms used for these in Cochiti, which the art historian recorded in a detailed key. In his 1923 lecture *Bilder aus dem Gebiet der Pueblo-Indianer in Nord-Amerika* (Images from the Region of the Pueblo Indians of North America) Warburg used this sheet to explain the mythological figures of the "snake as weather deity," which "in its lightning-like form is magically/causally associated with lightning," and described in detail the structure drawn by Yurina: "The roof of the world house is supported by a stepped gable. The rainbow spans the wall, and small streaks of rain can be seen flowing out of the dense clouds. In the middle–as the real ruler of the storm/world house–is the fetish, which does not bear a snake figure, Yaya or Yerrik."[7]

In the absence of the spoken commentary, which Warburg only recorded in brief notes, many of the cosmological scenes outlined in the drawings are hard to interpret. This is also true of his drawing of the creation myth ("How the Indians were created"), in which–very probably on the basis of information provided by Cleto and Anastacio Yurina–an inscription on the lower edge of the circular shape ("Shipapu") only states that the ancestors of the Cochiti originally came to the earthly world via the access known as *sípàapuni* (older spelling: *sipapu*), symbolized in the kivas by a lockable opening in the floor.[8] Yet in view of the fact that the Pueblo were–and are–very reluctant to divulge anything of their religious beliefs, it is astonishing that the two informants entrusted their secret knowledge to the visitor from Germany and even let him see the kiva shrine.[9]

The Dancer

On January 10, 1896, Anastacio Yurina drew the dance mask and the dancer in a secret ritual ("secret corndance outdoors below trees hidden from the Mexicans") and gave the sheet to Aby Warburg. Despite their sometimes clumsy execution, the two motifs, drawn in ink with highlighted colors, are very expressive. The attached key ("Shi-wa-na") allows the depicted figure to be clearly identified as a Katsina (*Shíwana* in Keres language) with accompanying weather symbols.[1] The feather-trimmed mask on the upper edge of the sheet displays geometrical painting, with yellowish, black, blue, and reddish-brown patches of color dividing the cylindrically constructed head; and the cosmological/meteorological symbol of steps can again be seen here. The dancer's headdress–a leather mask ("Ķá'ponaía")–has the same shape, but details of its painting cannot be detected in the dark shading. The figure is wearing a short, blue outer garment and holding a barely identifiable gourd in its right and a pine branch in its left hand, and hanging from its leg–though this is also hard to distinguish in the dense web of lines–is a rattle made of tortoise shell and the hooves of smaller animals.[2]

We do not know exactly how Yurina explained his drawing to the art historian, but in the reports by the French missionary Noël Dumarest, who had been working in the Catholic community of Cochiti since 1894, we have reliable testimony on how the Pueblo saw these and other masks: "The *shiwanna* are gods who give rain, health, and life, in short everything that makes for the welfare of man. It is mostly in their visits to the pueblos that they bring an abundance of benefits ... The men all know that the *shiwanna* do not come from *wenima* [heaven] since all have danced in the *Katsina* [dance mask]. But they think that in putting on the sacred mask on their head they take on the holy personality. They think the spirits of the *shiwanna* are within these masks and thus they visit the pueblos."[3]

The *Shiwana* dances were organized at the request of village elders, who approached the priests (*nahia*) with gifts. If the priests consented, young men were selected as dancers in the various kinds of masks. First they had to spend a few days fasting and learning the sacred songs in the kiva or some other undisturbed place; but the embodiments of the rain god, who only communicated in pantomime, remained mute during the ritual. The dances, which continued until sunset, were concealed from outsiders and, exactly as noted by Warburg, were performed in hidden places; the inhabitants of Cochiti Pueblo performed them under an avenue of trees located a long way outside the village on a piece of land belonging to the priests near the Rio Grande.[4] The impressive power of the masked dancers ("I am making the thunder, I am sending down the rain") is clearly displayed in Anastacio Yurina's drawing.[5]

34 Anastacio Yurina (with commentary by Aby Warburg): *Dance mask and dancer*, 1896, crayon, pencil, and ink on paper, 25.3 × 20 cm

35 Aby Warburg: *Zia creation myth*, 1895–1896, pencil and ink on paper, 26 × 12.3 cm

The Myth

During his stay in America, Aby Warburg read, besides other ethnological and cultural history works, Matilda Coxe Stevenson's fundamental treatise on the Zia (Ts'íiy'am'é) people, a small Pueblo community that speaks East Keres and is famed for its often colorful pottery.[1] The members of this people reside in Zia Pueblo, which in the seventeenth century was one of the biggest Pueblo villages, located some thirty-five miles north of the city of Albuquerque, whose flag, like that of New Mexico, is decorated with the cruciform sun symbol of the Zia. Through this study Warburg got to know the local creation myth, which evidently fascinated him so much that he attempted–perhaps as early as the fall of 1895, but in any case by January 1896, when he asked Cleto and Anastacio Yurina for cosmological information–to present the multilayered stories in a chart.

Stevenson's research revealed the following legend. In the beginning the spider woman Sûs'sĭstinnako's singing created all life, starting with the two women Ût'sĕt (the mother of all the Indigenous peoples of America) and Now'ûtsĕt (the mother of all other peoples).[2] When the spider had almost completed her creation, she wanted to create rain, and produced the cloud, lightning, thunder, and rainbow creatures, for which in the four realms of the world as well as the zenith and the nadir six springs burst forth on high mountains with huge trees growing on their peaks. The world was divided into the earth (Ha'arts) as well as–invisible to humans–the middle kingdom (Ti'nia) and the upper kingdom (Hu'waka). Ût'sĕt and Now'ûtsĕt brought light to people by placing the sun in the sky by day and the moon at night. In the middle kingdom they created Ko'shairi (the mediator between people and the sun) and Quer'-ränna (the mediator between people and the moon) as well as the Ka'-tsuna (creatures with human bodies and monstrous heads, embodied by the masked dancers). After long, eventful, and turbulent years the twins Ma'asewe (Masewa) and U'yunyewě (Oyoyewa), sired by their father the sun to help people, were eventually born; they also instated the six warriors in the mountains of the world to watch over the earth.[3]

Warburg set out the protagonists in this highly complex creation tale in a chart that starts with the symbol of the spider Sûs'sĭstinnako ("a body like crystal"), with the layers of the world continuing all the way down to the earth.[4] Finally he included the names of the sacred objects that mediate between the earth and the creatures of the higher spheres ("fetishes," "Yaya," and "Hä'chamoni"), and outlined people's ritual access to the higher beings through religious practice ("heroes / animal gods - fetish sacrifices - dance").[5] Here we can already detect his ideas of seeing sacrificial gifts and dance rituals as a "sublimated, spiritualized form" of archaic animal and human sacrifices, cultural phenomena whose origins Warburg could also study with reference to the mythical tales of the Zia.[6]

The Altar

Aby Warburg had probably already come across the study of the Zia people, published by the ethnologist Matilda Coxe Stevenson only in 1894, while he worked on Pueblo culture at the Smithsonian Institution in Washington.[1] The co-founder of the Women's Anthropological Society of America was the scientist commissioned by the Bureau of Ethnology to do field research in the region of the Pueblo communities. Following numerous stays and years of empirical investigations on the spot she was particularly famous for her studies on the Zuni, as well as other peoples. We do not know if Warburg had read her publication *The Sia* when he arrived in New Mexico in December 1895. However, he did have an illustration that he had copied at some point from the *Eleventh Annual Report of the Bureau of Ethnology*, in which the treatise had appeared.[2] Like Stevenson's published original, his sheet also shows an altar of the Knife fraternity from Zia Pueblo, which Warburg had reproduced precisely in pencil and had then partially colored: In a wooden structure decorated with dragonflies and another insect we can see some carved and painted representations, partly in the form of snakes, partly with jagged bodies and headdresses.

During his conversations with Cleto Yurina in Santa Fe in January 1896, Warburg showed him the drawing and evidently asked him to identify the figures for him and give them their correct names. Yet, as he noted on the sheet, altars of this kind were "not customary" in Cochiti, and so the alleged local kiva guard could only give a few clues as to the meaning of the illustration ("Cleo Jurino only knew the gods of the cardinal points"). Although Stevenson's study described the ritual acts performed before

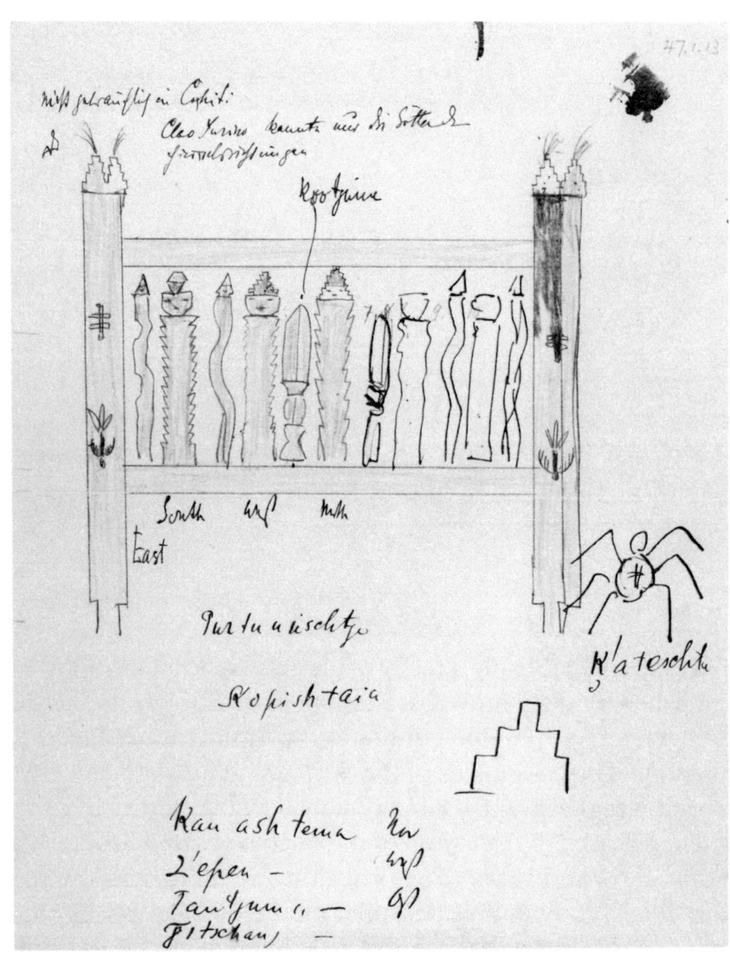

36 Aby Warburg (with explanations by Cleto Yurina): *Altar of the Knife fraternity in Zia Pueblo*, 1895–1896, pencil, crayon, and ink on paper, 20.2 × 25.5 cm

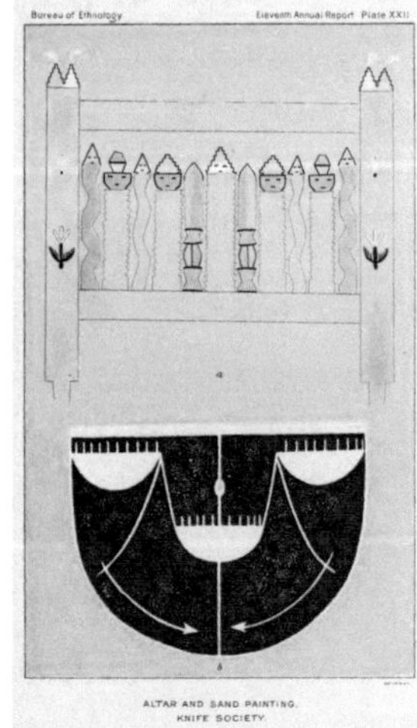

37 Anonymous artist: *Altar of the Knife fraternity in Zia Pueblo*, from Matilda Coxe Stevenson: *The Sia*, in *Eleventh Annual Report of the Bureau of Ethnology to the Secretary of the Smithsonian Institution, 1889-1890*, Washington DC 1894

the altar in every conceivable detail, she did not explain to her readers the design of the altar, which must have interested Warburg, given the snake and stepped figures shown here. On the site of the altar, with in front of it a sand painting and all manner of sacred objects, such as the "Yaya fetishes," the initiated members of the fraternity, in a complex ceremony lasting several hours, called upon the "cloud people of the north, west, south, east, and all the cloud people of the world" to "gather and send rain to water the earth."[3] The animal spirits allocated to the four realms of the world, whose name Warburg likewise recorded on the sheet ("Kopish-taia"), were also asked for assistance during the ritual.[4] Although Yurina was able to name the "gods of the cardinal points" inserted into the figurative decoration of the carving, other features of the sheet–the name of the "lightning creature" (*pûr'-tu-wish-ta*) from the rain songs of the Snake fraternity, or the spider with the cruciform sun symbol of the Zia, drawn with parallel double lines–remain a mystery as far as the viewer of the illustration of the altar is concerned.[5]

[III.47.1.1]

UNITED STATES INDIAN SERVICE,

Pueblo & Jicarilla Agency,

Santa Fe, N.M. Jany. 22, 1896.

The Governor of San Ildefonso Pueblo, N.M.

Dear Sir:-

The bearer of this is Dr. Warburg who wishes to witness the dance tomorrow and possibly may remain a day or two as he is engaged in the study of the language and customs of the Pueblo Indians. Will you kindly see that he obtains the assistance of Donaciano Pino son of Juan Jose Pino, who I understand speaks English as he will need an Interpreter.

Respectfully

John L. Bullis,

Capt. 24th Infy. Actg. Indian Agent.

38 John L. Bullis: *Letter of recommendation to Alfonso Vigil, governor of San Ildefonso Pueblo*, January 22, 1896

The Letter

Within a few days of arriving in New Mexico, Aby Warburg began studying the dance rituals, which he hoped would enlighten him about symbolism in the Pueblo communities, which, as he believed, were still largely untouched by civilization. In January 1896 he saw the first such events in Acoma Pueblo and Pueblo de Cochiti, and then decided to also visit the dances in San Ildefonso Pueblo, a settlement some twenty-five miles northwest of Santa Fe in the Rio Grande valley. Inhabited by members of the Tewa language group, the village rich in tradition had been exposed to–at first fairly unsuccessful–Christian missionary efforts ever since the seventeenth century, until a blend of local and Roman Catholic rites emerged in the nineteenth century. To this day the traditional Buffalo Deer Dance is performed in San Ildefonso Pueblo each year on January 23, the feast of St Ildefonsus of Toledo, a dance which particularly interested the art historian because he wanted to compare the various representational forms during his journey.[1]

As Warburg was evidently not sure if he would be allowed to view the performances first hand and perhaps also wanted to use his stay in the village for some days of study, he looked up John L. Bullis in Santa Fe, from where he initially organized his trips, and asked him for a letter of recommendation to the governor of San Ildefonso Pueblo. Captain Bullis, a US army veteran who had fought in, among other things, the American Civil War and the "Indian Wars" and from 1893 to 1897 had been the Indian Agent for the Pueblo and Jicarilla Apaches, complied with his request and drew up a letter to the governor, Alfonso Vigil (who was not specifically named in it). Bullis also requested that Donaciano

Pino, a local resident who spoke English, serve as the young scholar's interpreter. One day later, on the saint's feast day, Warburg did indeed see the dances in San Ildefonso Pueblo, in illustrious company that included the former governor of New Mexico LeBaron Bradford Prince and the Indian Agent's wife Josephine Bullis.[2]

While he was there, "after a long palaver with the chief and with reference to the Indian Agent's letter of recommendation," Warburg was granted permission to take photographs during the ritual.[3] His recollection of these negotiations, which he recorded in 1897 on the occasion of his first lectures on his trip to America, makes very clear that the Pueblo were by then already trying at least to control media access to their religious ceremonies; and from the early twentieth century onward this would lead to increasing restrictions and eventually an outright ban on photography for some of the ceremonies.[4] In his lectures, Warburg focused on the specific features of the ritual as compared with other masked dances that he had previous seen: According to his summary of his observations, the performers were attempting "somehow to bewitch the animal world and make it a intercessor with the weather deities, not through symbolic adornments and actions, but through traditional imitation of deer and antelopes."[5]

The Transformation

By the late nineteenth century, performances of local dance rituals in the various Pueblo communities of the southwestern United States had become tourist attractions. And on January 23, 1896, when the annual Buffalo Deer Dance took place in San Ildefonso Pueblo (now called P'ohwhóge Owingeh), "a large delegation of sight-seers" came to the small village from nearby Santa Fe, as one of the regional daily newspapers reported.[1] Among these visitors was Aby Warburg, who had joined a tour group of society ladies and some local dignitaries ("enjoying the trip and the Indian dances very much").[2] Yet the art historian, armed with his letter of recommendation to the governor of the village, did not want to treat the ritual as a mere spectacle. Instead, as he stated to the *Santa Fé Daily New Mexican*, he had come to New Mexico to study "rustic life as seen in the homes of the Pueblo Indians," to collect "pottery, blankets and other Indian products," and to study the "origin and significance of the Indian dances."[3]

For this reason Warburg had determined to document the dances with his camera; but he would not be the only one to do so. Indeed, by 1900 the influx of picture-hungry visitors during the various rituals, in San Ildefonso and elsewhere, could hardly be controlled; and it eventually led to a complete ban on photography in some villages.[4] And from a scientific standpoint this development was also highly questionable–for, as the photographer and journalist George Wharton James had already observed, the dancers were changing their traditional choreographies in response to the presence of cameras, and even found themselves compelled to conceal some of their ritual acts from the curious eyes of the

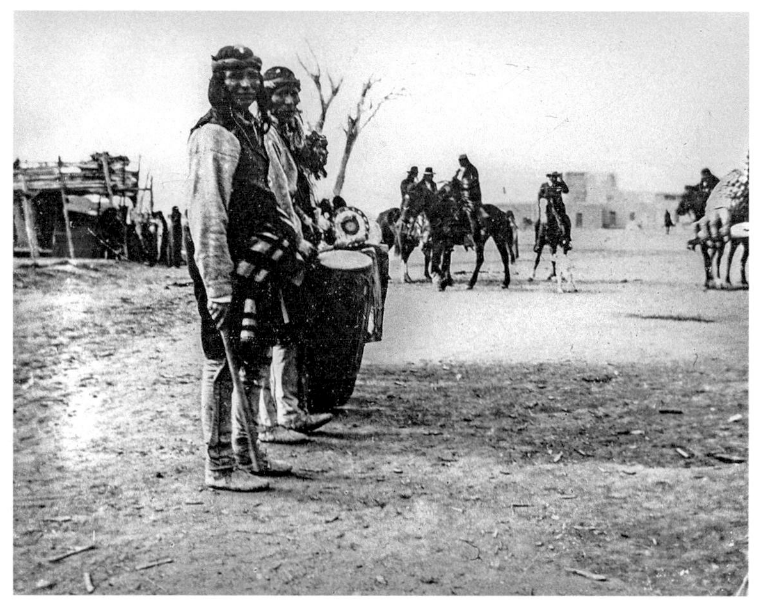

39 Aby Warburg: *Governor Alfonso Vigil and other Tewas with drums*, 1896, photograph

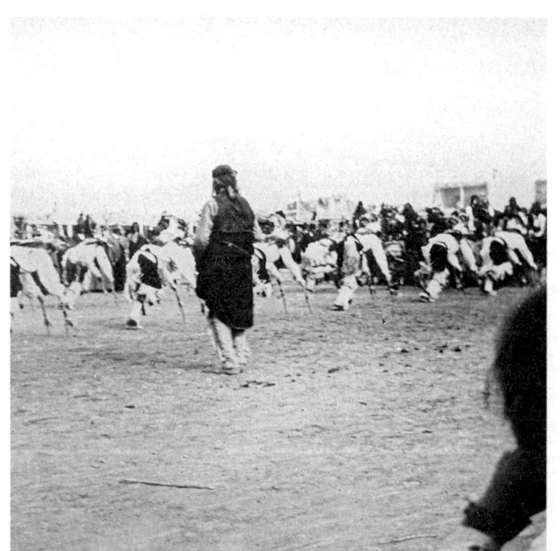

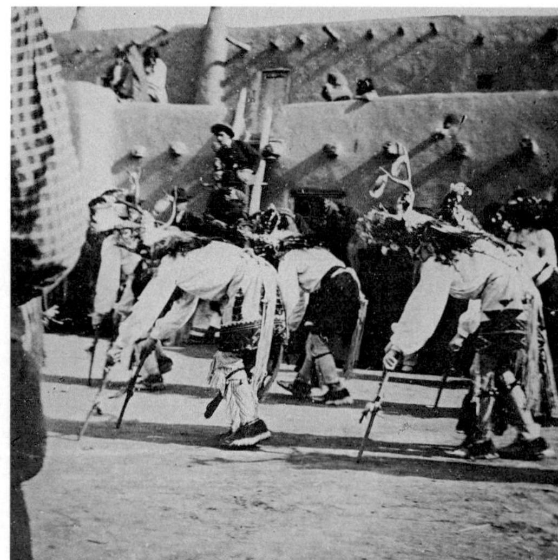

40-43 Aby Warburg: *The Buffalo Deer Dance in San Ildefonso Pueblo*, 1896, photographs

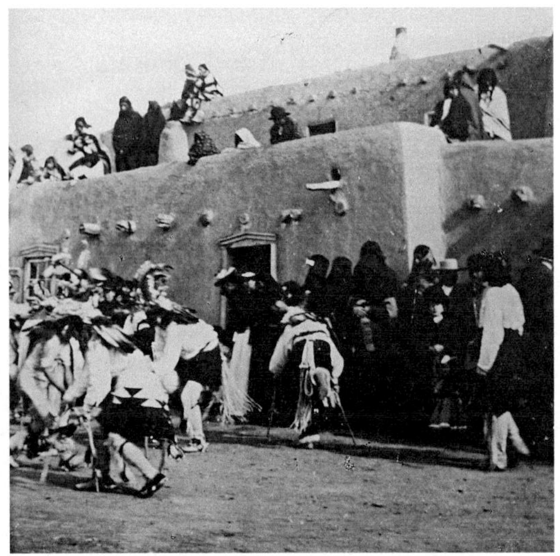

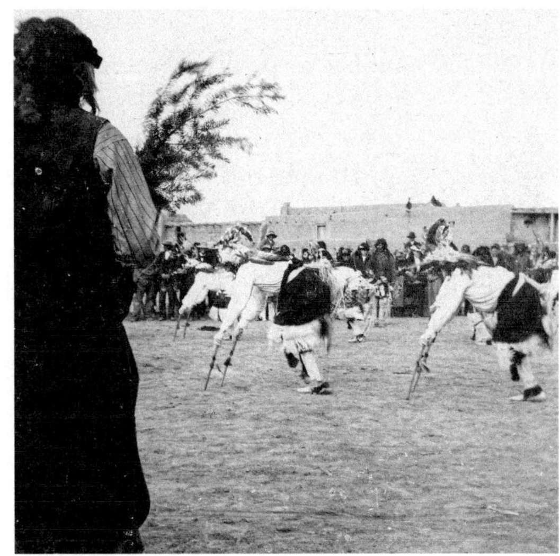

40-43 Aby Warburg: *The Buffalo Deer Dance in San Ildefonso Pueblo*, 1896, photographs

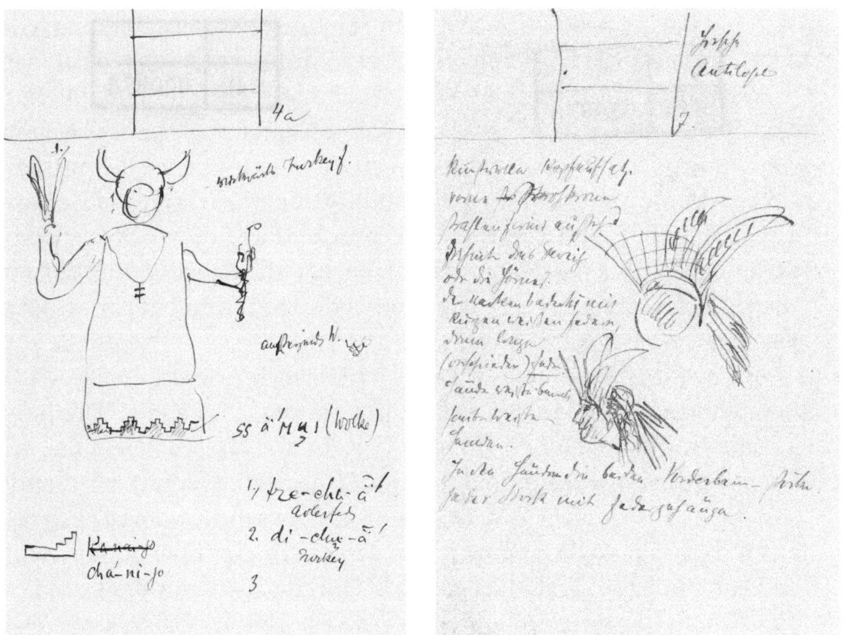

44-45 Aby Warburg: *Notes on the Buffalo Deer Dance in San Ildefonso Pueblo*, 1896, sheets 4a and 7, manuscript with drawings, ink on paper, each 16 × 10.6 cm

public: "... it will be not long before one can write a learned and accurate paper from the standpoint of scientific ethnology on 'the change in religious ceremonies owing to the camera.'"[5]

Nonetheless, the Indian Agent John L. Bullis's letter of recommendation enabled Warburg, despite initial hesitation by the village leader, to bring his camera as close as possible to the event, the "mysterious mimetic transformation."[6] In a series of shots he recorded the performers, the deer and buffalo dancers with their characteristic movements, but also the onlookers that had gathered in front of the buildings or even on the roofs of the village.[7]

While the dance was still going on (or immediately afterwards) Warburg began hastily writing down in barely legible script what he had seen on the village square. He soberly outlined the nature and number of the dancers, their masks and costumes, and the complex choreography of the sequences of steps, and interspersed his notes with small sketches that carefully recorded the details of interest to him. In many places he referred to some of his photographs, which makes clear that he must have continued his work some days later in Santa Fe, as he evidently could already see the prints. On January 27, Warburg added to his notes some more terms from the Tewa language, which he said he had obtained from Victoriano Sisneros, probably the later governor of Santa Clara Pueblo: "Without having seen the festivities in San Ildefonso, he named each item to me ... always after brief reflection and with an earnest wish to help me."[8]

Warburg's notes on the dance ritual that recurred annually on the feast of St. Ildefonsus of Toledo, whose original purpose was to honor animal spirits from the surrounding areas and so influence the prosperity and subsistence of the village community, remained largely descriptive: "The animal dance in San Ildefonso proceeds as follows: A spruce tree is planted towards the center of the [square]; the dancers emerge from a house [Buffalo House] on the eastern side; the 5 or 6 old [inserted: percussionists and singers] have lined up with drums. ... The dance is performed by the two buffaloes with the buffalo girl (?) in the center, 10 deer, 10 antelopes, 2 young deer, the hunter, in total 26 people. The hunter, the buffalo and the buffalo girl walk upright, the rest walk bent like quadrupeds and with two supporting sticks [inserted: feathers on them] in their hands as front feet. The deer and antelopes move behind each other in two parallel rows. Dancing in the center are the three buffalo people, the hunter and the small deer calves."[9] Only occasionally did he indicate that the animals were embodied by "incorporation" (*Hineinverleibung*) or "accorporation" (*Anverleibung*), or consider iconographic details on the dance costumes such as the snake or the "intricate" ornament of the stepped symbols.[10]

Only in the lectures he gave after returning to Germany did Warburg outline a religious-psychological theory of the ritual event he had observed, and recognized in the Buffalo Deer Dance–in contrast to other dances–not a symbolic but a mimetic representation of the animals, which in this way would become "intercessors with the weather deities."[11] In his 1923 Kreuzlingen lecture, Warburg was to retrospectively outline a "psychology of the will for animal metamorphosis" based on such considerations: "For to primitive people the masked dancers mean in the process of interlinkage with the most extra-personal the most far-reaching subordination to an alien demonic creature. When, for example, the Indian in his mimetic masked costume imitates an animal's expressions and movements, he does not penetrate the animal for the fun of it, but by transforming his personality seeks to wrest from nature something he does not trust his unextended and unaltered human personality to do."[12]

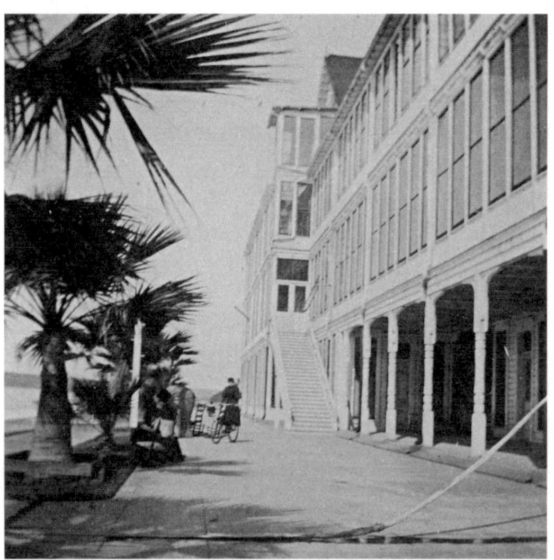

46 Aby Warburg: *View of the southwest facade of the Hotel del Coronado, with the Coronado Beach promenade on the left*, 1896, photograph

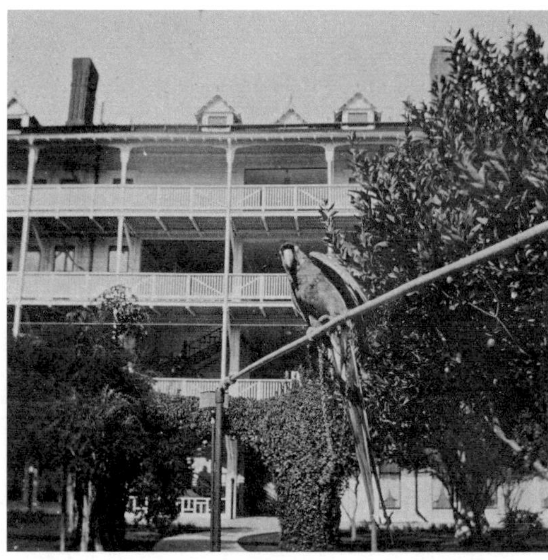

47 Aby Warburg: *Tame parrot in the inner courtyard of the Hotel del Coronado*, 1896, photograph

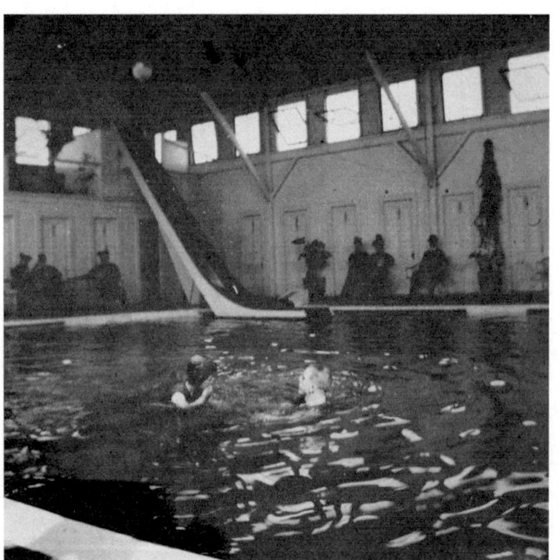

48 Aby Warburg: *Swimming pool in the Hotel del Coronado with water chute*, 1896, photograph

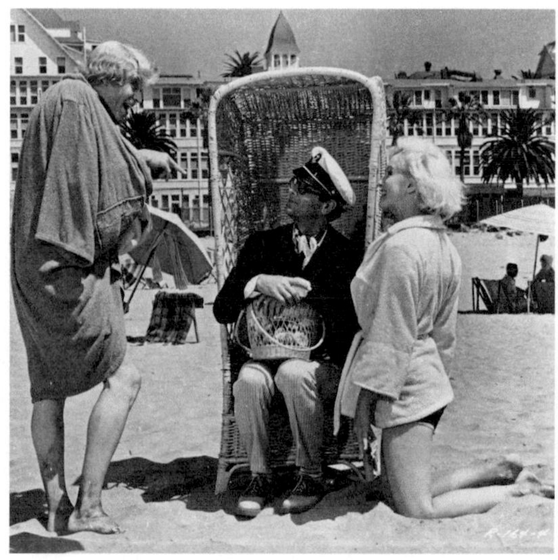

49 Billy Wilder (director): *Some Like It Hot*, 1959, film still (with Jack Lemmon, Tony Curtis, and Marilyn Monroe outside the Hotel del Coronado)

The Hotel

After spending the first weeks of 1896 in New Mexico, not only in Santa Fe but also in such villages as Acoma, Cochiti, Laguna, and San Ildefonso, Aby Warburg decided to go to California for some time, as he was finding his stay in the inhospitable Pueblo region rather exhausting: "I would like to spend fourteen days resting from the very strenuous past two-and-a-half months, especially as I am starting to suffer from dyspepsia because of the abominable hotel food in New Mexico."[1] In February Warburg therefore traveled to Pasadena, where he stayed at Hotel Green, the small town's best hotel.[2] And a few days later he went on to San Diego, where on February 17 he moved into room 127 in the Hotel del Coronado, right next to the Coronado Beach promenade.[3]

Opened in 1888 and already equipped with electric light and every conceivable amenity (including hydraulic elevators, a telephone, and a sprinkler system, as well as an ice machine that could produce fifteen tons a day), the 400-room Hotel del Coronado is to this day California's largest timber structure, consisting of extensively interconnected residential tracts erected around inner courtyards and gardens with countless bow windows, arcades, towers, and turrets.[4] Ballrooms, music rooms, and billiard parlors, as well as a restaurant wing, were in Warburg's time also available to guests in the Victorian-style building. Located on a peninsula that was developed for this very purpose, and divided from the city by San Diego Bay, the complex was surrounded by a separate suburban community with streets and parks, and with traffic and commercial features that were supplied with electricity from the hotel's private power station. Countless illustrious guests resided at the Hotel del Coronado or were honored there with banquets: American presidents from Franklin D. Roosevelt to Richard Nixon, and celebrities such as Charles Lindbergh, Douglas Fairbanks, and Charlie Chaplin. And the hotel soon became a film venue; Billy Wilder's 1959 *Some Like It Hot* would make its architecture world famous.

In Coronado Beach, as in Pasadena, Warburg devoted himself entirely to social life, getting to know hotel guests and making relaxed trips with them to the surrounding area, visiting the hotel swimming pool, and indulging in all kinds of other leisure activities: "I have a go at cycling, I take photographs, I go out hunting geese," he noted in his travel diary in February 1896.[5] Warburg was quite clearly enjoying his stay; he had wine brought daily to his room, bought a new suitcase at the hotel and had it specially lined, and made other uses of the Coronado's excellent service, as surviving–but only now discovered–account and guest books from the time make clear; among other things, he had his clothes laundered and repaired by the hotel's own tailoring department. And so, when he left on February 22 after a five-night stay, Warburg had accumulated a bill amounting to 42.95 dollars–around 1,300 dollars in today's money.[6]

Yet it is significant that the young scholar was seemingly not satisfied by this tourist existence. Just as after his arrival on the East Coast some months before, he was quickly disgusted by this life of leisure. And so he eventually also began to give an art-historical basis to the studies of ornamentation that he had already begun before his journey and had decisively extended both thematically and motivically in his pursuit of symbolic art in Colorado and New Mexico–which Warburg himself saw as a direct response to his worldly hotel life: "On the evening of February 18 (an unconscious response to worldly ferment?) I began to record in a book: 'Symbolism conceived as a function of gravity in the spiritual balance.'"[7] In a letter written to Mary Hertz, his later wife, on March 3, 1896, Warburg outlined the significance that his far-reaching work plans had assumed in his hours of Californian leisure: "In the midst of this idleness I still began to enter the beginnings of an immortal work in a fine, empty exercise book with a thick cover ... Actually, I should not write nonsense about this concoction, for it is in fact the quintessence of my thought. But I cannot help eventually finding it comical how I keep gnawing at these bones. My time in America gave me real-life experience of religious symbolism–but overall I still have to wait a long time until the whole thing is complete."[8]

This "fine, empty exercise book" has survived in Warburg's estate, and its title page indeed displays a motto dated February 18, 1896, and quoting the German playwright and poet Friedrich Schiller, written down in "Coronado Beach, Calif[ornia]": "This day must the bell be ready."[9] Up to March 1896 and then quite sporadically until 1901, the art historian entered notes and fragments in the notebook and in this way attempted to map his "arduous walk through the world of symbols."[10] Although some of his fragments of ideas revolve around such concepts as "symbol," "sense of distance," and the "grasping man," which Warburg used in the United States to interpret phenomena of the Pueblo culture, and the Hopi Snake Dance is mentioned at one point, a systematic representation of his art-psychological reflections was to fail just as much as in the *Grundlegende Bruchstücke zu einer pragmatischen Ausdruckskunde* (Fundamental Fragments for a Pragmatic Science of Expression) or other such collections of this kind of ideas as he created around and after 1900.[11]

By staying in the luxurious Hotel del Coronado, Aby Warburg had thus evidently acquired enough mental distance from the observations he had made in the Pueblo areas—we could also refer to this as "conceptual space"—so that he now felt ready to put the "quintessence" of his thinking on the symbolic foundations of art on paper. Yet even his already pessimistic assumption that he had to "wait a long time until the thing is complete" was not to be realized. In California, in any event, Warburg was unable to decisively pursue the recording of his reflections; instead, after his days of relaxation in April 1896, he again set off for the Southwest to gather other impressions.

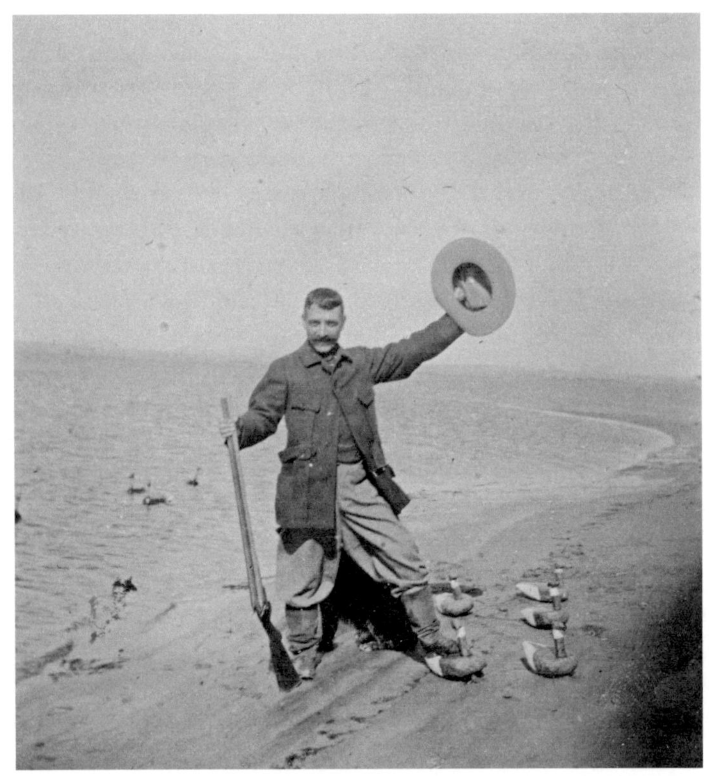

50 Anonymous photographer (taken with Aby Warburg's camera): *Aby Warburg during a hunting trip with gun and decoy ducks*, 1896, photograph

51 Donatello: *David with the Head of Goliath*, ca. 1445, bronze, height 158 cm, Florence, Museo Nazionale del Bargello

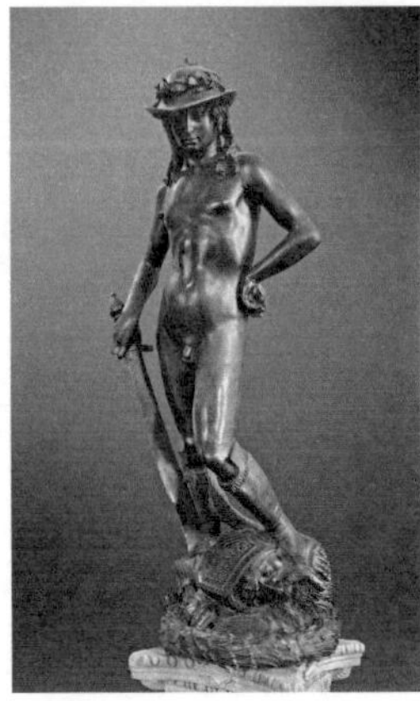

The Hunter

When Aby Warburg stayed at the sophisticated Hotel del Coronado outside San Diego in February 1896, he was invited for a hunting trip with a group of men and women, including some hotel guests, that took them to the coastal city's beach. He devoted a whole series of his photographs to this pastime and the people involved in it. The pictures show Captain James Robert Dunne, who ran the Coronado Boathouse in Glorietta Bay, putting some wooden decoy ducks into the water from a small sailboat. Warburg also took pictures of the hunters aiming their rifles at the birds flying past, made close-up portraits of some of the men and a boy, and also photographed a group of people who had come to the beach to watch.[1]

Although Warburg himself had little luck with his hunting ("am bringing 1 seagull home"), he did not pass up the opportunity to have himself photographed as a hunter.[2] The picture, which was taken by one of the party with his own camera, shows him almost standing in the water on Coronado Beach. He is dressed in a very rustic outfit, wearing a long jacket with patch pockets and wide trousers tucked into the tops of his boots. He is waving his hat triumphantly in the air, and in the other hand he is holding a shotgun, with the butt propped up on the sand next to his foot. In a parody of himself as a successful marksman he has placed his left foot in a victorious pose on one of the decoy ducks that had been lined up next to him. He added an ironically humorous commentary on this pictorial souvenir of the trip, and jotted a suitable title (in a comical mixture of German, English, and Hamburg dialect) for his portrait on the back of the print: "Aby amid the decoys, or the happy hunter with his prey" makes clear that Warburg did not take the picture too seriously.

Yet a dedication to his daughter Marietta, born in 1899, which the father subsequently wrote on the back of the photograph shows that its subject must have felt an emotional attachment to it at least many years later: "To his dear Detta after the lecture in Kreuzlingen on April 21, 1923. May the decoys lure her to Hamburg."[3] What the enigmatic dedication is supposed to mean will never be quite clear. But Warburg seems to have picked out the photograph as a present for his daughter in the hope of persuading the young woman, who was then taking a nursing course in Aschaffenburg, south of Frankfurt, to come home and perhaps care for him after he returned to Hamburg.

In any case, it may be assumed that it did the patient good during his grave mental illness to see himself in a victor's pose. His triumphant posture with his foot on the "prey" indeed recalls one of the pathos formulas that he closely researched in the final years of his life, for instance in his series of pictures *Urworte leidenschaftlicher Gebärdensprache* (Primal Words of Passionate Sign Language, 1927) or *Römische Antike in der Werkstatt des Domenico Ghirlandaio* (Roman Antiquity in Domenico Ghirlandaio's Workshop, 1929).[4] The art historian must certainly have been familiar with the Christian/ancient origins of this iconography of triumph. Thus the Old Testament tells us of Joshua's victory at Gibeon: "And it came to pass, when they brought out those kings unto Joshua, that Joshua called for all the men of Israel, and said unto the captains of the men of war which went with him, Come near, put your feet upon the necks of these kings" (Joshua 10, 24). Warburg undoubtedly knew such artworks as Donatello's *David with the Head of Goliath* (ca. 1445), which included the motif of the victor's pose: In the bronze sculpture the biblical hero, likewise with a propped-up weapon in his right hand, has placed his foot in a triumphant gesture on his conquered foe's severed head. When taking his portrait as a "happy hunter" Warburg probably did not have such iconographic references in mind, but his theory of the involuntary afterlife of ancient pathos formulas is well illustrated by the amusingly staged photograph.

The Chinese

"So now I'm sitting high up on the seventh floor of a huge hotel on the very edge of America," Aby Warburg wrote to Mary Hertz from San Francisco on March 3, 1896, "where you can hear the Chinese chattering ching-ching–and am still not the least bit homesick."[1] After spending some weeks in the southwestern United States, the art historian now reported to his future wife from the restfulness of California that he had made plans to travel on from there to Japan: "The Bohemian in me has awoken and simply longs to be taken to Asia, which is after all 'so nice and near.' A sixteen-day voyage is not sheer pleasure, but no matter–by the time you get this letter I hope to be aboard the *China*."[2] Yet not only was Asia itself "so nice and near," but Warburg could also visit San Francisco's historic Chinatown just a few blocks away from the Palace Hotel, an elegant building, later newly erected after the 1906 earthquake, which is located to this day at the intersection of Market Street and Montgomery Street.

From his hotel Warburg explored the to him alien world of Chinatown, and his walks took him through Geary Street, where at the corner of an commercial building he encountered two Chinese dressed in traditional worker's garb and calico shoes, whom he photographed along with other passers-by. To give his audience at the 1897 lectures on his journey in Berlin and Hamburg an impression of San Francisco's "colorful street life," he showed them this photograph, and commented on it in a surviving draft of the manuscript of his talk in the following mocking words: "... sons of the Celestial Empire who would not allow their repose to be disturbed".[3] However, this marginal and certainly jocularly

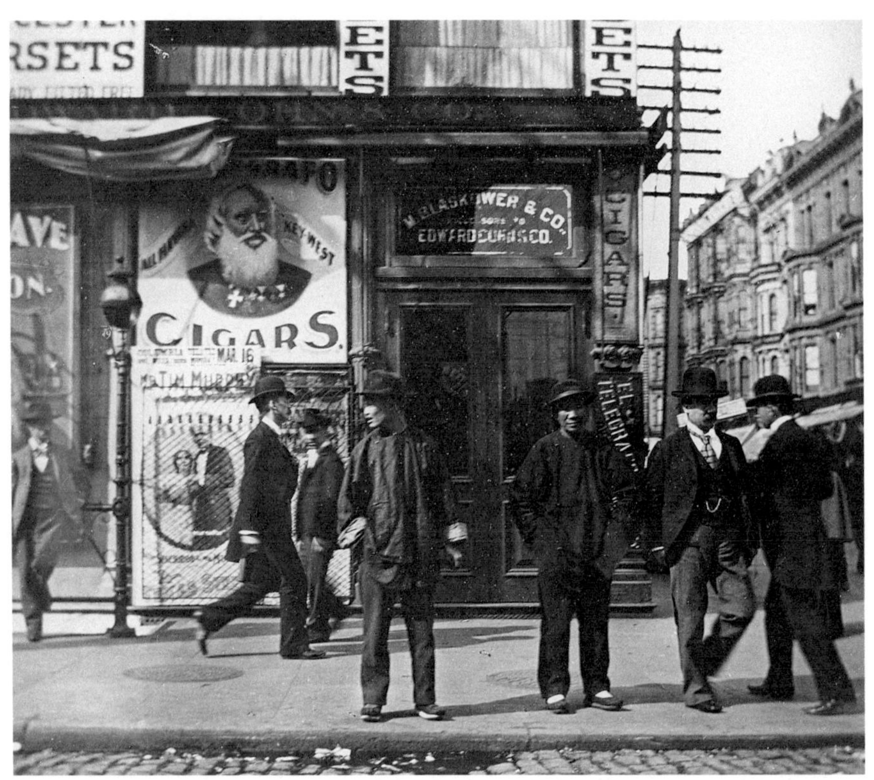

52 Aby Warburg: *Two Chinese workers and Euro-American passers-by*, 1896, photograph

intended comment, which refers to the traditional Chinese ruler's title 天子 (*tianzi*, son of heaven), makes clear that Warburg was by no means free from ethnocentric stereotypes at the time. Here he disparagingly perpetuates the myth of the supposed lethargy of the Chinese, a prejudice that had spread throughout Europe during the nineteenth century after the political and social decline of the cultured nation once so admired in the Western world.[4]

Yet Warburg's misgivings were not confined to the Chinese immigrants who had been brought to the country to work on the construction of the railways, but also extended to the Pueblo, Navajo, and Mexicans he encountered during his journey.[5] His sense of his own cultural superiority is sometimes so clearly apparent at many points in his lectures, as well as in his travel diary and individual letters, that we have to assume an essentially ethnocentric and evolutionistic attitude that the young Warburg, here again a child of his time, had yet to overcome. Although he indisputably embarked on his journey with the aim of studying what he considered the origins of symbolic forms of expression shared by all human beings, the intercultural tolerance and criticism of civilization that strongly emerged in his 1923 lecture are still largely absent in his earlier texts.

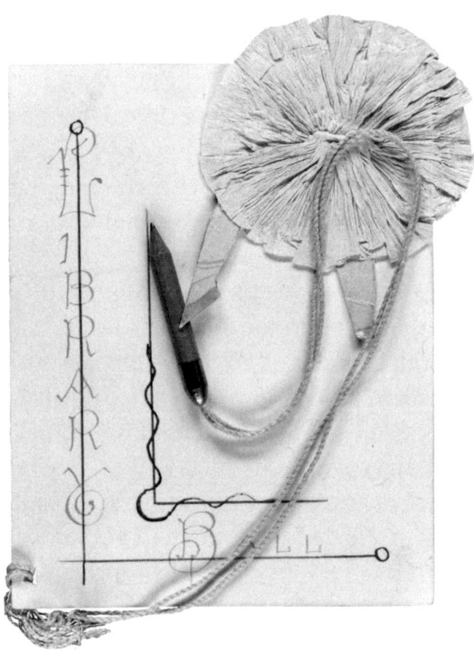

53 Library Association, Albuquerque: *Dance card*, April 6, 1896, folder with decorative band and glued-on paper flower, red and black ink, letterpress

The Dance Evening

Aby Warburg's journey to America was by no means a pure research expedition that took him solely to remote regions of the country. Instead, this son of a wealthy banker's family always stayed in the most renowned hotels in the cities he visited, and frequented the best circles. His explorations of the archeological sites, villages, and dance rituals of the Pueblo took up just over twelve weeks of his in total eight-month stay in the United States. He was usually accompanied by acquaintances, as well as small tour parties made up of members of the urban elites who were charmed by Warburg's appealing demeanor ("a most agreeable and entertaining young gentleman").[1] Nor did the young scholar deny himself such private pleasures as dinner parties, excursions, and dance evenings during his trip to America.

However, the art historian—who had abandoned his plans to travel on to Japan—broke off his luxurious sojourn in California, and in the spring of 1896 he instead returned to the lands of the Pueblo. Yet social pleasures awaited him even in the "wilds" of New Mexico. At Eastertime in 1896 he was invited to a ball and dinner in Albuquerque by the local library association, which was based in the Commercial Club, a prestigious building in Gold Street.[2] Organized by the ladies who had founded the association, and whose names are unfortunately not recorded, the ball was sponsored by such local notables as Matthew W. Flournoy, vice-president of the First National Bank in Albuquerque; Frank W. Clancy, attorney and future attorney general of New Mexico; the former mayor William B. Childers; the post office director Ernest A. Grunsfeld, with whom Warburg had become friends; the businessman Noa Ilfeld; and the later

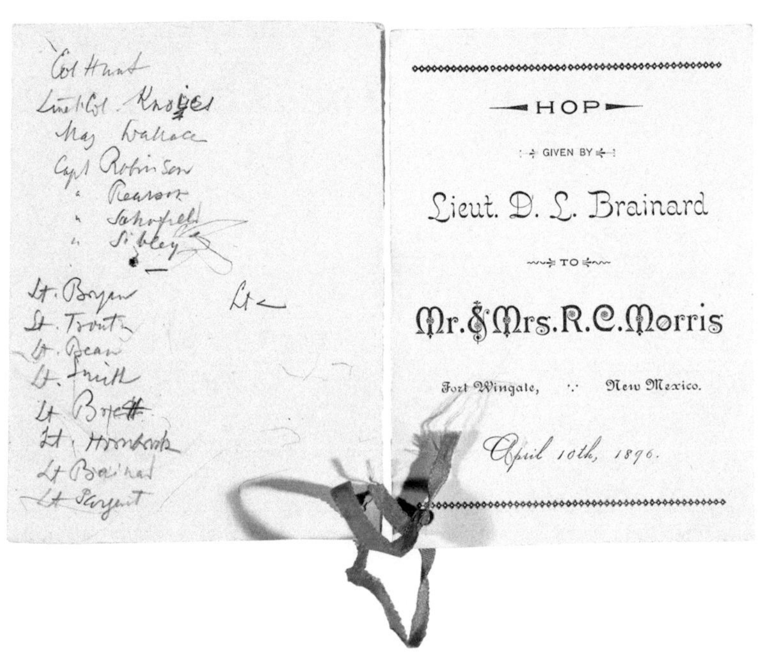

HOP

GIVEN BY

Lieut. D. L. Brainard

TO

Mr. & Mrs. R. C. Morris

Fort Wingate, New Mexico.

April 10th, 1896.

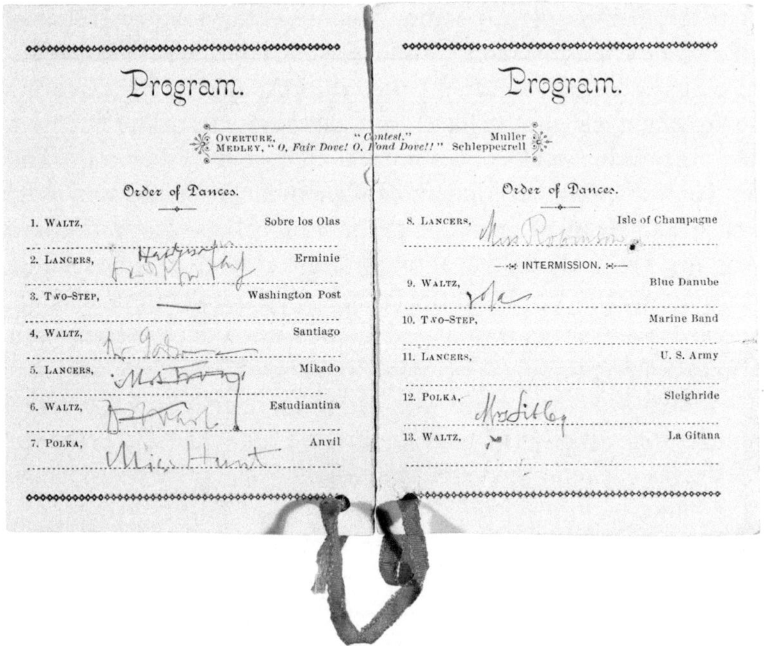

Program.

Overture, "Contest." Muller
Medley, "*O, Fair Dove! O, Fond Dove!!*" Schleppegrell

Order of Dances.

1. Waltz, Sobre los Olas
2. Lancers, Erminie
3. Two-Step, Washington Post
4. Waltz, Santiago
5. Lancers, Mikado
6. Waltz, Estudiantina
7. Polka, Anvil

Program.

Order of Dances.

8. Lancers, Isle of Champagne

INTERMISSION.

9. Waltz, Blue Danube
10. Two-Step, Marine Band
11. Lancers, U. S. Army
12. Polka, Sleighride
13. Waltz, La Gitana

54 Second U.S. Cavalry Regiment, Fort Wingate: *Dance card*, April 10, 1896, folder with decorative band, letterpress

commissioner of public lands Alphaeus A. Keen, whose wives Warburg entered on his dance card that evening along with other ladies. The ball ended with a cotillion, an ebullient swapping dance in which Warburg took part along with an otherwise unidentifiable Mrs. Schuster. As was then customary, he had probably kept the small blue paper flower glued to the folder as a "dance order" and as a souvenir of the ball.

A few days later, on April 9, 1896, Warburg traveled on to Fort Wingate, which he already knew from an earlier visit in December of the previous year. With letters of recommendation to the fort's commander George Gibson Huntt, he spent a carefree week there and made some trips into the surrounding area, including one to Zuni Pueblo, a day's travel away.[3] Set up in 1860 near the town of Gallup in McKinley County to control the surrounding Pueblo and Navajo areas, the garrison also had an exhilarating social life to offer. By December 1895 Warburg had been invited to a Christmas concert by the Second Cavalry Band in Fort Wingate.[4] During his second stay he enjoyed an evidently relaxed dance evening ("informal hop") organized in honor of Lieutenant Robert C. Morris by the cavalry officer and former Arctic explorer David L. Brainard.[5] Besides some garrison officers such as William H. Bean or Roger B. Bryan, who would accompany Warburg from Fort Wingate on his trip to Zuni Pueblo, some officers' wives of course also took part, and the art historian entered them in his card to dance waltzes, polkas, and quadrilles with them.[6]

The fact that the researcher of the ceremonial dances of the Pueblo, of Morris dances, and the dance culture of European courts was himself evidently also in demand as a dancing partner sheds a significant light on his interest in expressions of physical gesture: Again in his highly performative lectures in the 1920s Aby Warburg was to present the eloquence of his own body as a gesticulating teacher in the theater of his own cultural-research library.[7]

[III.47.1.1]

United States Indian Service,

Pueblo & Jicarilla Agency,

Santa Fe,N.M. Feby.1,1896., 189

The Governor of Zuni Pueblo,New Mexico,

Dear Sir:-

The bearer of this is Dr.A.Warburg who visits Zuni in the interests of scientific investigation. He wishes to study your ancient language,customs &c. Please be good enough to give him all the assistance possible in the pursuit of his studies,giving him all the information in your possession on the subjects he is interest -ed in.

Respectfully

John L. Bullis,

Capt.24th.Infy.Actg.Indian Agent.

55 John L. Bullis: *Letter of recommendation to Nick Dumaka, governor of Zuni Pueblo*, February 1, 1896

The Sorcerer

The soldier and Indian Agent John L. Bullis, whom Aby Warburg had met in Santa Fe, drew up two letters of recommendation to facilitate his access to the regional pueblos, their people, and their customs.[1] In the second of the letters, sent to the governor of Zuni Pueblo on February 1, 1896, Bullis emphasized the scientific interests that Warburg was pursuing on his visit to the village, and therefore asked for him to be given any information that could be of use to him in his research. The name of the recipient was hitherto unknown, as the successive Zuni governors' exact terms of office were not officially recorded. However, in his study *The North American Indian* the photographer and publicist Edward S. Curtis published an autobiographic sketch of a man who claimed to have been first elected governor of Zuni pueblo in 1895, but whose identity remained hidden behind the nickname "Zuñi Nick" that appears there.[2] In fact he was Nick Dumaka, who was born in 1864 and at times worked for Eugene A. Carr, the last military commander of the District of New Mexico, and in his native village as an assistant to the trader Douglas D. Graham. Besides his mother tongue, Dumaka spoke English and Spanish, always wore modern clothing, challenged traditional hierarchical structures and religious beliefs, and–according to sources–was headstrong and occasionally argumentative, which also led to conflicts within the village community.[3]

A few years before he was first elected governor, Dumaka was accused by members of a Zuni brotherhood of being a sorcerer; he was seized, interrogated, and harshly maltreated, which eventually even led to military intervention by soldiers from the nearby Fort Wingate east of the town of Gallup. The alleged sorcerer wrote down his memories of this incident at some unknown time (before 1910), and made his report available to Curtis: "In 1891 I was suspected to witchcraft because a woman gave up a rich husband for me, a poor young man. His sister made the first suggestion that I must be a sorcerer, and a Hopi visiting at his house made medicine and said I must be a sorcerer because I had learned English without going to school, while many others came back from school unable to speak the language. The two Bow Chiefs came for me at the store where I was working. I ran down into the cellar with a gun. They wanted to come down for me, but the owner of the store [Douglas D. Graham] warned them that I would surely shoot them. Naíuchi, the elder-brother Bow Chief, then asked if he could come down and talk to me. I told him to come alone and without a gun, and he did so. He tried to persuade me to go with him, but I refused. That night I got a horse and went to Gallup. Later I returned to the Pueblo, and one of the Bow Chiefs after many efforts got me drunk and took me to the kiva. I was hung up by the wrists, and so was my brother. He confessed falsely, and was cut down, and after a long time I was cut down ... A long time I lived in Gallup, then Naíuchi and the people begged me to return. I came back, and they wanted me to be governor, but I refused. But in 1895 they appointed me."[4]

In 1899, the journalist George Wharton James described this episode, evidently from other sources, in a series of sensational newspaper articles, with novelistic embellishments: "A few years ago Nick mortally offended some of the chief priests of Zuni, and they felt it was necessary to humble him in some way, and destroy his influence with the young men, or their own power would largely be lost. The evil fates favored them. For a couple of years crops were bad. Floods came and washed out their corn once; then a fierce wind came and blew all their growing peaches off the trees; a disease carried off a number of their sheep and goats, and, to crown all, an epidemic of smallpox slew a number of their baby boys and girls. Little by little it became whispered about–no one knew exactly how–that Nick was responsible for all this evil. Finally, it was openly stated that Na-u-che–one of the chief priests–accused Nick of being a witch ... Nick was rudely stripped entire naked, and his feet tied together. Then his arms were stretched behind him and his wrists so tied that his hands were back to back, with the thumbs upright. A stout rawhide rope was now fastened to his wrists and thumbs, the other end thrown over the crossbeam [on the village plaza], and several willing hands, upon a signal from Na-u-che, hoisted the unhappy victim of this merciless procedure several feet from the ground. As he there swung, suspended from

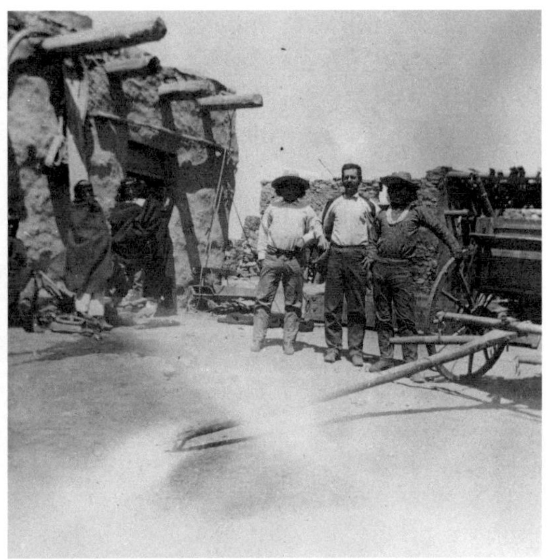

56 Aby Warburg: *Nick Dumaka, Roger B. Bryan, and other villagers in Zuni Pueblo*, 1896, photograph

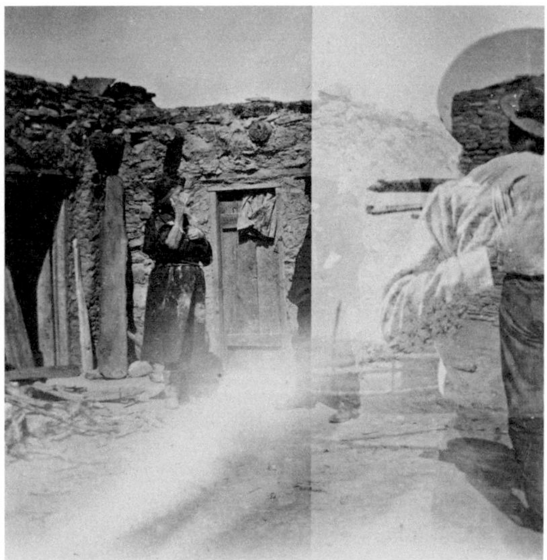

57 Aby Warburg and anonymous photographer (probably Roger B. Bryan): *Aby Warburg in conversation with a Zuni women, with a superimposed portrait of Nick Dumaka*, 1896, double-exposed photograph

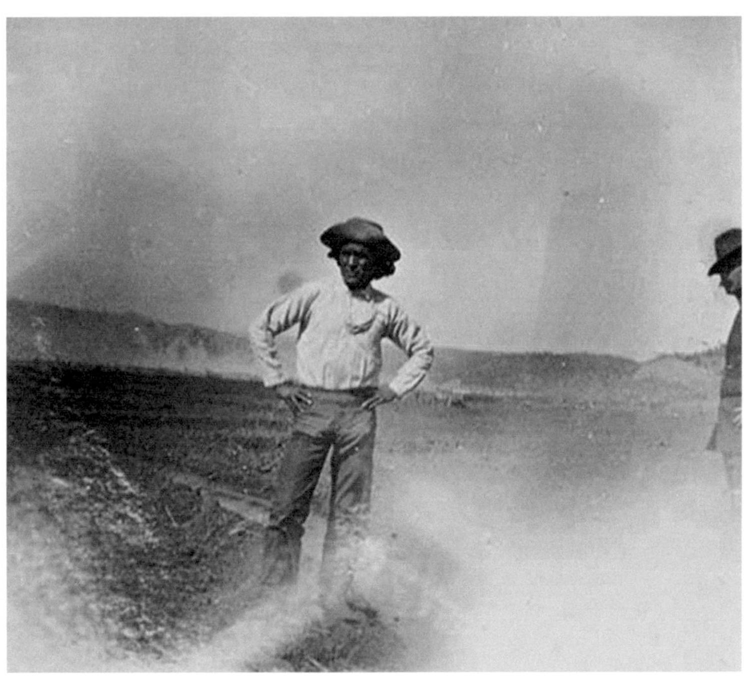

58 Aby Warburg: *Nick Dumaka and Roger B. Bryan in Zuni Pueblo*, 1896, photograph

the ground, the whole of his weight resting upon his thumbs and wrists, and the rope lacerating his skin and flesh to the very bone, he was asked—nay, commanded—to confess his witcheries."[5]

Until his death in 1927 Dumaka supported numerous explorers in their work, among other things reciting the myths and sacred songs of the Zuni for them. Not only Curtis, but for example also Franz Boas, who stayed in Zuni pueblo for a few days in 1920, and above all the cultural anthropologists Ruth Benedict, Ruth L. Bunzel, and Elsie Clews Parsons profited in their often multi-year field research in the 1920s from his outstanding knowledge of cultural and religious history.[6] Yet already by April 1896, when Aby Warburg visited the village, the charismatic man ("a person of great ability, of commanding presence") served as the visitor's guide and interpreter, and introduced him to individual villagers.[7] The visitor recorded him in several photographs that show Dumaka and Warburg's companion, Lieutenant Roger B. Bryan from Fort Wingate, touring the village. In an unintentionally double-exposed shot we can see Warburg talking to a woman with Nick Dumaka's help, superimposed with a blurred portrait of the man who had once been accused and maltreated as a sorcerer.

The Girl

On April 21, 1896, Aby Warburg wrote to his family in Hamburg from the very remote trading post of Bitahochee in Navajo County that, after a pleasant week in the company of US officers, he had set off to conduct more field research: "From Fort Wingate I made an excursion to Zuni Pueblo in a military vehicle, accompanied by my friend Lt. Bryan."[1] However, he was to be disappointed by his stay in the traditional village west of Albuquerque, as Warburg reported in retrospect in his lecture *Eine Reise durch das Gebiet der Pueblo-Indianer in New Mexico und Arizona* (A Journey through the Region of the Pueblo Indians in New Mexico and Arizona): "The excursion to Zuni did not have the desired success, for we were trapped at home for two days by a dust storm, and most of the Zuni Indians had left the village to till their fields."[2] But he did meet the charismatic governor Nick Dumaka, who acted as his guide and interpreter in his talks with the villagers, although he probably knew nothing about Dumaka's past; and neither his notes nor the few photographs taken on the spot show that the art historian obtained any noteworthy answers to the questions that concerned him.

However, one of the photographs makes clear that on his visits to the villages of the American Southwest Warburg's behavior was occasionally inappropriate, and even intrusive: The documented scene shows Roger B. Bryan together with the interpreter sweeping a Zuni girl's hair off her forehead so that Warburg can more easily capture her features in his photograph.[3] The girl looks trapped in the claustrophobic situation of the portrait, smiling gamely at the camera and submitting to Dumaka's embrace and the certainly unpleasant procedure, while a laughing older

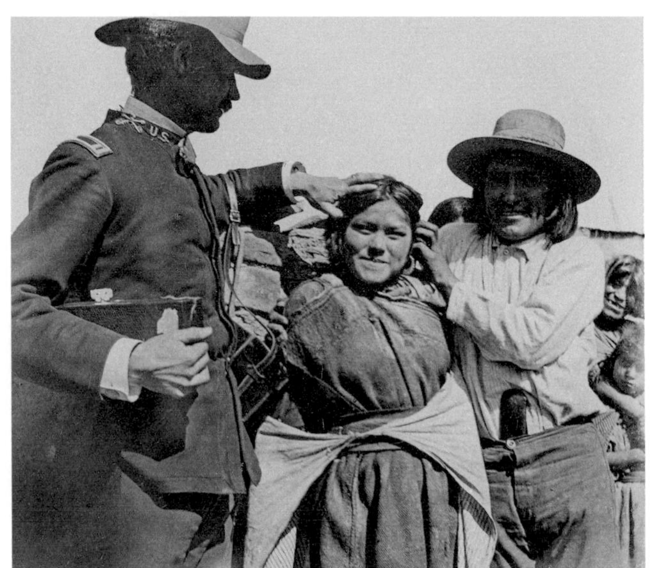
59 Aby Warburg: *Roger B. Bryan and Nick Dumaka with a Zuni girl*, 1896, photograph

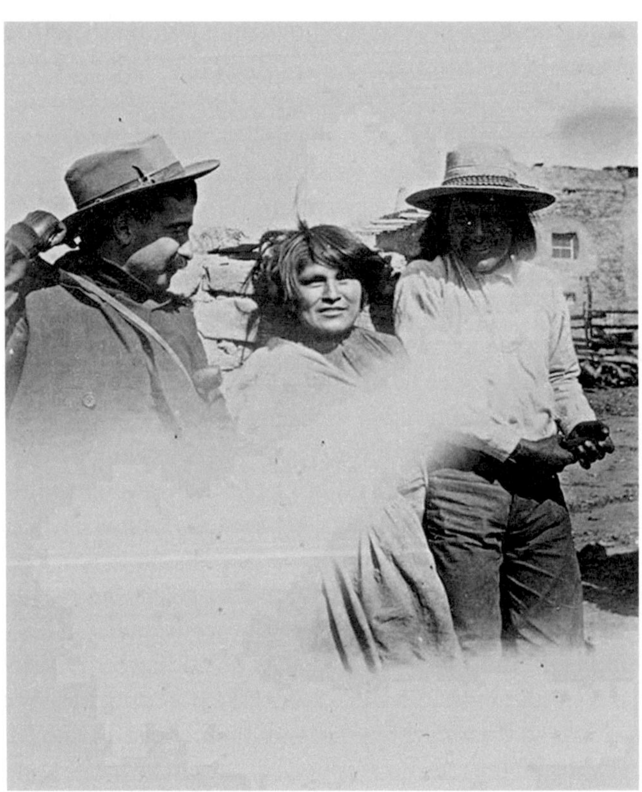
60 Anonymous photographer (probably Roger B. Bryan, using Aby Warburg's camera): *Aby Warburg and Nick Dumaka with a young Zuni woman*, 1896, photograph

woman in the background watches the whole process. The picture of the girl as she was harassed by his companions was displayed in the slide shows that Warburg organized in Berlin and Hamburg in 1897, and he made the following terse, laconic commentary on it in the manuscript of his speech: "Photography with obstacles. Lieutenant Bryan and interpreter Nick holding a Zuni girl."[4]

Yet it is telling that in a second picture, which must have been taken immediately afterwards, the art historian had replaced the officer so that he could be photographed together with another young woman whom he was facing with a friendly expression. We do not know if Warburg touched the woman so that she would look more favorably in his intended picture, for an unfortunate overexposure has made his left arm largely unrecognizable, while the gesture of his other hand, which may have been raised to his hat, remains unclear to the viewer. However, Warburg's comment shows that he was well aware of the earlier transgression, but did not have any problem with his companions' behavior.

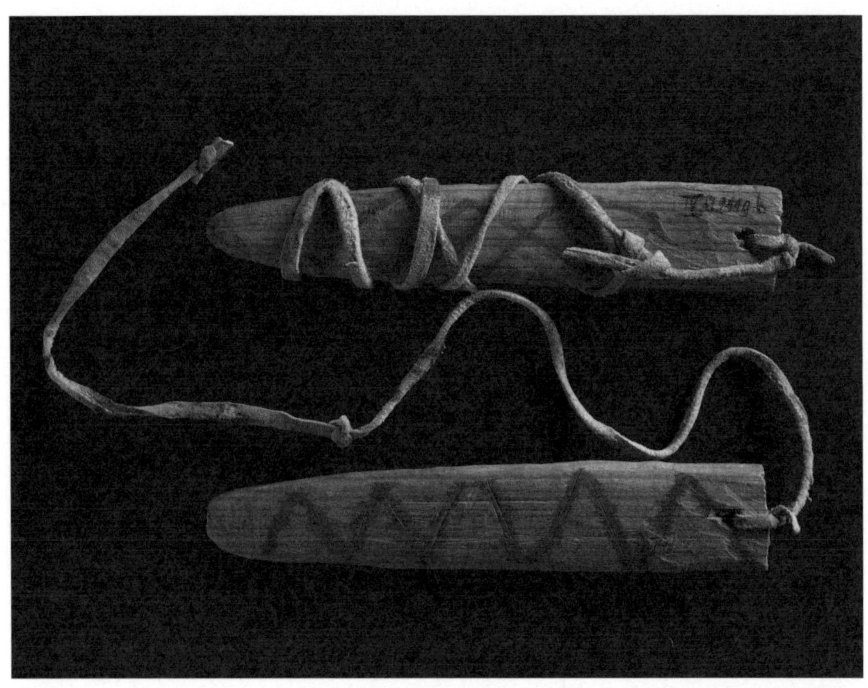

61 Anonymous maker: *Bullroarers*, ca. 1890–1896, wood, leather cord, and paint, respectively 14.5/14.8 × 2.7 × 1 cm, Berlin, Ethnologisches Museum

The Bullroarers

On his visits to the Pueblo in the American Southwest Aby Warburg was not only interested in the religious rites and symbols of the native population, but also tried to gain insights into their everyday lives. Some utensils, vessels, baskets, and tools purchased for this purpose on the spot or in antique stores, as well as trinkets or textiles, and even a paper-thin roll of cornbread (*piiki*), were included in his study collection.[1] Among these were a pair of so-called bullroarers (*tovokìnpi*), ancient instruments used in many cultures around the world, and hence also among the Pueblo, in some cases since prehistoric times. Whirling the small objects, which were made of wood or bone, on a cord produced sounds that could be used for a variety of purposes. Bullroarers, sometimes decorated with appropriate symbols, were originally used by the Pueblo to summon rain, for their roaring, buzzing sound recalled thunderstorms, but they were also, as in this case, used as children's toys.[2] A historical text from 1881 describes very graphically how the instrument was used when it was observed in Walpi: "The medicine-men twirled it rapidly, and with a uniform motion, about the head and from front to rear, and succeeded in faithfully imitating the sound of a gust of rain-laden wind. As explained to me by one of the medicine-men, by making this sound they compelled the wind and rain to come to the aid of the crops."[3]

Unlike with many items in his collection, the circumstances in which these objects (which were only crudely carved from wood) were acquired are precisely documented. While visiting Zuni Pueblo in April 1896, Warburg was able to obtain the pair of bullroarers from a boy, although the latter was reluctant to part with his toy. The art historian was probably interested in the objects because of their painted and partly carved zigzag lines (*hotsikve* or *hotsitsve*), which perhaps also here should be interpreted as symbols of snakes or lightning.[4] Warburg later recorded this detail, which seems to have amused him, in a list cataloging his collection: "I took it off a small boy in the Zuni village and gave him 25¢, but he began yelling so furiously that I let him keep it. The next morning, just as we were about to leave, his elder brother ran up, took the 25¢, gave me the bullroarer, and disappeared again."[5]

Although Warburg exchanged the modest artifact for a no less modest coin, this anecdote highlights how some Euro-American collectors came by the objects they coveted around 1900, and not only in the southwestern United States. Culturally or materially more valuable things also changed hands without a fair or voluntary transaction necessarily taking place; theft and fraud were common practice. However, the surviving documents show that Warburg himself did not indulge in such illegal forms of acquisition, but usually purchased the collection items that interested him from dealers in the region, and more rarely from the inhabitants, and always paid appropriately. After his return, in December 1896, for reasons or purposes unknown, Warburg donated his pair of bullroarers to the Royal Museum of Ethnology in Berlin, which considered them a valuable addition to its collection.[6] Its letter of thanks to him added hopefully that further gifts of this kind would be most welcome, as is also documented in a note for the files by Karl von den Steinen, the later head of the museum's American collection: "I leave it to you to decide whether a suggestion to that effect would be appropriate when thanking him for the bullroarers."[7] However, there would be no further donations to Berlin; from 1899 onwards Warburg transferred his collection in several stages to the Museum of Ethnology in Hamburg.

The Rock

In April 1896, Aby Warburg visited the small village of Walpi on the First Mesa, a rocky plateau in Arizona. Arriving Keams Canyon, the explorer photographed from a distance the outline of the narrow spur of the mesa (which had been inhabited for centuries) with its barren landscape, and then—as if in a slow traveling shot— approached the place picture by picture, recording a female inhabitant and some donkeys in the village street that led past the multistory stone houses, and finally focusing on the architecture in close-up.

Yet the most interesting picture in the short series from Walpi in cultural history terms is surely the photograph of Warburg's driver Frank Allen, leaning on one disrespectfully raised foot, and two companions at the entrance (*kivàytsiwa*) to one of the sacred kivas in the village. The picture shows the Dance Rock around which the famous Hopi Snake Dance is performed every other August (in alternation with Oraibi).[1] Behind the bizarrely shaped rock, concealed in Warburg's photograph, is a thicket of small black poplars which during the ceremonies is covered with cloths to create an enclosure (*kìisi*) in which the snakes are kept until just before they are used in the dance: "The Snake Dance," wrote Jesse Walter Fewkes in 1894, "is an elaborate prayer for rain, in which the reptiles are gathered from the fields, intrusted with the prayers of the people, and then given their liberty to bear these petitions to the divinities who can bring the blessing of copious rain to the parched and arid farms of the Hopi."[2] The ritual, whose origins date back to well beyond its first mentions in sixteenth-century Spanish sources, was prepared for in an eight-day ceremony that partly took place in the underground assembly areas of the kiva. On the ninth day the dance was then performed in front of what by Warburg's day was already a vast crowd of onlookers who wanted to watch the Hopi priests carrying the poisonous reptiles (*tsuu'a*) in their mouths.[3] During the lecture he gave in Kreuzlingen in 1923, Warburg illustrated the end of the ritual with a series of photographs taken in Walpi by people that probably included the missionary Henry R. Voth. The influx of visitors initially led to some restrictions (after 1900 separate areas were created for photographers and camera crews), and eventually to an outright ban on visual documentation.[4]

For Aby Warburg this "most pagan of all ceremonies" was of great interest, for the animal and the dancer formed a "magical whole" and were not only mimetically (as in the Buffalo Deer Dance in San Ildefonso) or symbolically (as in the spring dance of the Hemikatsinam in Oraibi) connected: "So the snake ceremony in Walpi is a blend of imitative mimic empathy and bloody sacrifice, for in it the animals themselves appear in the crudest form as performers in the cult, and not in order to be sacrificed but–like the Paho–to act as petitioners for rain by being sent back into the earth."[5] Yet, apart from the Dance Rock, nothing of all this can be seen in Warburg's photographs from Walpi: In May 1896 the cultural historian traveled back to Europe, and he never saw the Snake Dance–today so closely associated with his research into the psychology of religion–with his own eyes.

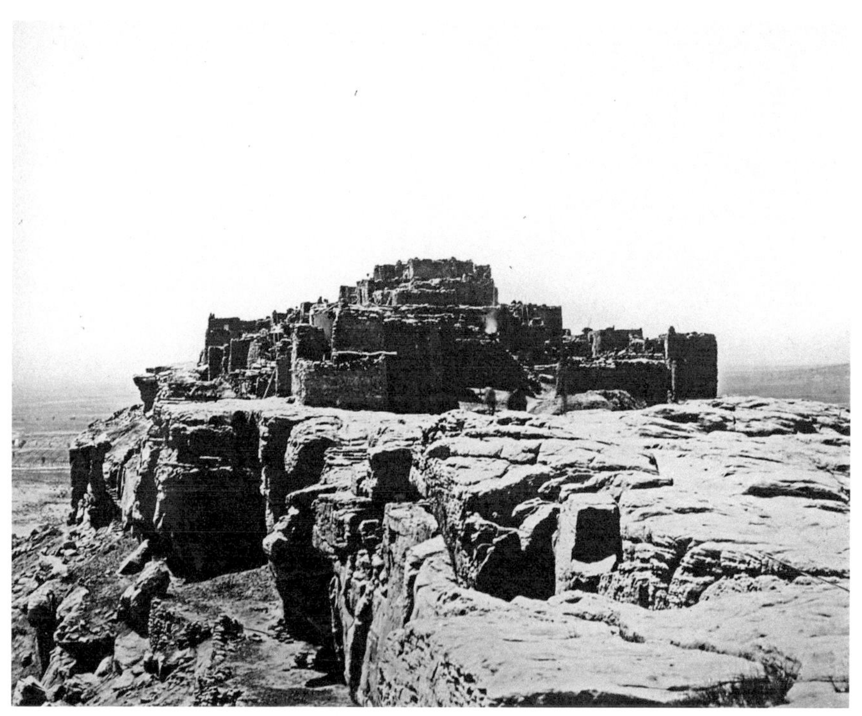

62 Aby Warburg: *View of the village of Walpi*, 1896, photograph

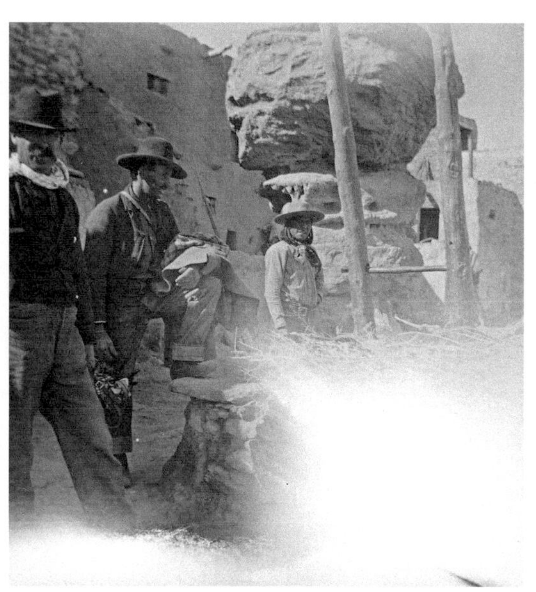

63 Aby Warburg: *Frank Allen with an unidentified traveling companion of Warburg's and a Pueblo in front of the Dance Rock in Walpi*, 1896, photograph

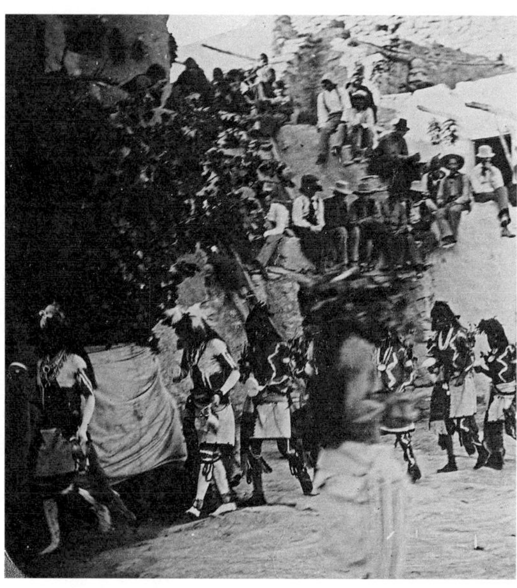

64 Anonymous photographer (probably Henry R. Voth): *Priest of the Antelope fraternity during the Snake Dance in Walpi*, ca. 1890–1895, photograph

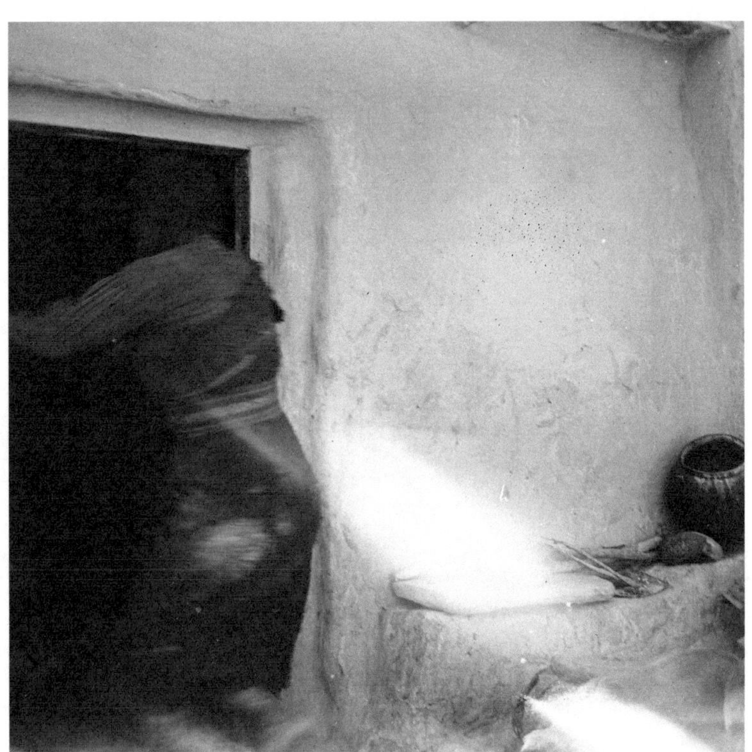

65 Aby Warburg: *A woman fleeing from Warburg's camera into a house in Walpi*, 1896, photograph

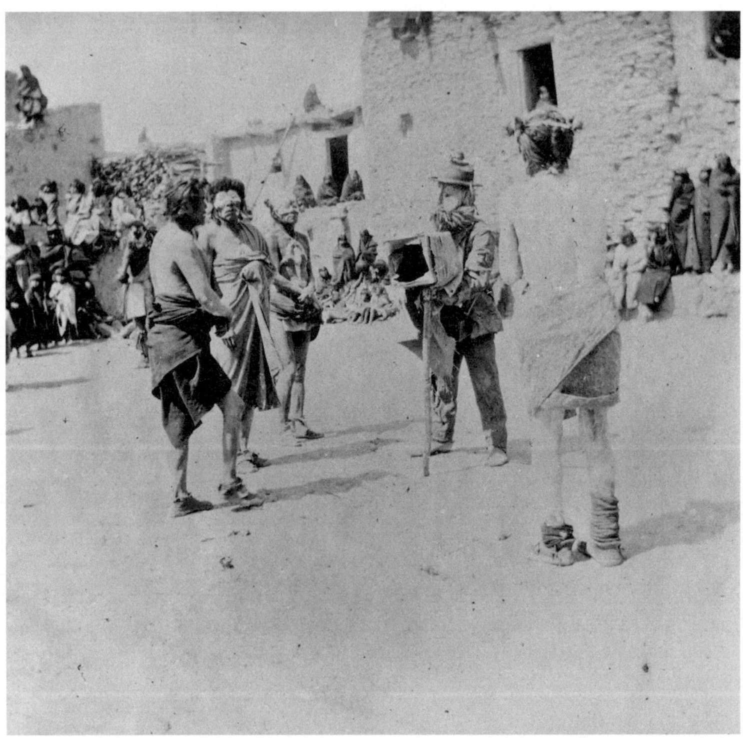

66 Karl von den Steinen: *Parodic depiction of a "white" photographer during the Hehey'a Katsina dance in Oraibi*, 1898, photograph, Berlin, Ethnologisches Museum

The Fleeing Woman

With a swift movement the woman turns away from the photographer, fleeing from him into the darkness of her home, her body leaving a shadowy, indeed even ghostly figure of blurred gray tones in the photograph, while the dazzlingly bright wall of the house and the wide-bellied clay jug and other everyday utensils in front of it are captured in clear detail. The photograph, which Aby Warburg took in this way in the cliff village of Walpi in 1896 and seemingly yielded little substantive interest, was undoubtedly a failure; yet the art historian kept a copy of this remarkable snapshot throughout his lifetime. The reason why he considered such a terribly blurred picture worth preserving at all can only be understood when we read his comments on the indigenous population's "superstitious fear" of the photographic medium which the researcher scattered through his lectures on his stay in the American Southwest.[1] Warburg kept the image precisely because of its failure: If the photographer's incompetence had been the only reason why the picture was ruined, it would probably never have been printed in the first place, or would subsequently have been destroyed; and only this provides any certainty that the woman in Walpi actually wanted to avoid being photographed–and did not flee into her home for any other reason–and that the blurring of the image, which of course was by no means intended when the picture was taken, thus became its real subject. The art historian was therefore not mainly concerned with a faultless technical and compositional result, but rather with the cultural-psychological essence of an iconophobia that was, as it were, documented with unerring acuity in the blurred image.

And yet it must be wondered whether the supposed "superstitious fear" was really due to the new pictorial medium imported by the Euro-American settlers and explorers, or rather to the intrusive manner in which they only too often took their pictures.[2] Adam Clark Vroman, who undertook a whole series of photographic campaigns in Arizona and New Mexico between 1895 and 1904, noted in his diary that he could dispel the Hopis' suspicions by explaining to them how the camera worked and letting them see for themselves how the photographs came into being: "One of the best ways of ingratiating one's self to their confidence, I found, was first to always sit down and try to explain the camera to them, then stand it up and look through it, pointed away from them, and have them look through and see [the] picture in the ground glass and, after all had seen, go out and let them see me standing on my head. It was amusing to see their surprise when [they] would put the focusing cloth back and see I was not on my head. They would look again and then come out and smile and call others to look and then they would smile too. Mothers, babies, all had to go through it, and after I had shown them all I could they never refused to allow me to make pictures of them."[3] Warburg, however, had not been able–or willing–to take such time with many of his photographs, for he was mainly concerned to quickly capture the moment, the instant that was so fruitful for him; and his only more than fleeting encounters with the Indigenous population were in any case with selected individuals such as Cleto Yurina, Nick Dumaka, or Loololma.[4]

Within a few years of the invention of photography, the new reproductive medium was already playing a key role in making images of remote parts of the world and their inhabitants available regardless of their location, and hence spreading knowledge of the "discovered" cultures, which were often considered "exotic." In the hope of technically and objectively recording an extract of reality in a specific time, photography was therefore also used in ethnology from the mid-nineteenth century onwards; but in addition to its documentary function it soon also developed colonialist, ethnocentric, anthropometric, and indeed racist tendencies. A purely scientific photograph was–and is–hard to distinguish clearly from such excesses. In any case, traveling ethnologists and anthropologists claimed, especially when acting on behalf of the emerging ethnological museums, to be using photographic and other resources to preserve an endangered cultural stage of humanity, which they usually saw as "primitive," in the historical memory of their fields of study.[5]

Even Warburg, who had, however, realized that the Pueblo were by no means leading such entirely pre-civilizational lives, seemed convinced of the acute threat to the symbolic culture ("between magic and logos") in the pueblos.[6] The population responded variously, with derision and resistance, to the photographers who wanted to record their way of life and ceremonies. Thus the German ethnologist Karl von den Steinen watched, from a respectful distance, the performance by a *piptuqa*, a masked jester who parodied the (present) white photographers and their behavior during a Hehey'a Katsina dance in Oraibi in 1898. Disguised as a Euro-American tourist or researcher, with a hat, false beard, and false spectacles, he carried a mock camera and tripod that were clearly made from wood and cloth, as well as a similar hand camera–the kind that Warburg had–and gave a burlesque performance of all the actions he had observed among the photographers visiting the Hopis, from making contact with their models to producing their portraits and paying them with fake bills.[7] However, the immediate reflex of avoiding an unwanted photograph becomes clear in the photograph in which Warburg–whether or not deliberately–documented the Pueblo's iconophobia: The woman he observed in Walpi could only escape from the camera by fleeing into her home and leaving the art historian with an amorphous illusion instead of a portrait.

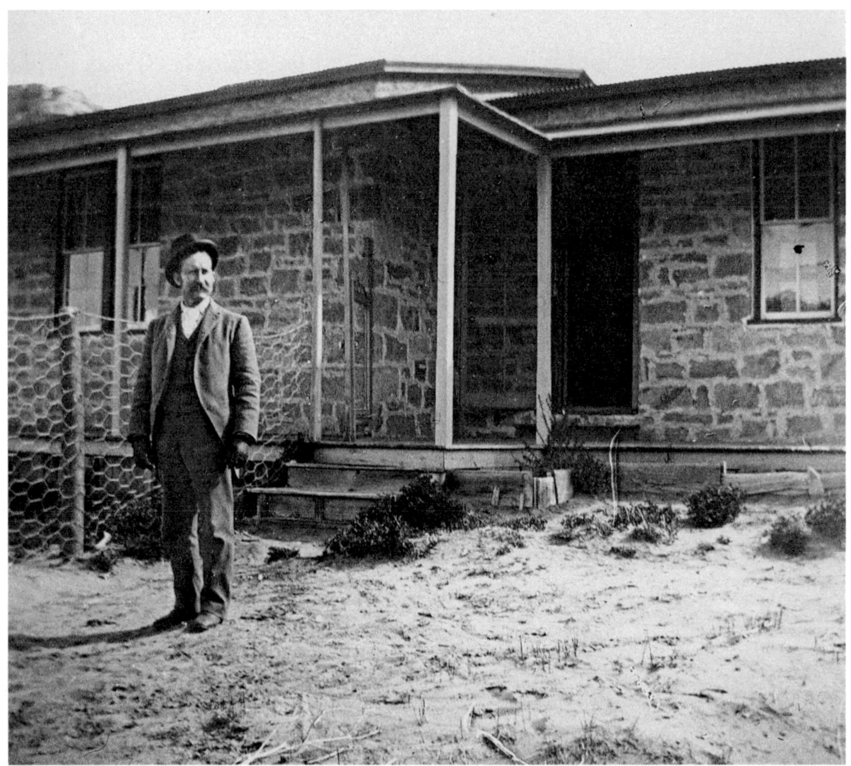

67 Aby Warburg: *Thomas Varker Keam outside a building in his trading settlement*, 1896, photograph

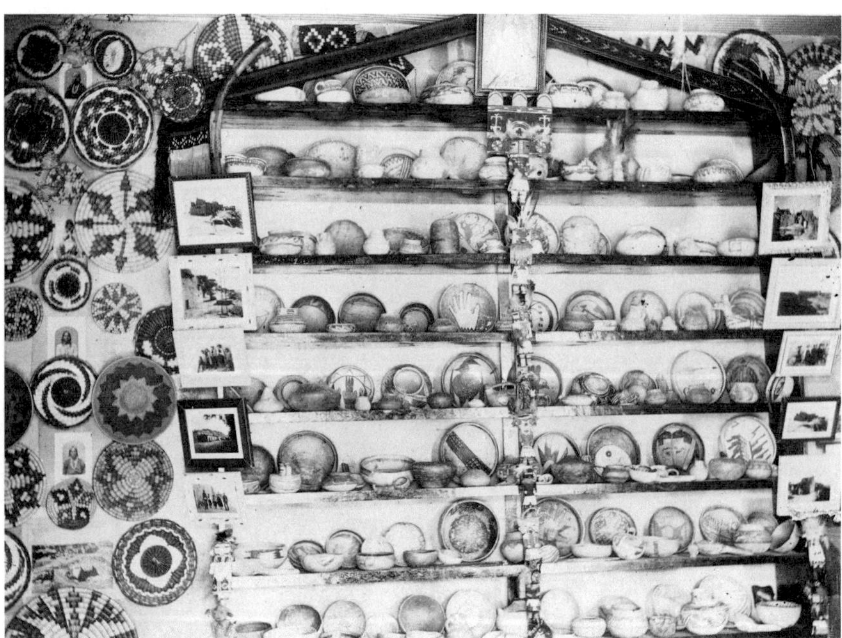

68 Anonymous photographer: *View of Thomas Varker Keam's collection*, ca. 1890–1900, London, British Museum

The Trader

After a two-day stagecoach ride in which he was at times exposed to a violent sandstorm, Aby Warburg arrived in Keams Canyon from Holbrook on the afternoon of April 22, 1896. There the art historian visited a trading settlement located east of the mesas whose pueblos were the real goal of his new trip to the southwestern United Sates. The settlement, "a homestead consisting of a series of farm buildings, dwellings, and a store in which goods are bartered with Indians," was run by Thomas Varker Keam, who had taken over the management of the business from his brother in 1880.[1] The anthropologists Jesse Walter Fewkes and James Mooney, who were aware of Keam's knowledge of regional culture and his astonishing collection of Pueblo artifacts, had drawn Warburg's attention to the owner of the Tusayan Trading Post only a few weeks earlier.[2] After his arrival Warburg described the trader, with whom he was to have important conversations, and recorded him and his settlement in a number of photographs: "Mr. K[eam], a stocky man, longish oval face, small eyes, blond mustache, strong chin, a self-assured (but not vain) smile on his energetic face, carefully dressed; ... intelligent, practical man not without understanding of and training in theoretical matters ..."[3]

Born in 1842 as the son of a ship's master from Kenwyn in the English county of Cornwall, Keam soon joined the British merchant navy. In 1862 he came to San Francisco, and at first became a cavalryman in the US army. After deployments in Arizona and New Mexico, from 1869 on he worked first as an interpreter from Spanish, and later as a special representative for the Navajo Agency in Fort Defiance, where he gained the Navajo's trust, learned their language–he later added Hopi, which he was also said to have spoken fluently–and married a young Navajo woman in accordance with native rites, thus wrecking his hopes of a career in the Bureau of Indian Affairs. In 1873 he founded his first trading firm near Fort Defiance, and despite political conflicts and intrigues continued to seek employment as an Indian Agent. As an interpreter for the military in Fort Wingate and Ojo Caliente he also defended the interests of the Apaches, but his hopes of a government job eventually came to nothing, and Keam moved to his second settlement, opened as early as 1875 and run by his brother William until his death in November 1880. In Keams Canyon Thomas Varker Keam expanded the settlement, which eventually comprised over a dozen buildings and a separate dwelling; there he traded with the Hopi and the Navajo and sold their handicrafts, which also helped him expand the collection whose basic items he had probably taken over from his brother. Keam played a key role in the ideological clashes among the Hopi, which would eventually lead to the "Oraibi Split"; he thus helped the conciliatory Hopi faction around the local leader Loololma obtain a school that used Euro-American teaching methods, and in 1887 he let the school have all the buildings in his trading settlement in Keams Canyon (at first on a leasehold basis), and built new dwellings and farm buildings a few miles further west.[4] Hopi and Navajo were likewise ever-present there, as Warburg documented in his travel diary and also in photographs. In May 1904 Thomas Varker Keam returned to England, where he soon died.

The trader not only had an extensive stock of ceramics, basketwork, and other artifacts, but also a library and a collection of photographs, and had conducted archaeological, cultural-history, and iconographic studies; and as early as 1883 Keam published the first eyewitness report of the Hopi Snake Dance.[5] He was gradually able to sell his stocks, which eventually comprised several thousand items, to collectors and museums; among others, the Field Museum in Chicago and the Peabody Museum of Archaeology and Ethnology in Cambridge today possess numerous works that once decorated the walls of the dwellings side by side in Keams Canyon.[6] In particular, however, the Berlin Royal Museum of Ethnology, facilitated by Eduard Georg Seler and Karl von den Steinen, in 1901 purchased over 2,500 items from his collection, hundreds of partly pre-Columbian and partly modern ceramics, dozens of Katsina figures, and much else besides.[7]

Aby Warburg also bought a whole series of objects by Indigenous artists from Keam's stocks, including a bowl presumably made by the most famous Pueblo female ceramic artist, Nampeyo ("Num-pa-yu", Tewa for

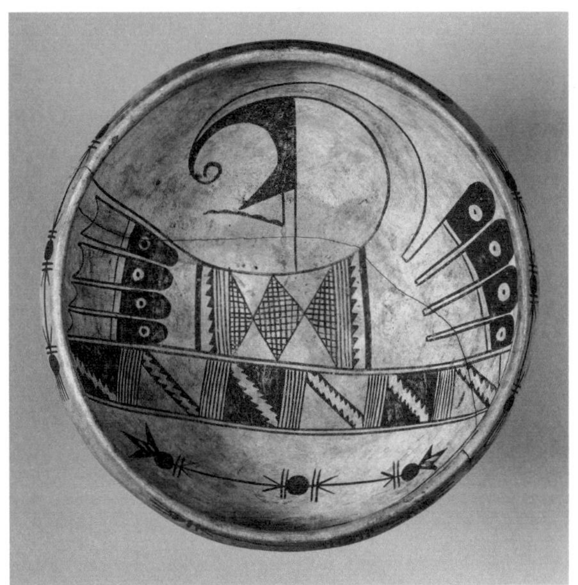

69 Nampeyo (ascribed): *Bowl*, ca. 1895, painted clay, 11 × 25 cm (acquired by Aby Warburg from Thomas Varker Keam)

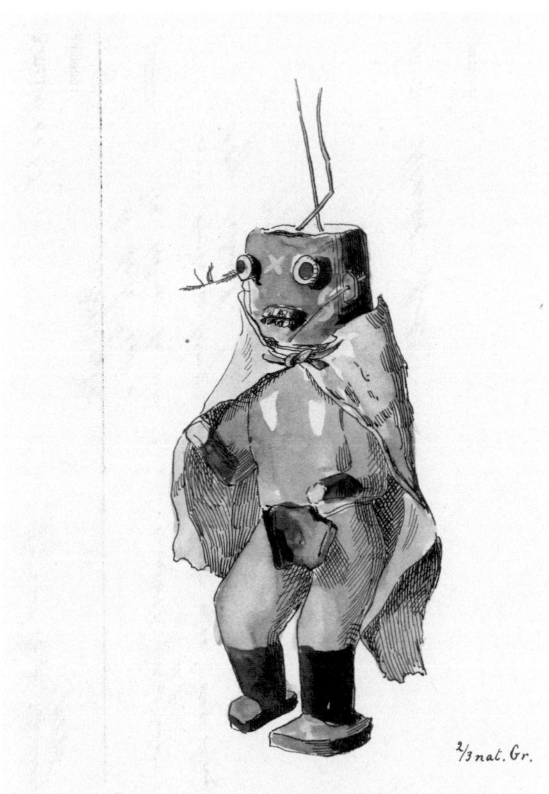

70 Anonymous artist: *Katsina figure (probably Atoshle tihu)*, ca. 1890–1896 (acquired by Aby Warburg from Thomas Varker Keam), index-card drawing, after 1907

"The snake that does not bite"), who was born on the First Mesa in 1859, as well as some Katsina figures he owned personally ("I saw each one hanging on the wall in his room").[8] The art historian stayed for some days with the famously hospitable trader ("is excellent at playing the host"), was able to study his collection at close hand, consulted some volumes of research literature he found there, and also obtained numerous tips from Keam, above all about iconography and the names of the purchased items in the original languages, which Warburg later included in his collection list.[9] The art historian was thus able to use his stay in the trading settlement to prepare himself for his most important encounter with the Hopi culture, the spring dance in Oraibi, in which the Hemiskatsinam also performed. On April 27, 1896, Warburg finally left Keams Canyon to ride to the small village on the Third Mesa ("the ultimate goal of my journey").[10]

The Navajo

The pictures Aby Warburg took during his stay in the southwestern United States not only document the villages and settlements, the people he encountered there, their architecture, living conditions and customs, but also provide an interesting idea of the researcher's photographic practice. Carefully, literally step by step, Warburg approached new places and situations, often first recording what he saw from a distance, before moving on to further details and eventually above all the people he was particularly interested in. This resulted in entire sequences of pictures, for example when he visited the cliff village of Walpi in April 1896, or moved slowly through the small village of Oraibi in May, in order to reach the scene of the dance with its spectators and eventually record what happened there with as many close-ups and abundant details as possible.[1] On some occasions Warburg finally gave his camera to one of his companions and asked him to take a picture showing himself with the people he had previously photographed.

Before reaching the trading settlement in Keams Canyon on April 22, 1896, Warburg first recorded its situation in the landscape from a distance, then photographed some of the simple, single-story buildings, portrayed their owner Thomas Varker Keam, and finally focused on a group of Navajo camped outside one of the buildings. They had probably come to the place to deliver or collect goods, for Keam's firm, located in the middle of one of the historical Navajo settlement areas, sold, among other things, artifacts produced by the native population. Warburg also only gradually approached the men who had sat on the ground around a woman cooking food. Together with Keam the visitor approached the resting group, gradually changing his focus from long shot and medium long shot to some close-ups of the people that had aroused his curiosity.[2]

Here Warburg changed the camera perspective with every shot, first photographing from a standing position, and finally capturing the bodies and faces more and more closely from a crouch, seeking–and making–direct eye contact with the people shown, who in turn also observed the visitor with curiosity and friendly smiles. In the pictures we can see some cooking utensils, as well as the jewelry and in some cases poor clothing of the Navajo, who call themselves Diné and, after many centuries of bloody oppression first by the Spanish *conquistadores* and then by the US government, to this day mainly live in the surrounding Navajo Nation Reservation. Finally, Warburg also handed over his camera and had his picture taken (probably by the owner of the trading settlement) together with one of the Navajo, an older man who was rolling a cigarette, as we can tell from the thin sheet of paper he is holding between his lips. The result was a truly 'cinematographic' series of pictures; and it is only a seeming coincidence that the very next day Thomas Alva Edison presented for the first time in public one of his Vitascope films in New York.[3] However, Warburg concluded the vitascopic sequence of his own shots, which similarly document the need to record temporally extended processes in the medium of photography, with the very scene that shows him smoking a cigar beside a Navajo, whose sitting and bodily posture was imitated by the visitor.

The photographs taken in Keams Canyon also make clear that Warburg by no means only acted as a neutral observer who pursued the greatest possible objectivity; he often also sought the personal and sometimes even physical proximity of the people he photographed or spoke to. However, such behavior can hardly be interpreted as "participatory observation" (as in the case of, for instance, the ethnologist Frank Hamilton Cushing, who lived with the Zuni for many years); Warburg's encounters with the Pueblo and Navajo were too sporadic for there to be actual participation by the researcher in and with the communities he studied. Instead, his photographic practice occasionally led to clear intrusions, or even violations of taboos. In taking his photographs, the art and cultural historian abandoned the due scientific detachment and on such occasions

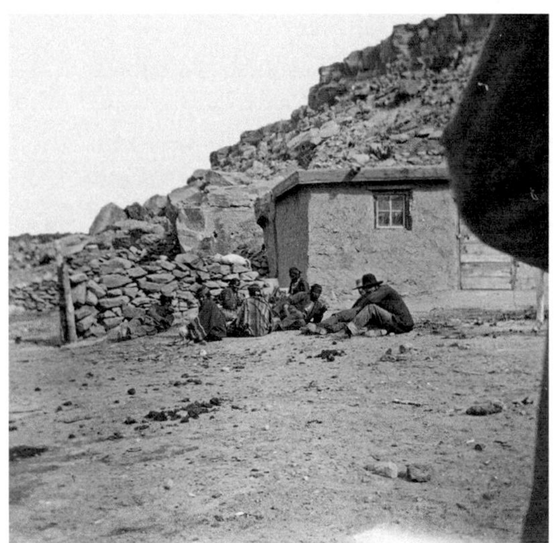

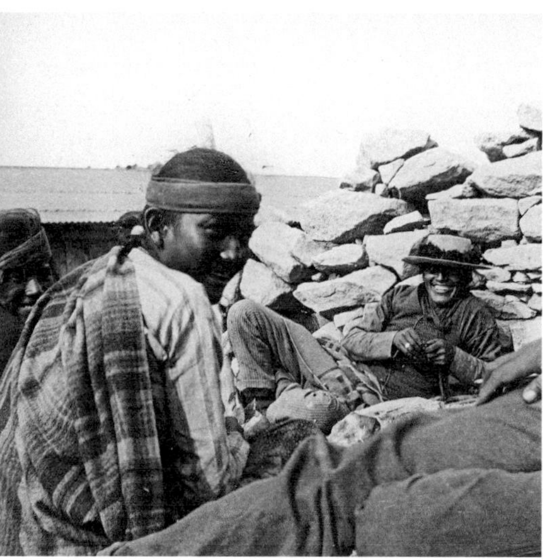

71–72 Aby Warburg: *A group of Navajo in Thomas Varker Keam's trading settlement*, 1896, photographs

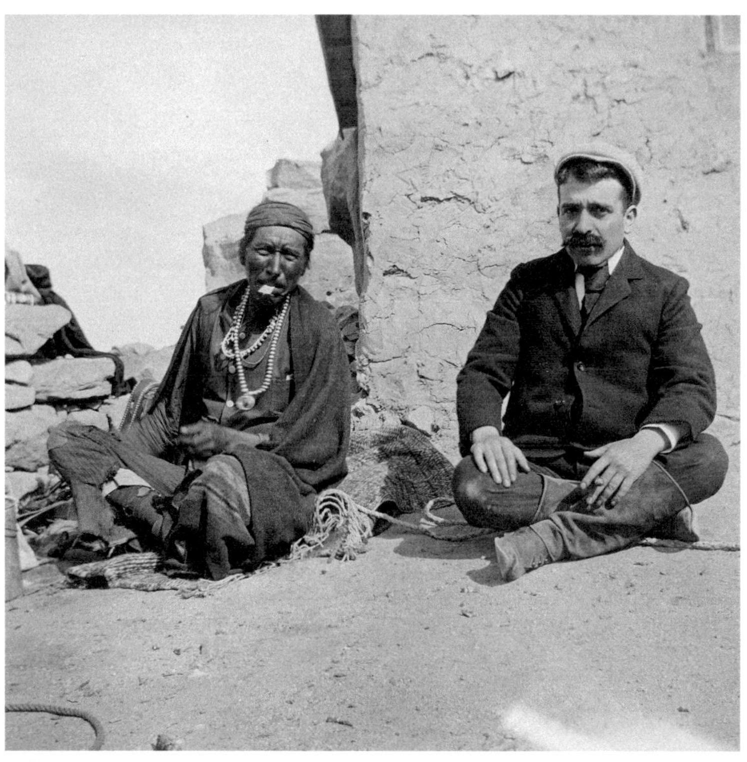

73 Anonymous photographer (probably Thomas Varker Keam, using Aby Warburg's camera): *Aby Warburg with a Navajo in Thomas Varker Keam's trading settlement*, 1896, photograph

did not objectively record in situations, but maintained his own subjective viewpoint. Photographic sequences of this kind thus show, beyond reproduction of the motif that interested him, the essentially personal role that every observer, in Warburg's day and also now, plays in his ethnological and cultural-history studies.

The Schoolchildren

The Keams Canyon Boarding School was founded in 1887 by the Bureau of Indian Affairs in Navajo County just a few miles east of the mesas inhabited by the Hopi. Originally attended by some fifty children, it was modeled on the state-run Carlisle Indian Industrial School in Pennsylvania and had been built on the site of the settler and trader Thomas Varker Keam's first settlement.[1] For this purpose Keam, who believed in any form of assimilation, had sent the US government a petition from representatives of the conciliatory faction of the Hopi ("Friendlies") calling for the school to be founded so that their children could learn "the Americans' tongue and their ways of work."[2] But it might also protect them from being sent to other boarding schools as far away as California, Kansas, or Pennsylvania, as often happened at the time.[3] The boys and girls of the Pueblo communities were required to attend such schools, which sometimes led to drastic coercive measures and even kidnappings, including in Keams Canyon. The political and ideological conflicts among the Hopi, which in 1906 would culminate in the "Oraibi Split," the secession and foundation of the new village of Hotvela by the traditional faction ("Hostiles"), also became visible with regard to this system of education, which was first introduced in the late 1870s.[4]

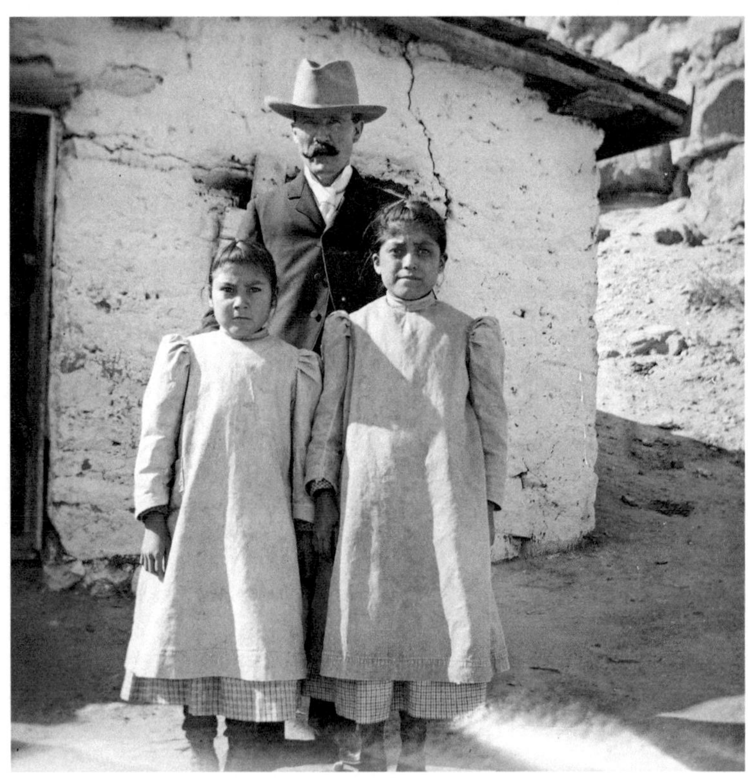

74 Aby Warburg: *The teacher Francis M. Neel with Hopi schoolgirls from the Keams Canyon Boarding School*, 1896, photograph

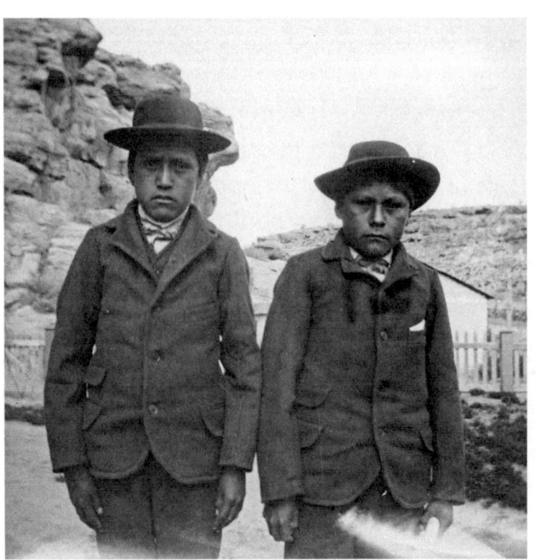

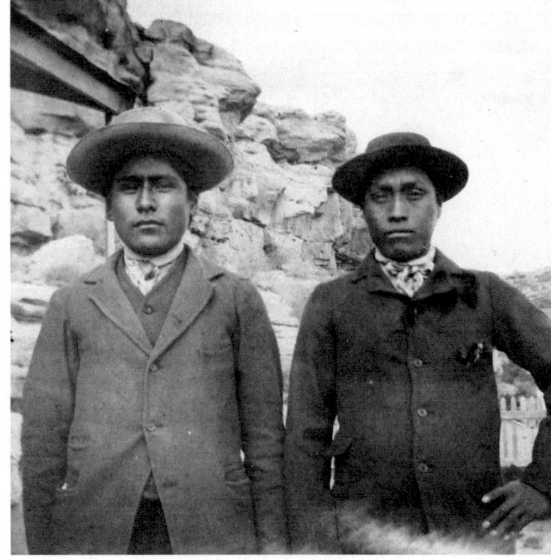

75–76 Aby Warburg: *Hopi schoolboys from the Keams Canyon Boarding School*, 1896, photographs

Although some parents–as well as their children–entirely favored education in the boarding schools, the advocates of a more conservative way of life, in particular, attempted to hide their sons and daughters from the authorities, who often came armed.[5]

The teacher Francis M. Neel, who had a good command of the Hopi language and spent many years working at various boarding schools run by the US Department of the Interior and was employed at the school until December 1896, later, in his capacity as superintendent of the Navajo Agency Boarding School in Fort Defiance, described the guiding principles of this type of school, and reported that there (unlike in Keams Canyon, where there were at least exceptions) the children were forbidden to speak their mother tongue during lessons: "The school was conducted on the principle that it is much better for an Indian child to learn to labor and to form habits of industry, where hand and muscle are required, than to spend so much time in schoolroom studies. The industrial force assisted greatly in compelling pupils to speak English. After every task performed each day the pupil was required to give an English sentence, and during work hours speaking Navajo was forbidden."[6]

When Aby Warburg visited the school in Keams Canyon in April 1896, he welcomed the progressive educational ideals conveyed there, for, as he wrote afterwards, the children "no longer believe in the pagan demons." Yet he also recognized the danger of imminent loss of their cultural identity: "This may certainly be progress. But I am not sure it will do justice to the Indians' visually oriented–or, shall we say, poetically and mythologically anchored–souls."[7] And Warburg was even fully aware of the violent conflicts associated with the introduction of the Christian-oriented education system, noting in his travel diary: "The Oraibi children are to be forced to attend school."[8] The very threat to their cultural identity caused him to have an experiment carried out in order to discover whether the now missionary-trained boarding-school pupils would still depict the natural phenomenon of lightning in the traditional cultural form of a snake. He therefore got the pupils to illustrate a story in which a thunderstorm was also mentioned; and two of the children did indeed draw the lightning in symbolic form.[9]

Warburg also photographed thirteen male and female pupils of the boarding school, who had been dressed in clothes appropriate to their adaptation to a modern lifestyle and had lost their traditional hairstyles.[10] Accompanied by their teacher in one of these portraits, the children are standing stiffly and timid before the photographer in high-necked suits or linen dresses, and looking either skeptically or with a slight smile, but some of them also with a degree of self-assurance, into the camera. However, in their evidently predetermined postures and the strict frontal view, designed to guarantee maximum objectivity, these photographs are compositionally very similar to anthropometric photography of the nineteenth and early twentieth centuries, which had not remained free of racist implications. Yet the modern observer cannot escape the fascinating idea that the children in these awkward portraits–who are not known by name–may have included the makers of the drawings that were so important to Aby Warburg.

The Lightning

Observing the various artifacts that he studied during his stay in the southwestern American pueblos, Aby Warburg repeatedly came across the lightning motif. He quickly learned that lightning was often represented by a snake symbol, for the similarity of the lightning and snake forms in Aztec art had already led to a causally interpreted magical connection between the meteorological phenomenon and the reptile. In April 1896, convinced that the Indigenous people of the villages he visited were at a cultural level in between a magical and a rational interpretation of the world, he took the opportunity to arrange at the Keams Canyon Boarding School an experiment suggested to him by the educationalist Earl Barnes during a visit to Stanford.[1] In his Kreuzlingen lecture Warburg described to his audience what his intention was: "I once tried to get the children of this very school to illustrate a German fairy tale that they did not previously know, *Johnny Head-in-the-Air*, because there was a thunderstorm in it, and I wanted to see if the children would draw the lightning realistically or in the form of a snake."[2] Warburg had assumed that in this way he could prove his theory of a lasting afterlife of predetermined motifs, for the school, in which the children were exposed to progressive educational ideals, seemed to him the right place for this. And, as he had expected: "Out of fourteen very vivid drawings that were influenced by the American school, twelve were drawn realistically. But two still showed the indestructible symbol of the arrow-headed snake that is found in the kiva."[3]

Some years after his return Warburg donated these sheets, which were so important to him, as well as the photographic portraits of some schoolchildren, to the Museum of Ethnology in his native city, where

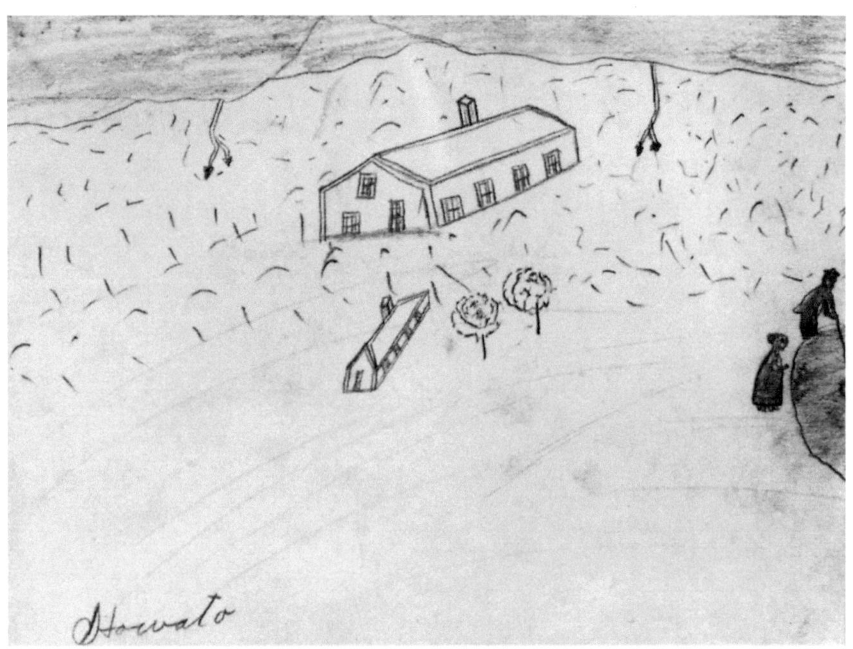

77 Goshoeneva Howato: *Buildings and people, as well as lightning in the form of double-headed snakes*, 1896, whereabouts unknown (formerly Hamburg, Museum für Völkerkunde)

78 Wí-ki (priest of the Antelope fraternity): *Sand Painting with Rain Clouds and Lightning in Snake Form from the Moñ'-kiva in Walpi*, 1891, drawing from Jesse Walter Fewkes: *The Snake Ceremonials at Walpi*, in *A Journal of American Ethnology and Archaeology* 4/1894, pp. 1–126, after p. 18

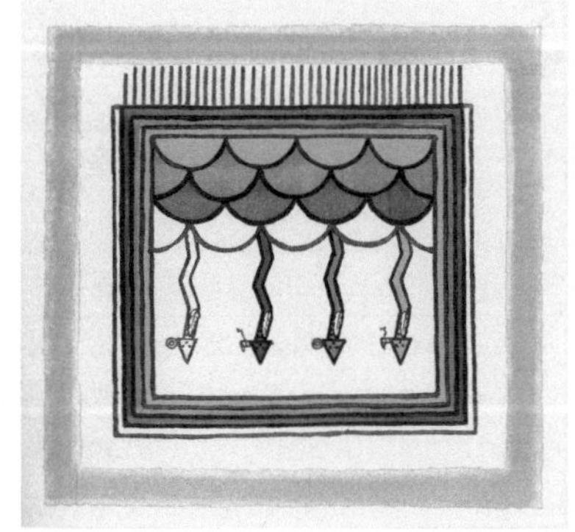

they were still traceable up to 1939.[4] Previously, however, he submitted the drawings to an exhibition organized in 1898 by the Hamburg Kunsthalle under the title *Das Kind als Künstler* (The Child as Artist), and commented on them in the catalogue published on that occasion: "It is ethnologically interesting that individual children drew the lightning as an arrow or as a snake with an arrow-tipped head, and also the clouds in the same stylized manner as their pagan fellow tribespeople still depict them during the Snake Dance in sand paintings on the floors of their underground assembly areas."[5] The depiction of lightning in the form of a snake from a kiva in Walpi to which Warburg is referring here was also, in photographic reproduction, among his donations and unfortunately, like the drawings themselves, was lost during or after World War II. Luckily, an admittedly not very successful black-and-white reproduction was made of one of the two sheets that supported Warburg's theory of "afterlife of Pueblo symbols,", so that we at least still have an approximate visual impression of the depiction.[6]

Although the name of the boy who signed his drawing in the bottom left-hand corner was not mentioned either in Warburg's texts or in the research, he has recently been identified.[7] In all likelihood he was Goshoeneva Howato, who was born around 1885, probably came from Polacca near Keams Canyon, and was later enrolled at the Grand Junction Indian Training School in nearby Mesa County. What is notable about Warburg's human interest in the children is that he did not just collect and scientifically assess their illustrations, but also recorded the young artists' names: In a notepad there are two columns listing twelve names–not fourteen, as he may have misremembered in 1923–including that of Howato, who had evidently misunderstood a word when the story was being read out ("heard 'log,' not 'dog'").[8]

What Warburg had arranged to have read out to the children in both English and their mother tongue was an amended and greatly abridged version of *Die Geschichte vom Hanns Guck-in-die-Luft* (The Story of Johnny Head-in-the-Air) from Heinrich Hoffmann's popular 1845 children's book *Struwwelpeter* (Shock-Headed Peter), to which he had added a thunderstorm: "It was a dark, cloudy day with a lot of lightning. A mother told her son not to leave the house, but still he went out into the storm. The storm became so violent that he went back and tripped over a dog he had not seen, and fell into a pool, where his father found him and pulled him out with a long pole."[9] Goshoeneva Howato incorporated these details almost literally into his drawing, which has probably only partly survived in the reproduction; on the right-hand edge of the detail that has come down to us is a scene in which the parents, with the father wielding the pole referred to, are trying to pull the submerged boy out of the pool, and above the landscape with the two structures captured from scholarly angles we can see the dark clouds, from which two bolts of lightning are flashing onto the ground.[10] These are again depicted as two-headed snakes, so that here too we see "the snake in the form of lightning, magically and causally connected to it."[11] So, despite his Euro-American education, the schoolboy depicted "the snake as a lightning symbol," thereby confirming Aby Warburg's assumption that traditional imagery still determined at least how some Hopis thought even under changed cultural conditions.[12]

The Missionary

On the morning of April 28, 1896, Aby Warburg arrived at the Mennonite mission founded near the Third Mesa by the German-Russian pastor Henry R. Voth. The traveler had evidently not announced his arrival ("he has been referred to me from various quarters"), but Voth took the visitor under his wing, helped him with his studies, and on the very first evening and in the coming days accompanied him to Oraibi, some three miles from the mission post.[1] There the two men descended into one of the underground kivas and observed the preparations for the spring dances—the reason why Warburg had traveled to the ancient village, which had been inhabited for around two thousand years. Voth had assembled large stocks of Pueblo artworks in his modest home through barter with the Hopi; Warburg examined them on the two days after his arrival ("Dr. W[arburg] thinks my collection is valuable").[2] Although the art historian immediately recognized the knowledge that Voth, "the most adroit and best observer of Indian ceremonies," possessed about Hopi art and culture, his reservations about what he called the "quirky" and "selfish" missionary grew during his stay.[3] When Warburg wanted to purchase some items from Voth's study collection and offered a sum for selected Katsina figures that was evidently deemed insufficient, the two men fell out. Warburg accused his host of "the basest pursuit of profit," and eventually purchased fewer objects than he probably at first intended, but these did include five painted prayer sticks (*pahos*) that were decorated with feathers.[4]

The later missionary was born under the name of Heinrich Richert Voth into the originally West Prussian Mennonite colony Alexanderwohl at Molochna in southern Russia in 1855. He emigrated to the United States in 1874, and was a pastor in the Oraibi area from 1893 to 1902, after working for ten years as both a missionary and an ethnologist among the Cheyennes and the Arapahos.[5] Besides his missionary activity, Voth,

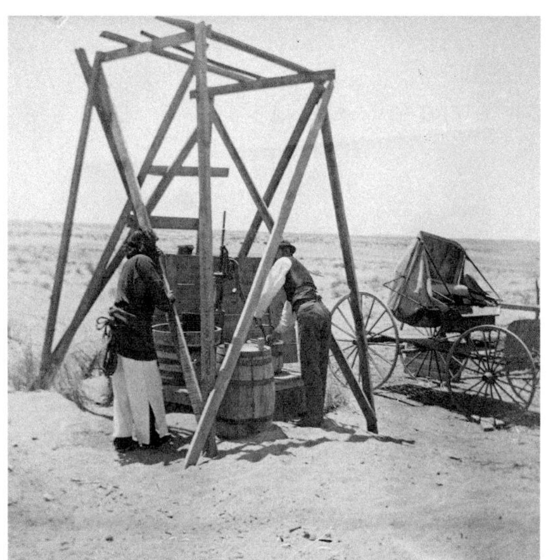

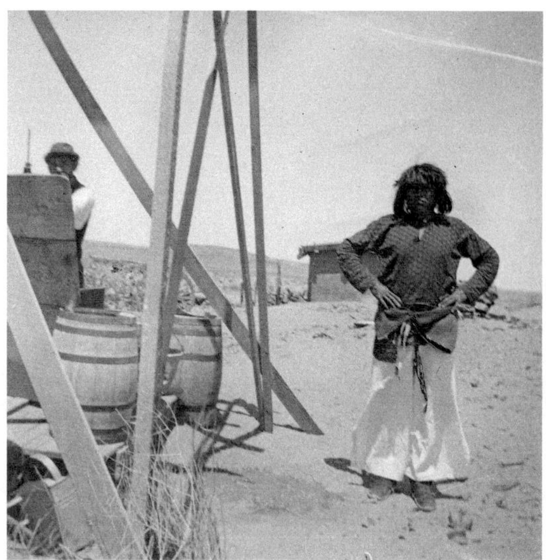

79–80 Aby Warburg: *Henry R. Voth with a Hopi at the well in the grounds of the Mennonite mission post*, 1896, photographs

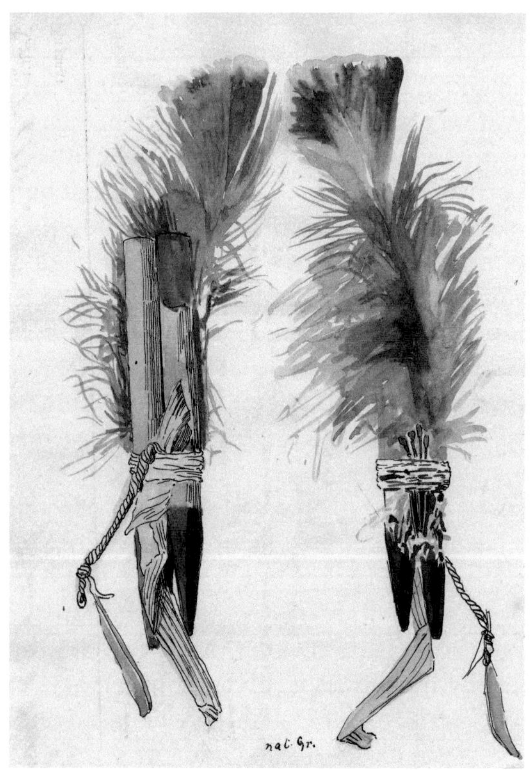

81 Anonymous artist: *Prayer intermediary (paho)*, ca. 1890–1896 (acquired by Aby Warburg from Henry R. Voth), index-card drawing, after 1907

together with his wife Martha, provided the Pueblo people with medical care, took lessons in the Hopi language, researched local myths, dances, and songs, and received repeated visits from not only American scientists because of his outstanding cultural and religious knowledge. He himself published important papers on the rituals he observed in the surrounding villages, including the 1903 book *The Oraibi Summer Snake Ceremony*.[6] And his descriptions of the various ceremonies were so detailed and accurate that in at least one case they were even used by the Hopi in later years to reconstruct and suitably revive forgotten ceremonial processes–a most ironic twist in view of his persistent efforts to suppress such "pagan" rituals.[7] During his time in Arizona, with its privations, concerns, and disease, Voth furthermore documented life in the mission and the surrounding villages in hundreds of photographs, some of which he also left to Warburg.[8] And even though it was officially forbidden by his church, he at least occasionally traded in the artworks and ritual objects he had acquired from the Hopi; and after abandoning his missionary work he sold many items from his collections to museums both in the United States and abroad.[9]

Voth's work as a missionary and researcher is nowadays much criticized, for among other things he gained access to the Hopi sanctuaries without permission and is said to have acquired some of the works in his collection illicitly. The main source of such charges is the memoirs of Don C. Talayesva, who grew up in Oraibi and described Voth and his conduct as follows in his autobiography: "The land was very dry, the crops suffered, and even the Snake dance failed to bring much rain. We tried to discover the reason for our plight, and remembered the Rev. Voth who had stolen so many of our ceremonial secrets and had even carried off sacred images and altars to equip a museum and become a rich man. When he had worked here in my boyhood, the Hopi were afraid of him and dared not lay their hands on him or any other missionary, lest they be jailed by the Whites. During the ceremonies this wicked man would force his way into the kiva and write down everything he saw. He wore shoes with solid heels, and when the Hopi tried to put him out of the kiva he would kick them."[10]

Yet Voth's actions, as well as his personality, were a good deal more complex than these accusatory lines imply. The diaries that Heinrich and Martha Voth kept after arriving in Arizona record that he was remarkably often allowed to enter the kivas. There he took part in gatherings, repeatedly used the places for missionary lectures in which he also showed pictures, or attended Hopi rituals. But the diaries also note times when he was refused access: "Hein[rich] was again on the mesa, but returned home early[,] [the Hopi] no longer wanted him in the kiva, where he had already spent some days observing and studying the preparations for the dance."[11] On February 17, 1895, for example, Voth made a drawing of the snake altar in the Antelope priests' kiva in Oraibi ("which did somewhat amaze them"), and then wondered "whether they will now let me attend their ceremonies later on."[12] There are also details of extensive theological discussions with some Hopis, in which the missionary tried to win them over to Christian beliefs; and finally Shókhunyoma, the old high priest of the Soyal fraternity, even gave Voth's son Albert Cornelius, who was born on October 10, 1895, the name Honanshokioma (abbreviated to Honchoki)–a clue that the family was accepted into the social structures of the Hopi community.[13] In other ways, too, the missionary enjoyed the trust of some Hopis, even including members of the "Hostiles" faction, acted as their interpreter and advocate on official occasions, and admired their culture, although as a Mennonite missionary he of course had to reject their religious convictions: "What a pantheon, what a religious system, what a rich language, what traditions, what organization! And yet how utterly little to satisfy the longings of the soul, to give peace to the heart for this life and a hope for eternity."[14]

The portrait of Henry R. Voth that can be drawn from this–and other–sources thus remains as indistinct as the only pictures Warburg took of him during his stay at the mission: In one of the two snapshots, accompanied by an anonymous Hopi at a well on the property, the pastor has turned his back on the photographer, and his head is obscured by a beam; and in the other, which is blurred, he is peering out from behind some wooden planks. So it was not only in his diary notes that Warburg provided a contradictory picture of this controversial man.

The Cane

Among the ritual instruments that Aby Warburg acquired during his visits to the Hopi, one occupies a very special place: a 43-centimeter wooden rod, bent at the end, to which a second, blade-shaped carved piece was lashed with a cord–according to Warburg's notes a "weeding knife."[1] Henry R. Voth, from whom he had purchased the object, also told him its exact local name, which Warburg wrote down, noting on the occasion that he had seen such an object as an attribute of a Katsina figure in the missionary's collection ("the female Kats[ina] doll carrying the ngö-lösch-hoya, the crook").[2] Warburg had probably not fully grasped the various religious functions of such wooden rods, for he saw the item in his collection purely as a prayer stick, a *paho* (older spelling: *baho*), like the specimens he was also able to acquire from Voth.[3] However, unlike these artifacts, which were painted and decorated with feathers and parts of plants as vehicles of various petitions and, for example, were stuck into the earth near fields or wells or deposited as gifts, the *ngölöshoya* acquired by Warburg was only coated in white, today largely faded, paint (though it cannot be ruled out that one or more attached feathers have been lost) and hence looks extremely plain.[4]

Why the art historian bought the aesthetically none too attractive object in the first place can only be explained by what Warburg assumed was the unusual shape of what he took to be a *paho*. In the collection list which he drew up for the items he had taken back to Germany he assumed that this was a "crooked walking cane used as a baho."[5] Ever in search of hybrid forms that displayed exchange between different cultures–forms that Warburg likewise sought in European visual arts–he probably also saw the bent wooden rod as a "product of encounter."[6] The art historian

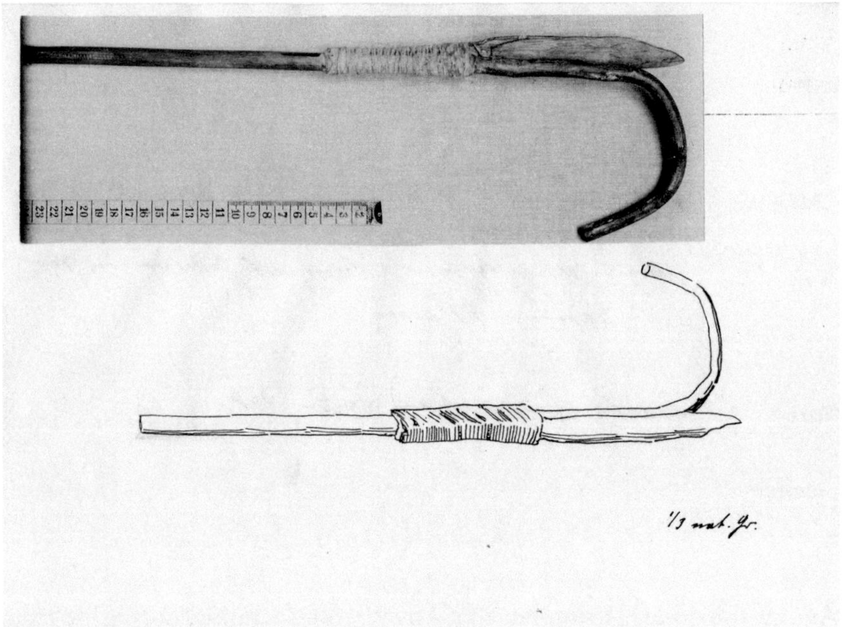

82 Anonymous artist: *Ritual implement of the Maraw society (probably owned by Kuwanwikvaya)*, ca. 1890–1896, index-card drawing with pasted photograph, after 1907

used this term, which he only coined later, in an attempt to describe the relationship between individual and traditional, native and migrating forms of expression that was inherent in each artifact.

Such crooked rods, which have survived in various lengths, were used for a variety of purposes: As tangible vehicles of the wish for a long, happy life they were carried in Katsina dances and other ceremonies, they served (like *pahos*) as prayer intermediaries in the open country, or they were placed on altars for the same reason; but they could also be used as badges of membership of religious societies.[7] However, Warburg's association with a "walking cane" was by no means incorrect, for the Hopi did indeed see the crooked form as a symbol of age: "... the crook (ñwelü'kpi) [signifies] the bent old men who walk with their heads bending over and looking down toward the Below from whence people came and where all must return."[8] The specimen acquired by Warburg probably came from the Maraw society, and was presumably made by its high priest Kuwanwikvaya, who often worked for Voth and, as his diary reveals, mainly ran errands for him.[9] However, the man whom Martha Voth called one of their best friends in the Oraibi area also sold Voth other artifacts, discussed with him religious questions not only about the Hopi ("When I explained that the staff of Moses turned into a snake, he said Moses must then have been a snake priest"), and finally was one of the very few inhabitants of Oraibi to convert to Christianity, though only after the missionary had ceased to work there.[10]

Thus the supposed "walking cane" can by no means be seen as a reused, spiritually charged everyday object that was used by Euro-American settlers and then assigned a new cross-cultural religious function, as a fascinated Warburg appears to have assumed. Instead, the crooked wooden rod, as a purely autochthonous object, is further material evidence of the Hopi ritual culture in all its complex organization.

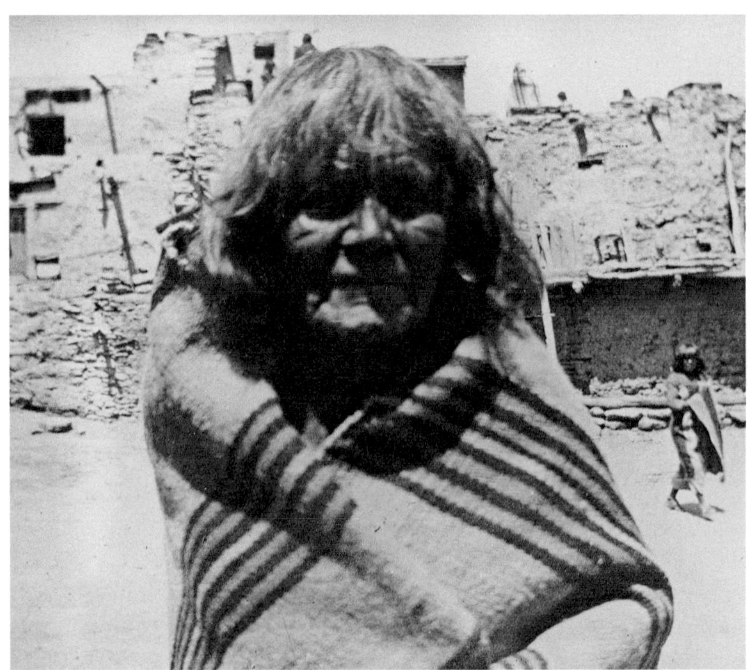

83 Aby Warburg: *Loololma, Hopi local leader in Oraibi*, 1896, photograph

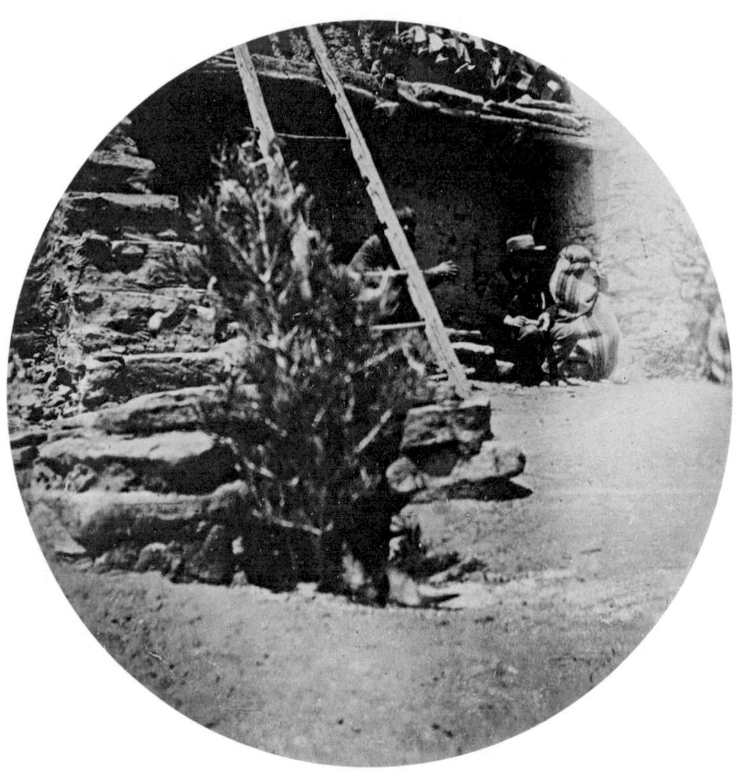

84 Henry R. Voth: *Stone altar and Douglas fir decorated with feathers, and in the background on the right Aby Warburg with local leader Loololma*, 1896, photograph

The Chief

The man is looking attentively at the visitor with deep-set eyes that are shaded by the sun. His face, marked with the signs of age, is fringed with graying hair that just reaches down to his shoulders; his upper body is wrapped in a thick, close-fitting, striped blanket, probably made of sheep's wool. The hands, clutching the inside of this cloak, cannot be seen. Compositionally the photograph is focused entirely on the person; only in the background do we see some houses on the edge of the large village square that is being crossed by a second Hopi, houses whose weather-beaten facades, like some architectural echo, have captured the passing of time that has also shaped the man's face. Aby Warburg, who took this picture in Oraibi in May 1896, must have sensed that this photograph would display the man in his full dignity and statuesque pose, as a monument to his people and its recent history.

We do not know if Warburg had been told that the old man, whose name he recorded in his notes as "Lelohmai," was an important and famous Hopi leader.[1] In all likelihood he had been introduced to the visitor by Henry R. Voth, who accompanied the art historian to Oraibi; but Warburg must have misunderstood the name quoted to him on this occasion. The man was in fact Loololma, chief of the Bear Clan, whose biography is one of the most fascinating tales from the American Southwest. As village chief (*kikmongwi*) from 1880 onwards, Loololma, who died in or shortly before 1904, played a key role in the "Oraibi Split," the schism between ideologically conflicting factions within the Hopi.[2] Whereas the "Friendlies" (or "New Hopi") that he led supported many of the US government's measures, their conservative opponents, the "Hostiles," rejected Euro-American influences on principle, and in 1906, after bitter clashes, they quit the village community to found one of their own.

Loololma had also advocated the establishment and teaching methods of the Keams Canyon Boarding School, and in June 1890 had traveled to Washington to meet high-ranking government officials, if not (as is often rumored) the US president.[3] Thomas Varker Keam acted as an interpreter for the delegation, which spent a month visiting cultural and educational institutions on the East Coast and in Indiana, including the Carlisle Indian Industrial School in Pennsylvania. According to official documents Loololma, who actually had the support of a large part of the population, took the opportunity to lament his own special position within the Hopi: "My people are blind. Their ears are closed. I am the only one. I am alone. They don't want to go in the white men's way, although I am Chief."[4] Conflicts over forced school attendance and land surveying, resettlement and other assimilation plans gradually came to a head, and threatened to end in outbreaks of violence. US troops eventually came to the aid of Loololma's faction in Oraibi, and in November 1894 they arrested some leaders of the "Hostiles" and interned them on the prison island of Alcatraz in San Francisco Bay.

Aby Warburg and Henry R. Voth, who lived only a few miles away, had come to Oraibi to watch the spring dances there. The missionary knew Loololma well, and so he could translate the conversation which Warburg reported in his lecture *Bilder aus dem Gebiet der Pueblo-Indianer in Nord-Amerika* (Images from the Region of the Pueblo Indians of North America). The visitors had been struck by a "small temple," a young Douglas fir decorated with special feathers (*nakwakoci*) to which some of the dance figures were oriented: "We therefore went to the old chief who was sitting at the end of the square and asked him why the tree was so small. To which he replied: 'We used to have a big tree, but now we have a small one, for the child's soul is pure.'"[5] Warburg thereupon considered the feather-decorated tree as part of a "tree and soul cult" of a kind also found in Germanic pagan rites, and compared its function to that of a petition.[6] Voth then photographed this "temple," together with Warburg, a notebook on his lap, as well as Loololma sitting on a low stone bench, as they calmly watched the dances.

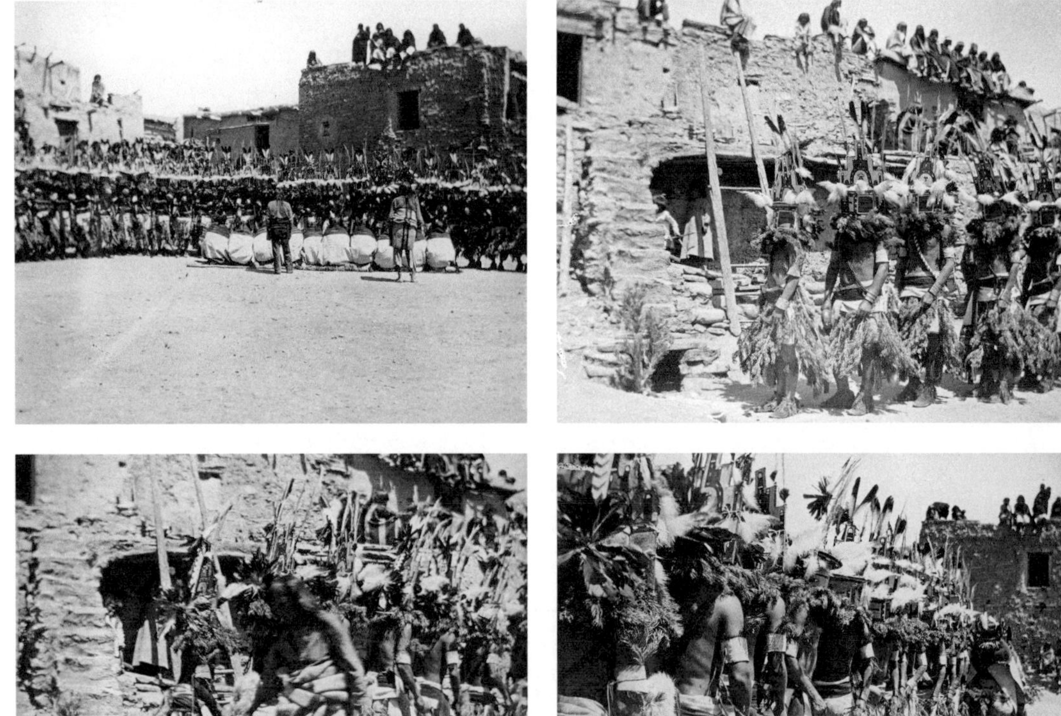

85–88 Aby Warburg: *Hemiskatsinam during the spring dance in Oraibi*, 1896, photographs

The Ritual

The Katsinam (singular: Katsina) are spiritual beings that embody all the life forces of the cosmos. They visit the pueblos from the end of winter until July, when their departure is celebrated in the Nímaniw ("Home Dance") ceremony. During these months various dance rituals based on the calendar of the vegetation and seasonal cycle take place. Through their multiple beneficial influence–they bring rain, ensure a good harvest and much else–Katsinam appear in countless anthropomorphic forms, as dolls known as *tithu* (singular: *tihu*), with whose help the girls to whom they are given learn to distinguish the various figures in the complex pantheon of Hopi mythology, but also in the masks of the dancers, who through their rituals do not simply act the roles of the Katsinam but, according to Pueblo religious beliefs, become one with them.[1]

Although in America Aby Warburg had already bought some *tithu*, including from Thomas Varker Keam and Henry R. Voth, but also in the village of Walpi, the purpose and high point of his journey to America was to attend one of the Katsina rituals: "For I had come to Oraibi to see such a dance, which is ethnologically the most interesting."[2] On the evening of April 28, 1896, he therefore went with Voth to the old center of the village, a few miles from the Mennonite mission, and in the Wikiolabi kiva ("where the secret ceremonies take place") he was able to observe the preparations for the spring dances.[3] The two men repeated this visit in the coming days, saw some young Hopis painting their masks, and spoke to them, as Voth noted in his diary ("had a lively conversation with the Indians about the meaning of the signs on the masks").[4] Although the missionary was accused of occasionally obtaining access to the kivas by force, his visit with Warburg was evidently at least tolerated by the Hopi.[5] Voth was also able to obtain permission for other scientists, such as the Berlin ethnologist Paul Ehrenreich in August 1898, to study some parts of the ceremonial areas together with him ("I was the only white who was again allowed to see everything in the kivas").[6] On May 1, 1896, Warburg and his host then watched the Hemiskatsina ritual, whose purpose was to help the corn plants flourish. These deities were normally not due to appear until the seasonal cycle of the dances for the Nímaniw, the ritual departure of the Katsinam. However, the Hemiskatsinam occasionally appeared earlier, even outside the ritual calendar in mixed dances (perhaps the ritual known as *Hakitonmuya*), and reminded the Hopi of the forthcoming summer departure of the spirit beings from their villages.[7] It was only for this reason that Warburg, who left the United States by the end of May, could observe the dances of the Hemiskatsinam. After his return the art historian described his walk through the village, the audience that had gathered, and finally the actual dances, just as he documented his visit with the photographs he took in Oraibi on this occasion.[8] Warburg and Voth watched the event until noon, then returned to the village in the late afternoon and experienced the performance by some "almost stark-naked" clowns (*tsutskut*, singular: *tsuku*).[9] However, they perceived the gestures of the men and some dancers dressed as women as "highly obscene," and immediately ended their visit.[10]

In 1923, Warburg described the dance ritual in his lecture *Bilder aus dem Gebiet der Pueblo-Indianer in Nord-Amerika* (Images from the Region of the Pueblo Indians of North America) in full detail, and also wove some interpretative comments into his report: "The dance was performed by some twenty to thirty men and some ten female dancers, i.e. men representing females ... The chorus performs two different acts. Either the girls sit in front of the men and make their music with a piece of wood on rasps, while the men's dance figure consists of them simply rotating on their axis one after the other, or else the women rise and accompany the men's revolving movements. Two priests were sprinkling them with consecrated flour."[11] Warburg also described the actual dance masks, the "Katsina Friends" (painted helmets with tall *tablitas*–Spanish for "tables," *kopatsoki* in Hopi–which were decorated with feathers and grasses), the costume, and the paraphernalia carried by the dancers, and particularly drew his audience's attention to the various meteorological symbols: "The dancers' mask is green and red, diagonally bisected by a white stripe along which three dots are placed. These, I was told, were the raindrops, and all the symbolism on the helmet primarily shows the stratified universe with the bringer of rain, always marked by semicircular clouds and lines extending from them. The same symbolism is found on their very gracefully woven body wraps, red and green ornaments on a white background. The male dancers are each holding a rattle made of a hollow gourd with stones inside it. And around their knees a tortoise shell with stones hanging down from it, so that rattling sounds also come from the knees ... The women's dance costume consists of a cloth that completely envelops the figures, so as not to show that these are men. On the sides at the top of the mask are the curious bindweed-like hairstyles so typical of Pueblo girls. Red-dyed horse hair hanging down from the mask symbolizes the rain, and rain ornaments are also to be seen on their shawls and body wraps."[12]

Yet the lecture at the Kreuzlingen sanatorium was not the first time that Warburg dealt with documentation on his trip to America. In the months immediately after his return he had additional photographs forwarded, got in touch with German ethnologists and museums of ethnology, tried to arrange purchases from the United States, and among other things asked Voth to let him publish his studies on the Snake Dance.[13] As he wrote to the missionary on October 2, 1896, he himself was then preparing an essay on the Hemiskatsina dance; but the questions he asked him make clear that Warburg had not yet made much progress with the scientific penetration of his observations. Besides information on nomenclature and certain details of the ritual, he particularly wanted to know from Voth what exactly the terms "Hemis" and "Katsina" meant.[14] The dances the art historian had seen in Oraibi in May 1896 had a very special relevance för Warburg, for they confirmed his assumption that the Pueblo culture was "midway between magic and logos."[15]

In his 1923 lecture he drew far-reaching cultural history conclusions from this, not without thinking of his own illness. Unlike in the Aztec ritual of the Chicomecoatl, in which "a woman representing a corn deity was worshiped as a goddess for forty days, and then sacrificed," whereupon a priest was clad "in this poor creature's skin," he did believe that the Hemiskatsina dance had shown itself to be a surviving phenomenon, but the former bloodshed in Mexico had been domesticated among the

Hopi by symbolic acts: "Although everything that can be observed in the Pueblo corn dance is basically related to this most elementary, insane (schizophrenic) attempt to approximate the deity, it is no longer cannibalistic–although frankly there can be no guarantee that sap does not secretly rise from the bloody roots of the cult."[16]

The Grasping Man

Many of the pictures that Aby Warburg took in his encounters with the Pueblo and the Navajo make clear that the art historian did not only want to observe his models from a distance. When he photographed the Hemiskatsinam dance in Oraibi in early May 1896, Warburg likewise crossed the boundaries of the purely recording scientist. During a pause in the dance he approached the men in a place of rest (*katsìnki*). Since they embodied the Katsinam, seeing them unmasked would mean death, as he wrote in retrospect in the manuscript for his Kreuzlingen lecture: "Anyone who sees a dancer without a mask dies."[1] And yet Warburg grasped the arm of one of the men who had interrupted their ritual, and had himself photographed with the Hopi man, probably by Henry R. Voth, who had accompanied him that day. The man's unmistakably skeptical gaze shows just how awkward the situation must have been for him.[2] The fact that the visual essence of Warburg's journey to America, and specifically its problematic aspects, were somehow concentrated in this highly delicate photograph was long overlooked by researchers–and so the picture of the art historian with the resting Katsina dancer was often used as an illustration for publications and events.[3]

Beyond the controversial nature of this scene, the photograph can also be interpreted in terms of its cultural-historical depth–for the grasping motif captured in it shows just how much the researcher, who had abandoned his only permitted spectator's role, was carried away by the extraordinary situation. He accordingly responded with a primitive tactile reflex, while the dancer himself was wearing on his chest the abstract

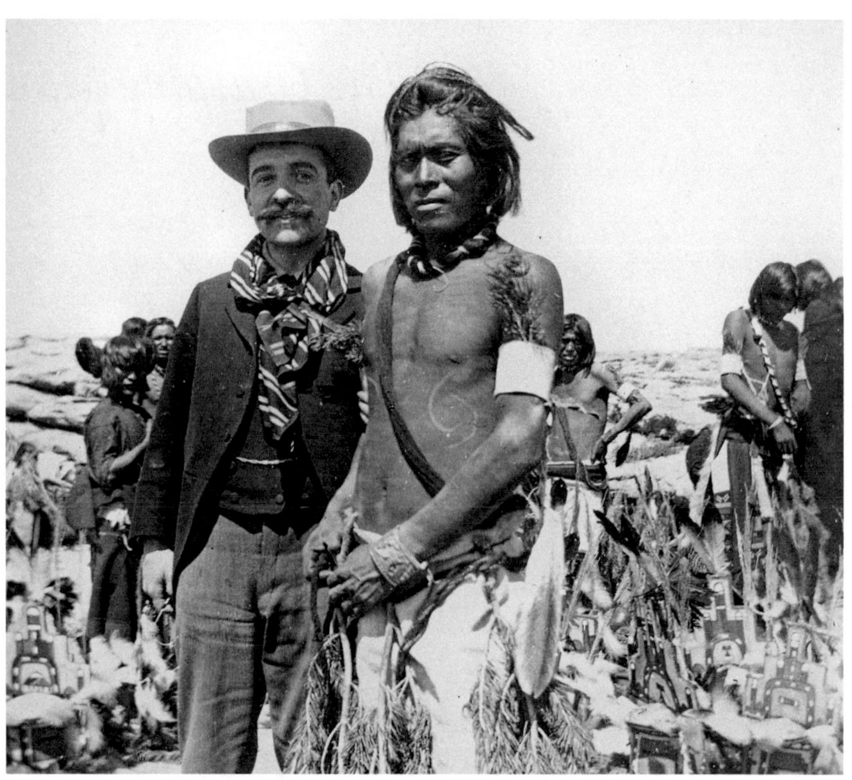

89 Anonymous photographer (probably Henry R. Voth, using Aby Warburg's camera): *Aby Warburg with one of the Hemiskatsina dancers in Oraibi*, 1896, photograph

symbol of two entwined hands, "the so-called sign of friendship" (*nakwatsveni*) of the Hopis: In the preparations for the ritual the semicircles, which are only faintly visible in the photograph, had been traced in the scorched-corn powder applied to the body.[4] Warburg himself, who could have likened the symbol to the Roman-medieval *mani in fede* (hands clasped in faith) motif of friendship or marriage, must not have noted this inversion of the cultural behavior he had postulated either in the actual situation or when looking at the photograph. Yet his study of symbolism in Pueblo art would later help him formulate the beginnings of a theory of cultural development. The suppression of magic by logos, the cultural and civilizational shift from what Warburg calls "having to apprehend" to "seeking to comprehend," which among the Hopi had in his view already reached the intermediate stage of symbolism, was to preoccupy the art historian throughout his life, not least in his research into the history of astrology.[5]

Thinking about the relationship between primitive physical grasping and intellectual conceptual grasping would even help him recover from his own mental illness.[6] At the Kreuzlingen sanatorium in 1923, in order to overcome his bipolar affective disorder, which had left him in a state of "primitive," indeed "magical" connection between phenomenon and cause without mental detachment, Warburg made use of his experiences during his American journey, and described the cultural level of the Hopi with the cognitive word play that so typified him: "They are not truly primitive grasping men, for whom activity relating to the future does not exist, but nor are they yet truly technologically reassured Europeans, who look forward to future events as something organically or mechanically predictable. They are midway between magic and logos, and the instrument they use for orientation is the symbol. Between physically grasping men and intellectually grasping men stands the one who is linking by means of symbols."[7] It is quite remarkable how unexpectedly the photograph taken in Oraibi in 1896 is a visual reflection of the afterlife of primitive "having to apprehend" in his own gesture which Warburg had undoubtedly not planned, and which he must have understood as completely innocuous.

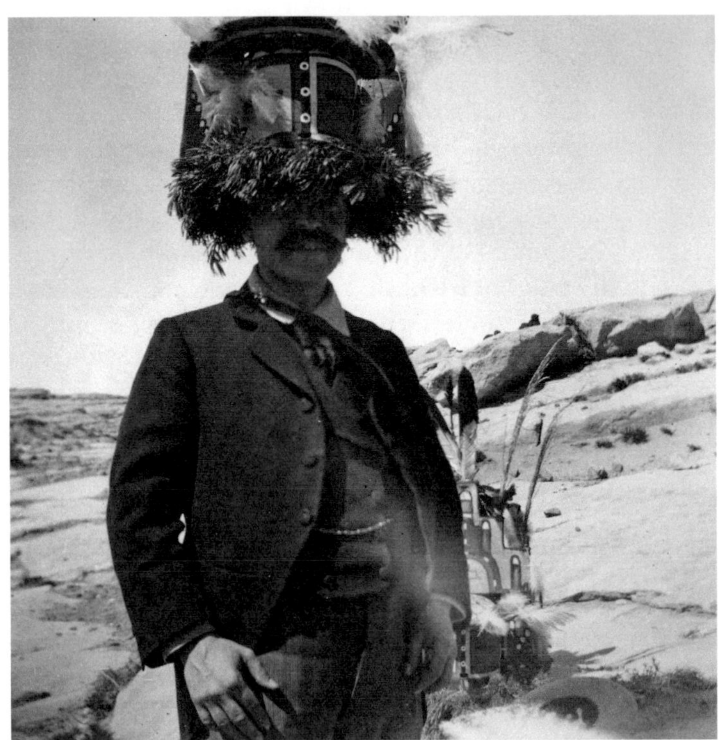

90 Anonymous photographer (probably Henry R. Voth, using Aby Warburg's camera): *Aby Warburg wearing a Hemiskatsina helmet mask in Oraibi*, 1896, photograph

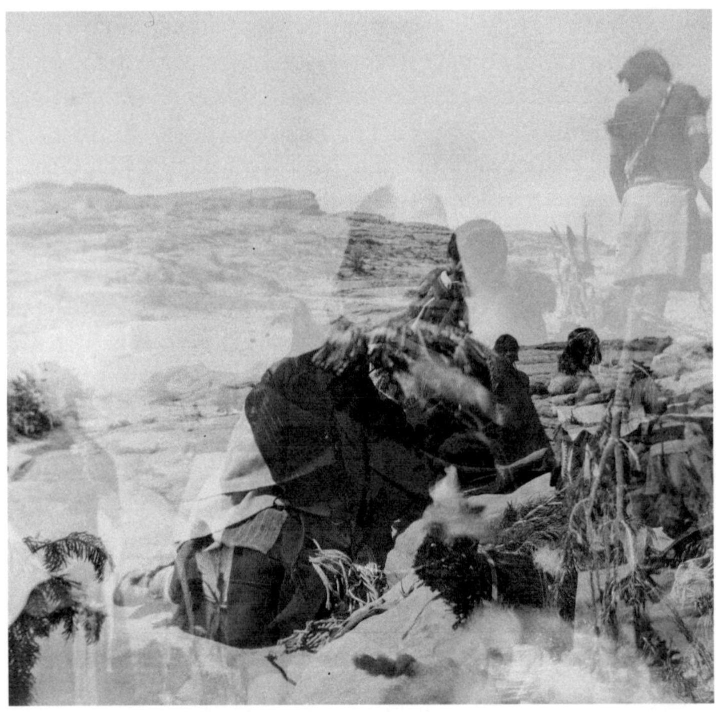

91 Aby Warburg and anonymous photographer (probably Henry R. Voth): *Hemiskatsinam at a place of rest in Oraibi, with a superimposed portrait of Aby Warburg*, 1896, doubly or multiply exposed photograph

The Mask

After observing the Hemiskatsinam in Oraibi on May 1, 1896, not only in their dance but also during a break in the ritual, when he did not shrink from approaching one of the Hopis in an inappropriate manner, Aby Warburg committed yet another irreverent act: As an intervening spectator he put on one of the helmet masks which the dancers had temporarily laid aside.[1] The photograph of this, which was to acquire some celebrity in the reception of his American journey, was reproduced again and again on posters and book covers, and as a text illustration.[2] If we look more closely at the picture of this scene, which was probably taken by Henry R. Voth, it is clear that Warburg must himself have realized how questionable his behavior was. His facial expression and tense posture show that he felt rather awkward about violating this taboo. Moreover, he was wearing the mask in an incorrect manner, revealing his face–and hence his own identity. Warburg had evidently sensed the temptation of surrendering to the magical ritual, the temptation of loss of self, of transformation and incarnation, but he had not succumbed to it. This may also explain why the picture, which showed the art historian as a wannabe Katsina dancer and would later become one of the icons of Warburg research, was never displayed at any of his lectures.[3]

In the photograph the helmet is cropped from the upper edge of the picture; otherwise we could have seen, above the colorfully painted cylindrical part with its wreath of fir twigs, which should normally have extended down to the wearer's shoulders, a wooden table (*kopatsoki*) in the form of a stepped gable with cloud, rain, and other weather and harvest symbols, as well as additional feather and grass decorations. In contrast, because of the incorrect use of the mask, the two eye slits are located a long way above the head, and are easily recognizable. Such masks–or rather, such face masks, for the mask itself actually includes the whole "costume" and such accessories as Douglas fir twigs or pumpkin rattles, and the accompanying bodily adornment–not only enable the dancers to represent the Hemiskatsinam when they appear in a village community, but above all ensure that the dancer, when he dons the helmet mask, which is interpreted as an animated "Katsina Friend" (*Katsina kwaatsi* in the Hopi language), actually becomes one of these spirit beings and completely assumes its sacred persona.[4] This also explains the rule that the dancers must not be seen during their "disenchanting" rest break, as well as the strict ban on any representation of the dancers and their dances, which applies to this day and came into force at different times in the various pueblos, but no later than the early 1920s.[5]

An unsuccessful, doubly or perhaps even multiply exposed photograph which was also taken in Oraibi during the break in the spring dances eerily shows the possible consequences of slipping into a mask and fusing with another, supernatural being. Here Warburg had again had himself photographed in front of the group of resting dancers; his face–and hence his physical existence–vanishes, with shadowy outlines and at least two other faces, as well as a section of the barren landscape and some of the fir twigs used in the ritual, superimposed on his face and upper body, so that the viewer is confronted here with a truly terrifying picture of a numinous composite figure. Of course, this involuntary configuration slipped into the repeatedly exposed negative by accident and in no way corresponded to the intended purpose (or the real content) of the situation in which the picture was taken. Yet photography is not just a technical objective process, but through its surreal power is able to summon up images that do not directly match observed reality. The ghostly portrait of Aby Warburg as a Hemiskatsina, produced by his own and another's hand, thus makes clear why not only the Pueblo had to treat the new medium with caution.

The Lecture

During his lifetime Aby Warburg battled with the demons in his own mind. From November 1918 onwards he received almost constant psychiatric treatment, sometimes entailing admission to an institution, and eventually the Bellevue clinic in Kreuzlingen, where his bipolar affective psychosis was initially misdiagnosed as incurable schizophrenia. With the collapse of the German Empire, the art historian–now also surrendering–had had to abandon all attempts to create the necessary reflective distance between himself and the oppressive news from the world war and the upheaval as it ended.[1] In September 1922, however, his physician Ludwig Binswanger urged his patient to attempt to write as a form of therapy; and, encouraged by his personal friend the philosopher Ernst Cassirer, who had been involved in work on his study *Die Begriffsform im mythischen Denken* (The Form of the Concept in Mythical Thinking), including Zuni mythology, Warburg had the study material he had assembled during his journey to America forwarded from Hamburg to him in Kreuzlingen.[2] Only by confronting the notes, sketches, and photographs, as he wrote to his wife, could he escape "from this spirit world into the world of health."[3]

On April 21, 1923, Warburg presented his lecture to the sanatorium patients and invited guests; despite the manuscript, it was largely extempore, and he by no means saw it as a completed–much less publishable–study. For three quarters of an hour he informed his audience about his travel experiences, offered reflections on the rituals he had studied at first hand, and related the Hopi Snake Dance to the cultic and iconographic

Ich will nicht, dass meine Bildvorführung aus dem Leben der Pueblo-Indianer in Nordamerika am 21.April 1923 in Kreuzlingen,Bellevue, etwa als "Ergebnisse" aufgefasst wird – ich nehme gegen diesen Ausdruck Stellung, weil Herr Dr.Kurt Binswanger unter diesem Titel Pfarrer Schlatter zu meinem Vortrag eingeladen hat – also nicht als Ergebnisse eines vermeintlich überlegenen Wissens oder Wissenschaft aufgefasst werden, sondern als verzweifelte Bekenntnisse eines Erlösungsuchers vom Verhaftetsein, des geistigen Erhebungsversuches von dem Verknüpfungszwang durch Verleibung. Die Katharsis des ontogenetisch lastenden Zwanges zur sinnlichen Ursachensetzung als innerstes Problem. Ich will, dass auch nicht der leiseste Zug blasphemischer Wissenschaftlerei in dieser vergleichenden Sache nach dem ewig gleichen Indianertum in der hilflosen menschlichen Seele gefunden werden kann. Die Bilder und Worte sollen für die Nachkommenden eine Hilfe sein bei dem Versuch der Selbstbesinnung zur Abwehr der Tragik der Gespanntheit zwischen Trieb und Hemmung. Die Konfession eines unheilbaren Schizoiden, den Seelenärzten ins Archiv gegeben.

92 Aby Warburg: *Reise-Erinnerungen aus dem Gebiet der Pueblo-Indianer in Nordamerika* (*Travel Memories from the Region of the Pueblo Indians in North America*), 1923, typescript with handwritten corrections, sheet 1

use of the snake motif in European culture ever since antiquity. With reference to the "symbolic ornamentation" and "masked dance art" of the Pueblo, he studied their worldview which, threatened by the rationalistic lifestyles of Euro-American immigrants, had maintained itself as a quite outdated and yet vivid form of antiquity.[4] Using the example of bird and snake motifs depicted on pre-Columbian ceramics to explain totemistic, animistic, and cosmological relationships to his audience, Warburg pointed to the hybrid nature of these well-nigh abstract images, which were located between directly grasping and symbolically detached representation: "What we have here is an intermediate stage between image of reality and symbol, between realistic reflection and writing. We can immediately tell from this way of treating ornamentation of such animals how this way of seeing and thinking can lead to symbolic picture writing."[5]

Warburg also showed one of the drawings made by Cleto Yurina in Santa Fe in January 1896, as well as pictures of the cultic dances, including George Wharton James's famous photograph of the Snake Dance, in the dining room of the sanatorium.[6] Yet unlike in the 1897 lectures, in which the snake and its meaning to the Hopi did not yet play any part, in his comments in Kreuzlingen Warburg compared the Indigenous ritual to practices from antiquity, especially the "orgiastic cult of Dionysus," in which "the maenads held snakes in their hands" as they danced and then "tore them apart in the ecstatic sacrificial dance in honor of the god."[7] The art historian pursued the iconographic use of the motif with examples such as the Laocoön group, which was personally so important to him, or Asclepius, via medieval miniatures to the afterlife of the pagan snake in modern churches. Combining magical and mathematical ways of thinking, ancient astrology had, like Pueblo symbolism, supposedly developed an early form of reflective detachment which unfolded through progressive enlightenment to the "conceptual space."[8]

In the closing passages of his lecture Warburg sketched the development from a magical/primitive approach to a terrifying universe and its demonic superstructure to the rationality of a modern worldview. Here he compared his own illness to humanity's persistent attempts to cast off magical bonds. He described his comments in the all too often convoluted twists and turns of a complex argumentation, as he explains at the start of one of the two versions of the lecture, as "desperate confessions by a seeker of release from detention," an "attempt at mental elevation against the compulsion to interconnect actual or imaginary incorporation."[9] That Warburg himself was on the threshold between illness and recovery is shown by an editorial detail of the punctuation of his text, whose seemingly incidental correction comprises all the hope that the patient could derive from working on the American materials. Warburg initially wrote a fatalistic characterization of his own, “incurable” situation. Yet on reviewing one of his drafts only a few days after the lecture he found the courage to make an optimistic self-diagnosis, corrected his findings, and inserted a–crucial–pair of brackets: “The confession of an (incurable) schizoid, for the psychiatrists’ archives.”[10]

Aby Warburg in fact repeatedly perceived his return to his art-historical and cultural studies as an act of self-healing. In much of his testimony from his time at the Kreuzlingen sanatorium–despite constantly burgeoning doubts about his recovery, as well as relapses that were to delay his discharge for over a year–he spoke of “self-liberation,” of “mental recovery through scientific work,” and diagnosed in himself a “growing intrinsic strength to break free from mental derangement.”[11] The scholar owed his rebirth in the spirit of science providing orientation to a topic which mentally took him back to Arizona and New Mexico, to the beginnings of his comparative cultural research whose study material he was now only evaluating in depth for the first time. His study of the hybrid cultural situation of the Pueblo ultimately led him in his lecture to an assessment of European culture as it oscillated incessantly between magic and reason, and eventually to reflections on his own endangered existence: His lecture thus ultimately became a cultural/psychological self-examination.

The Snake

On his journey to America Aby Warburg constantly came across snakes. They could be seen as a decorative ornament on ceramics that the art historian acquired during his stay in New Mexico and Arizona, in the drawings he had made by others–or made himself–and they also occurred in some rock drawings and murals, or in illustrations for the books he read about the mythological beliefs and cultic practices of the Pueblo. Yet as far as we know he never saw any of the living creatures with his own eyes, especially not the snakes that were the focus of his 1923 lecture *Bilder aus dem Gebiet der Pueblo-Indianer in Nord-Amerika* (Images from the Region of the Pueblo Indians of North America): Before his departure Warburg had not attended the Snake Dance in which the performers used the poisonous reptiles, and sometimes even carried them in their mouths.[1] He only knew the ceremony from reports and photographs and had obtained information from the literature about these dances, which are still performed in some pueblos to this day.[2]

Although the early lectures he gave soon after his return were indeed presented more as travel reports (and accordingly did not mention snakes with a single term), in the delicate situation of the Kreuzlingen sanatorium Warburg seemed truly obsessed with the cultural history designation of the snake as a symbolic form of ornamentation, a motif of pagan and Christian iconography, and a mythological creature: The term, alone or in combination with other words ("lightning snake," "snake god," "healing snake," "snake ruler/savior," and much else besides), appears well over a hundred times in the text of the lecture, and snakes are shown on ten slides in various motivic contexts. On the basis of his observation that the supposed decorative form of the snake in Pueblo art should be interpreted as a cosmological/meteorological icon, as a "lightning symbol" and representation of a "weather deity," Warburg devoted the central passages of his lecture to the three types of dance he had identified in the American Southwest: mimetic/pantomimic adoption of animals (the Buffalo Deer Dance in San Ildefonso), symbolic ritual (the Hemiskatsina dance in Oraibi), and finally the dance with snakes that were not merely represented but actually alive, which he called the "most pagan of all ceremonies" and a "more primitive stage of magical dance."[3]

The art historian started by explaining to his audience the environmental origins of such a ritual in a barren region with little rainfall: "For in August, a time of agricultural crisis because the very success of the harvest depends on rainstorms, a dance with live snakes which takes place alternately in Oraibi and Walpi is used to summon the salutary rain."[4] With reference to the available sources, Warburg described in detail the approximate course of the final day of the nine-day cultural acts (*tsu'tikive*), the use of the previously captured snakes in the preparations and in the actual dance, and their release to summon the much-desired rain.[5] He illustrated his commentary with some pictures taken by Henry R. Voth and a photograph in which George Wharton James recorded the dancers carrying the poisonous creatures in their mouths.

Warburg was convinced that the ritual turned the snake into a "provoker of lightning" or "producer of water," which is why he described the reptile as follows in one of his typical and inimitable neologisms: "It is a living (primal) rain-/snake-saint in animal form."[6] Although Warburg did also discuss the totemistic and mythological aspects of the ritual in his lecture, what impressed him above all was that–unlike in the orgiastic animal sacrifices of the ancient Dionysian cult–the snakes used in the Hopi dance did not have to die: "So the snake is not sacrificed in this Snake Dance, but is only, through consecration and influencing dance gestures, turned into a messenger and, having returned to the souls of the dead, is dispatched in the form of lightning to produce storms in the sky."[7]

At the end of his lecture Warburg's comparative cultural perspective, from which he pursued the iconography of the snake from pagan antiquity to medieval astrological representations and then on into eighteenth-century church decoration, culminated in some ideas about religious psychology that he only briefly touched on. Confronted with incomprehensible natural phenomena, the Hopi dancers used the snake as a creature with "demonic force" which they magically linked to menacing reality in order to influence weather and prosperity: "The Indians really take

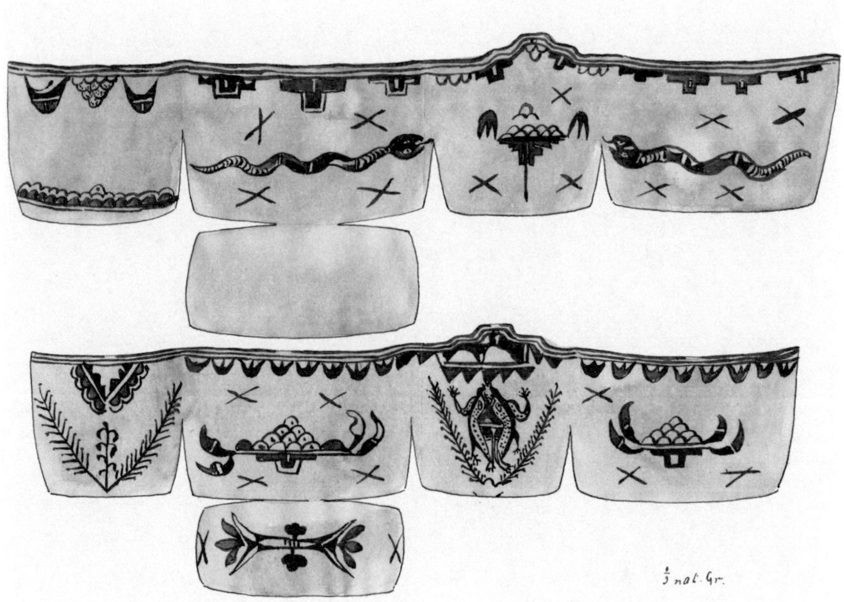

93 Anonymous artist: *Pseudo-ceremonial vessel with snake and cloud decoration*, ca. 1890–1895, index-card drawing, after 1907

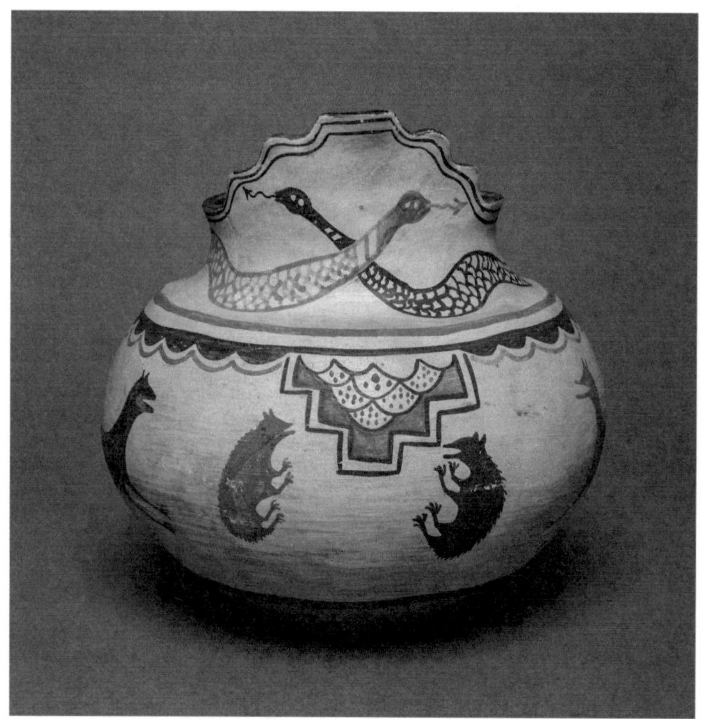

94 *Pseudo-ceremonial vessel with snake and stepped cloud decoration*, ca. 1890–1895, painted clay, 31.2 × 31 cm

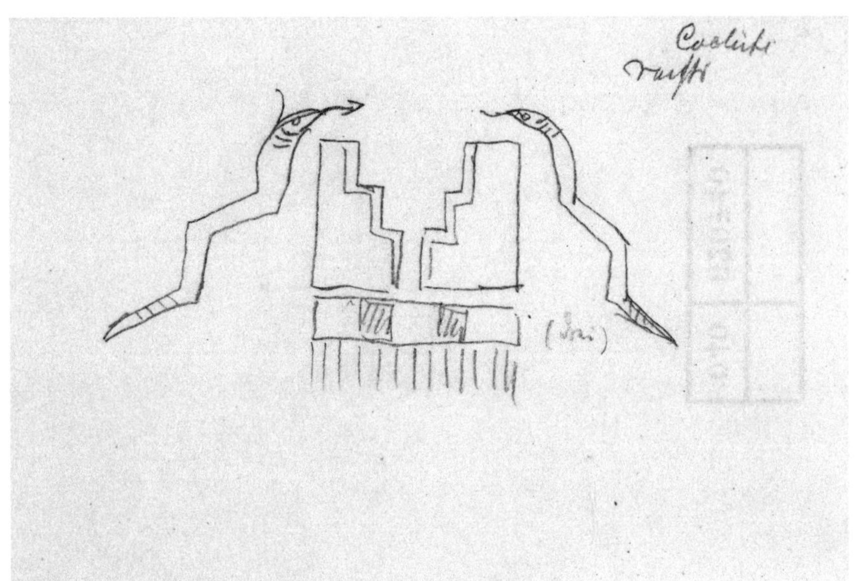

95 Aby Warburg: *Lightning snakes and stepped ornament (from an unknown model from Cochiti)*, 1896, pencil on paper, 9.6 × 15.6 cm

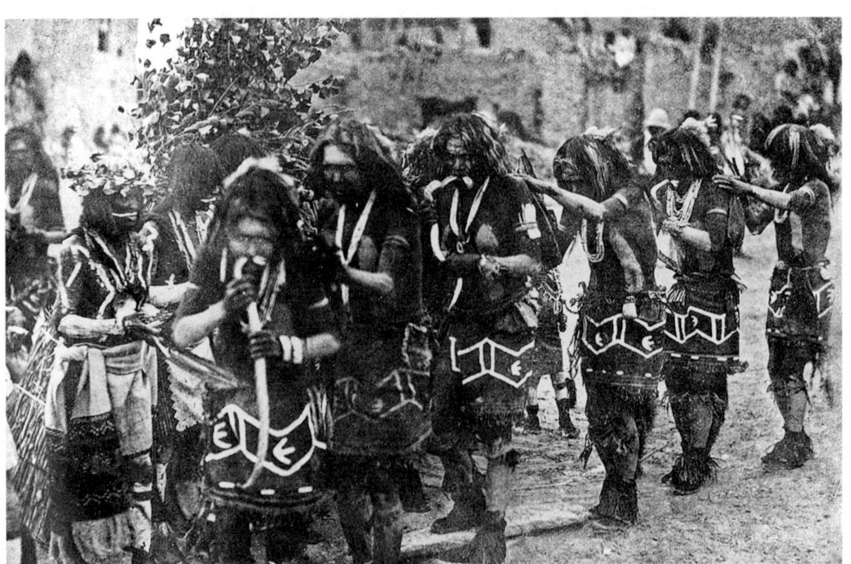

96 George Wharton James: *Hóveima and other priests of the Snake fraternity during the dance ritual in Oraibi*, 1898, photograph

hold of the snake and causally appropriate it as a living representative of lightning."[8] This grasping, this making-tangible, would in Warburg's view increasingly be sublimated in the course of cultural development into a (visual) symbol and (linguistic) concept, and so be replaced by a conceptual engagement with the world in which the snake motif would still have a long afterlife. Even in his enlightened technologized present, and no less in his own biography, the atavisms of a magical worldview accordingly remained operational, and thus for him the snake became the symbol of humans' persistent attempts to create an intellectual distance between themselves and elusive nature: "It was and is still to this day, as we see in these Pueblo cults, a manifest yardstick for the development of an instinctive/magical approach to spiritualizing detachment, which designates the poisonous reptile as a symbol of what humans must overcome both outwardly and inwardly in demonic natural forces."[9]

At the Kreuzlingen sanatorium Aby Warburg battled with these "demonic natural forces" and attempted to restore his own detachment from the phenomena that threatened him by scientifically examining the meaning of the snake and its role in Hopi religion. Yet the art historian had not seen the Snake Dance, with the dangerous creatures in the dancers' hands and mouths, during his stay in Arizona; he preferred to end his journey in May 1896 and return to Germany, although it must have been clear to him back in the United States that the ritual with the live snakes was probably the most important cultural event for his research. To be sure, as he indicated on several occasions, Warburg feared the sweltering southwestern American summer for health reasons.[10] But perhaps he was also instinctively afraid to expose himself to the threatening yet beneficent creature which he would then have to have grasped, at least in photographs.

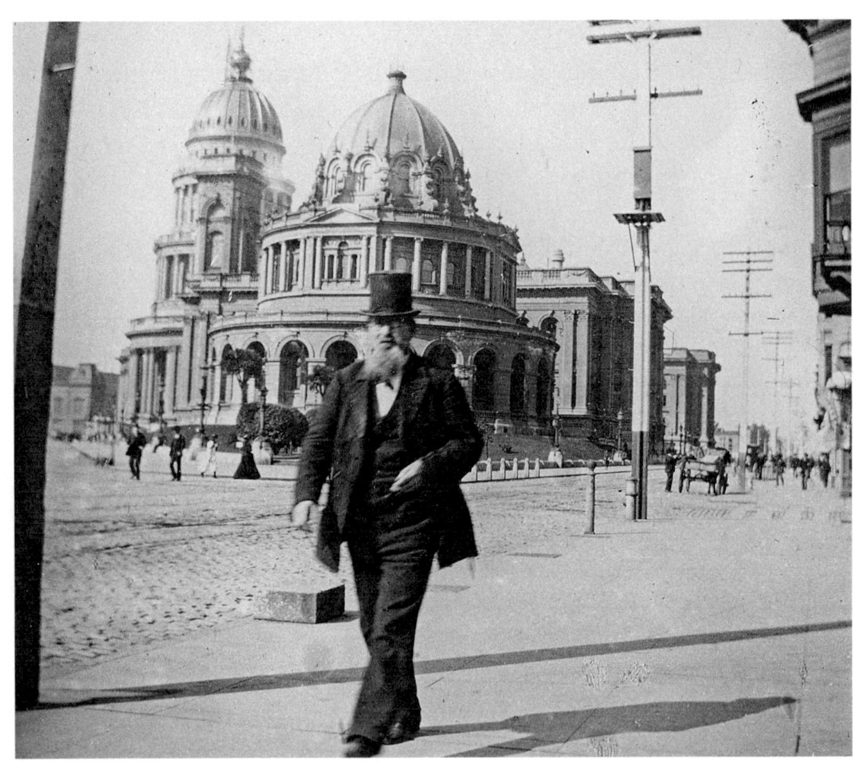

97 Aby Warburg: *Passer-by ("Uncle Sam") outside San Francisco City Hall, Hall of Records and Mechanics Pavilion, seen from McAllister Street*, 1896, photograph

The Telegraph Pole

When the unnamed passer-by, perhaps a businessman, as Aby Warburg thought, was photographed on San Francisco's McAllister Street in spring 1896, he could not suspect that his picture would many years later lead to a highly far-reaching reflection on cultural philosophy. Dressed in a dark suit with a waistcoat, and with a top hat on his head, the man strode past Warburg through the low Californian evening light, with behind him the magnificent historical buildings of San Francisco City Hall, the Hall of Records, and the Mechanics Pavilion in the heart of the city. Warburg had photographed this "archetype of Western civilization" because the bearded pedestrian reminded him of Uncle Sam, the popular personification of the United States, whose iconography dates back to the American revolutionary wars.[1] On returning to Germany, the art historian showed the picture of the man as the final slide at all his lectures, and briefly outlined the situation in which it had been taken. A draft of his 1897 lecture *Reise durch das Gebiet der Pueblo-Indianer in New Mexico und Arizona* (A Journey through the Region of the Pueblo Indians in New Mexico and Arizona) goes into somewhat more detail: "The final picture shows you a Californian businessman whom I quickly snapped just as he was passing the City Hall in San Francisco. I did not want to miss him, as he [seemed] to me to be the original for 'Uncle Sam,' known from American comic papers as an archetype."[2]

If this photograph were merely a humorous visual glimpse with which to conclude the lecture, it would hardly warrant further mention. But when looking through his American documentation in 1923 during his stay at Ludwig Binswanger's sanatorium to prove to himself and his physicians that he was once again capable of scientific work—and hence of the crucial detachment he needed to ward off the demons that so oppressed him—Warburg discovered a detail that he had evidently overlooked before: "Uncle Sam" was strolling down the sidewalk of a street edged by a long line of telegraph poles. In a famous passage from his no less famous Kreuzlingen lecture, Warburg then described the photograph taken a quarter of a century earlier, and lamented the loss of the "conceptual space" he had postulated in a completely technologized present: "I was able to symbolically capture the conqueror of the snake cult and the fear of lightning, the heir to the original inhabitants, and the gold-seeking supplanter of the Indians in a snapshot on the San Francisco street: Uncle Sam in a top hat, proudly walking down the street in front of an imitated ancient rotunda. Stretched above his top hat is an electric wire—lightning wrested from nature by Edison's copper snake. Today's Americans are no longer afraid of the rattlesnake—it is killed, or in any case not worshiped as a deity. What it faces is extermination. The lightning captured in the wire as electricity has produced a culture that puts an end to paganism. What does it replace it with? Natural forces are no longer seen in anthropomorphic or biomorphic terms, but as endless waves, invisible particles that yield to the pressure of a human hand. Thus does the culture of the machine age destroy what science so onerously wrested from myth, the meditation room that turned into the conceptual space."[3]

The dialectic of Enlightment that informs this idea was something Warburg had to experience for himself—for since the outbreak of World War I his mental illness had made him feel increasingly unable to create this "conceptual space" in a world gone awry. Following his physicians' eventually more optimistic diagnosis, Warburg gradually came to understand the source of his illness, and through this insight he also developed a fundamental cultural-philosophical diagnosis of his own times, in which such technical achievements as the lightning conductor, the airplane, and telecommunications were ever clearer impediments to humans' necessary reflective detachment from their environment: "The modern-day Prometheus and the modern-day Icarus—Franklin who captured lightning, and the Wright brothers who invented the steerable airship—are the ominous destroyers of our sense of distance who threaten to return our world to chaos. Telegraph and telephone are destroying the cosmos. In the battle for the spiritualized connection between humans and their environment, mythical and symbolic thinking creates space as a meditation room or conceptual space, which will be stolen by the instantaneous electrical connection unless a disciplined humanity restores the inhibition of conscience."[4]

Yet Warburg had also recognized the solution that would avert the dangers of the "instantaneous electrical connection," which had evidently struck him as the writing on the wall in his own photograph of the telegraph pole. He himself believed that a "disciplined humanity" could be restored by scientific work on his vital topics; and for humankind in general he also saw a return to mental confrontation as the only way not to lose the battle for the threatened orientation in the world. Warburg owed the fact that he could formulate these insights and overcome his psychosis not least to his study of the culture of the Pueblo communities he visited in the United States. Their mythical/symbolic thinking had taught him that between a magical and a rationalistic way of life lay the symbolical culture he had found in New Mexico and Arizona. It is certainly no accident that Warburg, who was fussy about his vocabulary, called the telegraph wire the "copper snake" and telegraphy as "lightning captured in a wire"–terms directly derived from his involvement with Pueblo art.[5]

It was in his photograph of the "conqueror of the snake cult and the fear of lightning" calmly striding beneath the telegraph poles that Warburg (as he later realized) encountered the symbol of these cultural-philosophical links, in front of "an imitated ancient rotunda," as if the afterlife of antiquity also had to be part of the picture. The art historian had set off on his journey to seek symbolical forms of expression in the Pueblo villages, but not only did he find them in the artifacts and rites of the Cochiti and the Zuni, the Tewa and the Hopi, he even captured such a symbol in a photograph taken in a San Francisco street. It hardly seems an exaggeration to see in Aby Warburg's study of the art and culture of the Pueblo communities and ultimately in the reception of his own photograph, of the symbol creating image, the genesis of a truly cross-cultural and in the best sense of the term "globalized" art history.

Notes

Notes

In Pursuit of Pueblo Art. Aby Warburg in Pueblo Territory

1 On the following, see also Uwe Fleckner: "Aby Warburgs amerikanische Reise. Vom 'illustrierten Tagebuch' zur kulturpsychologischen (Selbst)Betrachtung," in Warburg 2018, pp. 1–23. In contrast to the term "pueblos" (Spanish for "villages"), which designates the settlements of the sedentary Indigenous population of the American Southwest, the umbrella term "Pueblo" is currently used to mean their inhabitants.
2 Warburg 2018c, p. 65; see also idem 2018a, p. 25 ("illustrated diary").
3 Warburg's 1923 text, in which he prepared his nonetheless extempore lecture, was first published posthumously in 1939 in a version compiled for the purpose from Warburg's notes by his former colleagues Fritz Saxl and Gertrud Bing in collaboration with Edgar Wind; see Aby Warburg: "A Lecture on Serpent Ritual," in *Journal of the Warburg Institute* II/1938–1939, pp. 277–292 and plates 44–48; new edition: Warburg 2018e; see also idem: *Schlangenritual. Ein Reisebericht*, with an afterword by Ulrich Raulff, Berlin 1988 (Kleine Kulturwissenschaftliche Bibliothek, vol. 7); idem: *Images from the Region of the Pueblo Indians of North America* (Michael P. Steinberg, ed.), Ithaca and London 1995; idem: *Il rituale del serpente. Una relazione di viaggio*, Milan 1998; idem: *Le Rituel du serpent. Récit d'un voyage en pays pueblo*, Paris 2003; idem: *El ritual de la serpiente*, Mexico City 2004. The first reliable edition that also contains all the illustrations is Warburg 2018c. A selection of studies on the "Serpent Ritual" lecture in Fleckner 2018, p. 23 (note 64).
4 Apart from sporadically published individual pictures, a first selection of Warburg's photographs was presented in Benedetta Cestelli Guidi and Nicholas Mann (eds.): *Photographs at the Frontier. Aby Warburg in America 1895–1896*, London 1998. All of his photographs were published with captions related to their pictorial motifs in Warburg 2018, pp. 153–348 (picture W 1-196).
5 See Aby Warburg: *Werke in einem Band* (Martin Treml, Sigrid Weigel, and Perdita Ladewig, eds.), Berlin 2010, pp. 508–600; idem 2018, pp. 25–127 (with all the slides used by Warburg).
6 See Uwe Fleckner: "Aby Warburgs Schenkungen an das Hamburger Museum für Völkerkunde, 1899–1902," in Warburg 2018, pp. 355–455; for more on Warburg's collection, see also *Lightning Symbol and Snake Dance. Aby Warburg and Pueblo Art* (Christine Chávez and Uwe Fleckner, eds.), exhibition catalogue, Museum am Rothenbaum - Kulturen und Künste der Welt, Hamburg 2022–2023.
7 See draft of a letter from Aby Warburg to Karl Lamprecht, August 12, 1895, London, Warburg Institute Archive (WIA), General Correspondence (GC): "[After] my stay there I ... would probably like to make a longer trip to the other cities of North America, partly in order to get to know the universities and libraries there."
8 Quoted from Ernst H. Gombrich: *Aby Warburg. An Intellectual Biography*, London 1970, p. 88; for more on Warburg's scientific contacts in the United States, see Cestelli Guidi and Mann 1998, pp. 30 ff.
9 For more on the individual stages of his journey, see Aby Warburg: *Ricordi*, London, WIA, III.10.1 (excerpts in Cestelli Guidi and Mann 1998, pp. 150–155).
10 Letter from Aby Warburg to the Moritz Warburg family, December 14, 1895, London, WIA, GC; see Gustaf Nordenskiöld: *The Cliff Dwellers of the Mesa Verde, Southwestern Colorado. Their Pottery and Implements*, Stockholm and Chicago 1893.
11 Warburg 2018a, p. 36.
12 See Peter M. Whiteley: *Deliberate Acts. Changing Hopi Culture through the Oraibi Split*, Tucson 1988; David Freedberg: "Pathos a Oraibi. Ciò che Warburg non vide," in Claudia Cieri Via and Pietro Montani (eds.): *Lo sguardo di Giano. Aby Warburg fra tempo e memoria*, Turin 2004, pp. 569–611.
13 Warburg 2018a, p. 40.
14 A kiva is an often circular Pueblo sacred place of assembly, usually made of clay and with a wooden roof. Wholly or partly built below ground and reachable via a ladder, a kiva is used for the performance or preparation of various religious ceremonies, such as the Hopi

dance rituals. Some kivas have a closable aperture (*sípàapuni*) in the floor, symbolizing the underworld ancestors' access to the earthly world.

15 Aby Warburg: *Ricordi*, London, WIA, III.10.1, folio 58v (entry dated May 1, 1896); see Martha and Henry R. Voth's diary, North Newton, Bethel College, Mennonite Library and Archives, Ms. 21 (entry dated May 1, 1896); see ibid. (entries dated April 28–30, 1896).

16 See Cora Bender, Thomas Hensel, and Erhard Schüttpelz (eds.): *Schlangenritual. Der Transfer der Wissensformen vom Tsu'ti'kive der Hopi bis zu Warburgs Kreuzlinger Vortrag*, Berlin 2007 (Wissenskultur und gesellschaftlicher Wandel, vol. 16).

17 Quoted from Gombrich 1970, pp. 88–89.

18 Letter from Aby Warburg to the Moritz Warburg family, December 14, 1895, London, WIA, GC.

19 Warburg 2000, p. 3.

20 Warburg 2018a, p. 25.

21 Warburg 2018c, p. 84.

22 In addition, Warburg outlined a systematic/philosophical basis for his notion of symbolism (which he had already commenced in the US) in the fragments and aphorisms in his manuscript *Symbolismus als Umfangsbestimmung*; see Aby Warburg: *Fragmente zur Ausdruckskunde* (Ulrich Pfisterer and Hans Christian Hönes, eds.), Berlin and Boston 2015 (Gesammelte Schriften. Studienausgabe, vol. IV), pp. 295–320.

23 Warburg 2018c, p. 74.

24 Warburg 2018c, p. 94; for more on Warburg's notion of symbolism, see also Cornelia Zumbusch: *Wissenschaft in Bildern. Symbol und dialektisches Bild in Aby Warburgs Mnemosyne-Atlas und Walter Benjamins Passagen-Werk*, Berlin 2004 (Studien aus dem Warburg-Haus, vol. 8).

25 Anonymous: "Art of the Pueblos. Dr. A. M. Warburg, a Noted Florence Investigator, in the City," in *The San Francisco Call*, No. 86, February 24, 1896.

26 Warburg 2018a, p. 26; see Uwe Fleckner: "'Almost No Picture Is Free of Errors ...'. Distance and Its Loss in Aby Warburg's Photographic Practice," in *Lightning Symbol and Snake Dance* 2022–2023, pp. 140–145.

27 Warburg 2018a, p. 28; idem 2018b, p. 62; the last quotation from Cestelli Guidi and Mann 1998, p. 151.

28 Aby Warburg: "Arbeitende Bauern auf burgundischen Teppichen [1907]," in idem: *Die Erneuerung der heidnischen Antike. Kulturwissenschaftliche Beiträge zur Geschichte der europäischen Renaissance* (Horst Bredekamp and Michael Diers, eds.), Berlin 1998 (Gesammelte Schriften. Studienausgabe, Vol. I.1–2), 2 volumes, vol. I.1, pp. 221–229, p. 227; idem: "Italienische Kunst und internationale Astrologie im Palazzo Schifanoja zu Ferrara [1912]," in idem 1998, vol. I.2, pp. 459–481, p. 478.

29 Letter from Aby Warburg to the Moritz Warburg family, December 14, 1895, London, WIA, GC.

30 Aby Warburg: "Heidnisch-antike Weissagung in Wort und Bild zu Luthers Zeiten [1920]," in idem 1998, vol. I.2, pp. 487–558, p. 534.

The Ship

1 See Arnold Kludas: "Die deutschen Schnelldampfer. II. Die Augusta-Victoria Klasse. Anschluß an das Weltniveau," in *Deutsches Schiffahrtsarchiv* 4/1981, pp. 93–108; Matthias Trennheuser: *Die innenarchitektonische Ausstattung deutscher Passagierschiffe zwischen 1880 und 1940*, Bremen 2010, pp. 69 ff. and figures on pp. 448 ff.

2 See anonymous: "Arrivals from Europe. On the Fuerst Bismarck, from Southampton," in *The New York Times*, September 14, 1895; letter from John Maynard Harlan to Aby Warburg, October 25, 1895; letter from John Maynard Harlan to his father John Marshall Harlan, October 25, 1895, London, WIA, GC.

3 Anonymous: "The Fuerst Bismarck Has a Rough Trip," in *New-York Daily Tribune*, September 14, 1895.
4 See "SS Fürst Bismarck. List of Cabin-Passengers," in *Passenger Lists of Vessels Arriving at New York, 1820–1897*, Washington DC, National Archives and Records Service, microfilm (1957), roll 0648, folio 1, No. 10. This list mistakenly states Warburg's profession as "surgeon."

The Pioneer

1 See Alfred Vagts: "M. M. Warburg & Co. Ein Bankhaus in der deutschen Weltpolitik 1905–1933," in *Vierteljahrschrift für Sozial- und Wirtschaftsgeschichte* 45/1958, pp. 289–388, pp. 289 ff.; Jacob Rader Marcus: *United States Jewry, 1776–1985. Volume III. The Germanic Period*, Part 2, Detroit 1993; Stephen Birmingham: *"Our" Crowd. The Great Jewish Families of New York*, Syracuse, NY, 1996, pp. 83 ff.
2 Numerous newspapers report on the wedding of Paul Warburg and Nina Loeb; see, for example, anonymous: "The Week in Society [column]," in *New-York Daily Tribune*, September 29, 1895; anonymous: "Weddings Past and to Come [column],"" in *New-York Daily Tribune*, October 2, 1895.
3 See *The Jewish Encyclopedia*, New York 1906, under "Seligman" (Cyrus Adler and Joseph Jacobs); Hopper Striker Mott: "Isaac Newton Seligman," in *The New York Genealogical and Biographical Record* 49/1918, pp. 321–326; www.sekonassociation.com/Isaac.html (consulted on May 10, 2019).
4 Anonymous: "A Sensation in Saratoga," in *The New York Times*, June 19, 1877; see anonymous: "The Seligman Scandal, Antisemitism in Saratoga Springs," in www.adirondackalmanack.com/2009/09/the-seligman-scandal-antisemitism-in-saratoga-springs.html (consulted on May 10, 2019); Birmingham 1996, pp. 141 ff.
5 See www.sekonassociation.com/Timeline.html (consulted on May 10, 2019); the design of the house (by Brunner & Tyron, Architects) can be found in the *Catalogue of the Ninth Annual Exhibition of the Architectural League of New York*, exhibition catalogue, American Fine Arts Building, New York 1893–1894, n. p.
6 Isaac Newton Seligman also inserted numerous drawings in the lodge's guest book (1905–1915); see anonymous: "Upper Saranac Lake's Fish Rock Camp and Jacob Riis," in www.adirondackalmanack.com/2009/09/upper-saranac-lakes-fish-rock-camp-and-jacob-riis.html (consulted on May 10, 2019).

The Map

1 Aby Warburg, letter to the Moritz Warburg family, December 14, 1895, London, WIA, GC.
2 Ibid.
3 Ibid.
4 Moki (in Spanish: Moqui) is an old name, nowadays considered pejorative, for the Hopi, who call themselves Hopituh Shi-nu-mu ("peaceful people"). The spellings of the names of the villages, which vary considerably to this day, are taken from Kenneth C. Hill et al. (eds.): *Hopi Dictionary / Hopìikwa Lavàytutuveni. A Hopi-English Dictionary of the Third Mesa Dialect*, Tucson 1998.
5 See the photograph of the encampment in Warburg 2018a, p. 27 (fig. A 4), in which the stable hand "Jim" is mistakenly identified with James Loeb.
6 Aby Warburg: "MNEMOSYNE. Einleitung [1929]," in idem: *Der Bilderatlas MNEMOSYNE* (Martin Warnke and Claudia Brink, eds.), Berlin 2000 (Gesammelte Schriften. Studienausgabe, vol. II.1), pp. 3–6, p. 5; see Dorothea McEwan: "Aby Warburg's (1866–1929) Dots and Lines. Mapping the Diffusion of Astrological Motifs in Art History," in *German Studies Review* 29/2006, pp. 243–268.

The Railroad

1 Warburg 2018d, p. 107.
2 Warburg 2018c, p. 66; the photographs are published in Warburg 2018, pp. 240–241 (figs. W 88–89) and pp. 338 ff. (figs. W 186–188).
3 Anonymous: "Art of the Pueblos. Dr. A. M. Warburg, a Noted Florence Investigator, in the City," in *The San Francisco Call*, No. 86, February 24, 1896.
4 Warburg 2018c, p. 94.

The Rock Drawing

1 See Jerry J. Brody: "The Archaeological Society of New Mexico and the Rock Art of the Galisteo Basin," in *Archaeology Southwest Magazine* 4/2005, p. 5.
2 For more on Neef's life, see Warburg 2018a, p. 50 (commentary).
3 Ibid., p. 28.
4 See ibid., p. 49 (commentary); Warburg's photographs are published in Warburg 2018, pp. 154 ff. (figs. W 2–7).
5 Letter from Aby Warburg to Mary Hertz, November 8, 1895, London, WIA, GC; Warburg 2018a, p. 28. The "quadruped on the right" (see the illustration in this chapter) with its drawn-in stars has indeed been identified by researchers as a bear; see Polly Schaafsma: *Indian Rock Art of the Southwest*, Santa Fe and Albuquerque 1992, pp. 265–266.

The Photographer

1 See Uwe Fleckner: "Aby Warburgs amerikanische Reise. Vom 'illustrierten Tagebuch' zur kulturpsychologischen (Selbst)Betrachtung," in Warburg 2018, pp. 1–23, pp. 4 ff.; Warburg 2018a, p. 49 (commentary).
2 On Warburg's photographic competence, see Ian Jones: "Aby Warburg as a Photographer," in Benedetta Cestelli Guidi and Nicholas Mann (eds.): *Photographs at the Frontier. Aby Warburg in America 1895–1896*, London 1998, pp. 48–52, pp. 48 ff.; Karl Sierek: *Foto, Kino und Computer. Aby Warburg als Medientheoretiker*, Hamburg 2007, pp. 51 ff. (here Warburg's camera was erroneously identified as "Eastman Kodak No. 2 Bulls-Eye"); Uwe Fleckner: "'Almost No Picture Is Free of Errors ...'. Distance and Its Loss in Aby Warburg's Photographic Practice," in *Lightning Symbol and Snake Dance. Aby Warburg and Pueblo Art* (Christine Chávez and Uwe Fleckner, eds.), exhibition catalogue, Museum am Rothenbaum – Kulturen und Künste der Welt, Hamburg 2022–2023, pp. 140–145.
3 Warburg 2018a, p. 26, p. 36, p. 40 and p. 41.
4 See Elizabeth W. Easton: "Introduction," in *Snapshot. Painters and Photography, Bonnard to Vuillard*, exhibition catalogue, Indianapolis Museum of Art / The Phillips Collection, Washington DC / Van Gogh Museum, Amsterdam 2011–2012, pp. 1–11, p. 3.
5 Warburg 2018a, p. 25–26; see ibid., p. 31.
6 The Warburg Institute Archive in London includes a large stock of photographs and picture postcards that Warburg bought in the United States; at his lectures in 1897 and 1923 he showed, besides his own photographs, slides of photographs by Abraham Lincoln Fellows, Frederic Hamer Maude, George Wharton James, Thomas Varker Keam, Adam Clark Vroman, Henry R. Voth, and unknown photographers; see Warburg 2018a, pp. 26 ff.; idem 2018c, pp. 67 ff.

The Curiosity Shop

1 See Jonathan Batkin: "Tourism Is Overrated. Pueblo Pottery and the Early Curio Trade, 1880-1910," in Ruth B. Phillips and Christopher B. Steiner (eds.): *Unpacking Culture. Art and Commodity in Colonial and Postcolonial Worlds*, Berkeley, Los Angeles and London 1999, pp. 282-298, pp. 286 ff.; for more on Gold and the generation of the first "curio traders", see also idem: "Some Early Curio Dealers of New Mexico," in *American Indian Art Magazine* 3/1998, pp. 68-81; idem: *The Native American Curio Trade in New Mexico*, Santa Fe 2008, pp. 1 ff. and pp. 21 ff.; David S. Koffman: "Jews, American Indians Curios, and the Westward Expansion of Capitalism," in Rebecca Kobrin (ed.): *Chosen Capital. The Jewish Encounter with American Capitalism*, New Brunswick, New Jersey and London 2012, pp. 168-186.
2 Quoted from Koffman 2012, p. 177.
3 See ibid., p. 174.
4 Quoted from ibid., p. 172. "Germantown tools" refers to the famous firm Germantown Tool Works, founded in Philadelphia in 1871, which produced wrought-iron tools. For more on the mail-order catalogues, see Jonathan Batkin: "Mail-Order Catalogs as Artifacts of the Early Native American Curio Trade," in *American Indian Art Magazine* 2/2004, pp. 40-49 and p. 76; for more on Jake Gold, see ibid., pp. 46 ff.
5 See Uwe Fleckner: "Aby Warburgs Schenkungen an das Hamburger Museum für Völkerkunde, 1899-1902," in Warburg 2018, pp. 355-455, p. 377 (cat. no. 26), p. 378-379 (cat. nos. 28-29), p. 385 (cat. nos. 37-38), pp. 403-404 (cat. nos. 64-65), p. 406 (cat. no. 67), pp. 412-413 (cat. nos. 78-79) and pp. 448-449 (cat. nos. 127-128).

The Ornament

1 See Thomas V. McCalmont: *San José de la Laguna Mission and Convento, 1972-1973*, Washington DC, U.S. Department of the Interior, National Register of Historic Places; Marc Treib: *Sanctuaries of Spanish New Mexico*, Berkeley 1993, pp. 296 ff.
2 See Warburg 2018a, p. 30.
3 For more on the stair ornaments, see also the illustrations of the chapter "The Steps" in this publication.
4 Aby Warburg, notes on his visit of the San José mission church in Laguna, undated (December 1895), London, WIA, ZK 040/020698; see also the note on the corresponding drawing in the chapter "The Steps": "Understood by the priests?" ("Von den Priestern verstanden?").
5 Gertrud Bing: "Vorwort [1932]," in Aby Warburg: *Die Erneuerung der heidnischen Antike. Kulturwissenschaftliche Beiträge zur Geschichte der europäischen Renaissance* (Horst Bredekamp and Michael Diers, eds.), Berlin 1998 (Gesammelte Schriften. Studienausgabe, vol. I.1-2), 2 vols., vol. I.1, pp. XI-XIX, p. XIV.

The Steps

1 See the illustrations of the chapter "The Worldview" in this publication.
2 Warburg 2018c, p. 73. For more on San Esteban del Rey, see Marc Treib: *Sanctuaries of Spanish New Mexico*, Berkeley 1993, pp. 304 ff.; for more on the architecture of the village, see Peter Nabokov: *Architecture of Acoma Pueblo. The Historic American Buildings Survey Project*, Santa Fe 1986.
3 Warburg 2018c, p. 73.
4 For more on Juillard (b. 1867), also responsible for Acoma as a priest in the neighboring town of Gallup, see Warburg 2018a, pp. 30-31 and 51 (commentary).

5 Ibid., p. 31. The two photographs by George Wharton James referred to here by Warburg can be found in ibid., pp. 30–31 (figs. A 14 and A 14[a]).
6 Ibid., p. 30; see the illustrations of the chapter "The Ornament" in this publication.
7 Warburg 2018c, pp. 71 ff.
8 Ibid., p. 73.

The Forger

1 See in this publication pp. 96 ff., pp. 55 ff., p. 80, p. 116 and pp. 138 ff.
2 See Warburg 2018b, pp. 58 and p. 64 (commentary). At one point in his collection inventory Warburg also wrote "Cleto Jurino"; London, Warburg Institute Archive, III 46.2.2.1, no. 100. In the (partly contemporary) literature Cleto Yurina's names are occasionally also spelled as "Kleto," "Urina," or "Yulino"; see Patricia Fogelman Lange: "Cultural Collecting Fever in New Mexico: Figurines and Governor L. Bradford Prince," in *Journal of the Southwest* 40-2/1998, pp. 217-242. I am grateful to Christine Chávez, Hamburg, who drew my attention to this essay as well as the bust of Anastacio Yurina; see Christine Chávez: "The Origins, Afterlife, and Persistence of Symbolic Art. Aby Warburg's Pueblo Collection," in *Lightning Symbol and Snake Dance. Aby Warburg and Pueblo Art* (Christine Chávez and Uwe Fleckner, eds.), exhibition catalogue, Museum am Rothenbaum - Kulturen und Künste der Welt, Hamburg 2022–2023, pp. 68–77, p. 77 (note 13).
3 See John P. Harrington: *The "Stone idols" of Cochiti. A Remarkable Archaeological Forgery*, unpublished typescript, undated (ca. 1909), Santa Fe, Museum of Indian Arts and Culture, Laboratory of Anthropology, Hewett Files, No. 89ELH.080, p. 2. I am grateful to Diane Bird, Santa Fe, for providing me with the typescript. A set of notes that goes far beyond this text can be found in the National Anthropological Archives at the Smithsonian Institution, John Peabody Harrington Papers, NAA.1976-95, Cochiti, Ethnographic Notes / Notes and Drafts. Cleto Yurina's biographical data, as well as those of his wife and son, are extrapolated here from the (in some cases contradictory) documentation; see Jonathan Batkin: "Cleto Yurina, Folk Artist and Entrepreneur," in Robin Farwell Gavin and Donna Pierce (eds.): *Cultural Convergence in New Mexico. Interactions in Art, History and Archaeology*, Santa Fe 2021, pp. 243–255. Yurina's previously unknown year of birth can be approximately determined from the records of an 1887 census; see *The Indian Census Rolls, 1885–1940*, National Archives Microfilm Publication, M-595.
4 See Harrington (ca. 1909), p. 2; phonetic conversion of the Indigenous names in Harrington: Cochiti, Ethnographic Notes / Notes and Drafts, digitalisat, folios 88–89 and folio 218.
5 See Warburg 2018c, p. 71.
6 Warburg had recorded the son's name as "Anastasio" or "Anacleto"; see Warburg 2018c, p. 98 (comment).
7 See Warburg 2018, p. 160 (image W 8); other historical pictures of the hotel in Santa Fe, New Mexico History Museum, Palace of the Governors, Photo Archives.
8 See Benedetta Cestelli Guidi and Nicholas Mann (eds.): *Photographs at the Frontier. Aby Warburg in America 1895–1896*, London 1998, p. 152.
9 The bust was created as part of a series that also belongs to the collection of the Nationaal Museum van Wereldculturen in Leiden. For more on the anthropometric research by the now highly controversial scientist, see Frederick Starr: *Physical Characters of Indians of Southern Mexico*, Chicago 1902 (The Decennial Publications).
10 Warburg 2018b, p. 58. The room number is shown on a drawing by Cleto Yurina; see fig. 33 in this publication.
11 See Warburg 2018c, p. 71. According to Lange, Anastacio Yurina belonged not only to the Kwe'rena but also to the related Shi'kame society; see Charles H. Lange: *Cochiti. A New Mexico Pueblo, Past and Present*, Austin 1959, p. 465 and p. 514.

12 Warburg 2018c, p. 71. The description "keeper of the keys" ("Schlüsselbewahrer") is found on one of Yurina's drawings; see the corresponding illustration of the chapter "The Worldview" in this publication.
13 Quoted from Cestelli Guidi and Mann 1998, p. 152. For more on the two objects, see Uwe Fleckner: "Aby Warburgs Schenkungen an das Hamburger Museum für Völkerkunde, 1899–1902," in Warburg 2018, pp. 355–455, pp. 435–436 (cat. nos. 112–113); however, the term "stroking stone" (also testing or experimenting stone) noted by Warburg is inaccurate here; this was probably a stone (which may also not have been authentic) that produced its healing effect through contact with the patient; for more on Yurina's medical activities, see Harrington (c. 1909), pp. 3–4.
14 Harrington (c. 1909), p. 9. For more on Yurina's fakery, see Lange 1998, pp. 218 ff.; Robert W. Preucel, "Manufacturing Desire: Cleto Yurina and his Cochiti Figurines," in *Contexts. The Annual Report of the Haffenreffer Museum of Anthropology* 41/2016, p. 16; Batkin 2021, pp. 243 ff. (with numerous additional details).
15 In an essay on authentic stone figures Prince states that he was accompanied during his visit to the archeological sites by a "bright, active and intelligent Pueblo Indian," probably also Cleto or Anastacio Yurina; see LeBaron Bradford Prince: *The Stone Lions of Cochiti*, Santa Fe 1903, p. 3.
16 Batkin mentions over 1,600 items; see Batkin 2021, p. 243.
17 See *The Stone Idols of New Mexico. A Description of Those Belonging to the Historical Society*, Santa Fe 1896, p. 8, see ibid., panels 1–4.
18 Quoted from Batkin 2021, p. 246; see Lange 1998, pp. 222 f. As early as 1882 there was a report of a Cochiti called Cleto who apparently brought faked "magical" earth ("to keep out the wind and prevent storms") to Gold's store; see *The Southwestern Journals of Adolph F. Bandelier, 1880–1882* (Charles H. Lange and Carroll L. Riley, eds.), Albuquerque and Santa Fe 1966, p. 244.
19 See Lange 1998, pp. 226 ff.; Batkin 2021, p. 250 and note 45.
20 See Preucel 2016, p. 16.
21 See *Lightning Symbol and Snake Dance* 2022–2023, pp. 242–243 (cat. no. 126). A similar fetish figure, also acquired in Santa Fe in 1918, can be found in Washington DC, National Museum of the American Indian, no. 8/4588.
22 Warburg 2018b, p. 58.

The Worldview

1 Warburg 2018c, p. 71.
2 For more on the dissimulating strategies of some pueblos, see Adam Fulton Johnson: *Secretsharers: Intersecting Systems of Knowledge and the Politics of Documentation in Southwesternist Anthropology, 1880–1930*, PhD dissertation, University of Michigan 2018, pp. 105 ff.
3 We know that explorers often forced their way into kivas, but also that Henry R. Voth very often received permission to enter the sacred spaces in Oraibi (and that Warburg accompanied him on one such occasion); the local costums in Cochiti at that time are unknown; see this publication, pp. 143 ff.
4 For more on the term "Yaya" as used in Cochiti, see Noël Dumarest: *Notes on Cochiti, New Mexico*, Lancaster 1919 (Memoirs of the American Anthropological Association, vol. 6.3), p. 144; see also Matilda Coxe Stevenson: "The Sia," in *Eleventh Annual Report of the Bureau of Ethnology to the Secretary of the Smithsonian Institution. 1889–1890*, Washington DC 1894, pp. 3–157, p. 40.
5 See Dumarest 1919, pp. 216 ff.; Ruth Benedict: *Tales of the Cochiti Indians*, Washington DC 1931 (Smithsonian Institution. Bureau of American Ethnology, vol. 98), pp. 19–65 (passim) and pp. 210 ff.
6 For more on the stepped ornaments in Laguna and Acoma, see the illustrations of the chapters "The Ornament" and "The Steps" in this publication.

7 Warburg 2018c, p. 71. Warburg uses the term "Yerrik" (*i'ariko* in the East Keres language) for the figurative embodiment of the corn cob.
8 See Kenneth C. Hill et al. (eds.): *Hopi Dictionary / Hopìikwa Lavàytutuveni. A Hopi-English Dictionary of the Third Mesa Dialect*, Tucson 1998, pp. 504, under "sípàapuni."
9 See Benedict 1931, p. 201.

The Dancer

1 See Noël Dumarest: *Notes on Cochiti, New Mexico*, Lancaster 1919 (Memoirs of the American Anthropological Association, vol. 6.3), pp. 174 ff.; Ruth Benedict: *Tales of the Cochiti Indians*, Washington DC 1931 (Smithsonian Institution. Bureau of American Ethnology, vol. 98), pp. 41–42 and pp. 213 ff.
2 See Dumarest 1919, p. 180. For more on the identification of the objects, see Uwe Fleckner: "Aby Warburgs Schenkungen an das Hamburger Museum für Völkerkunde, 1899-1902," in Warburg 2018, pp. 355–455, p. 411 (cat. no. 77).
3 Dumarest 1919, pp. 174–175.
4 See ibid., pp. 175 ff. (including the exact sequences of the dance with its various masks).
5 Ibid., p. 175.

The Myth

1 See Matilda Coxe Stevenson: "The Sia," in *Eleventh Annual Report of the Bureau of Ethnology to the Secretary of the Smithsonian Institution. 1889-1890*, Washington DC 1894, pp. 3–157, pp. 26 ff.
2 The nomenclature here consistently follows Stevenson's not always uniform spelling.
3 See Stevenson 1894, pp. 43 ff. and p. 72.
4 Ibid., p. 69.
5 The Zia *hä'chamoni* are equivalent to the Hopi *pahos* (prayer intermediaries or prayer sticks).
6 Warburg 2018d, p. 119.

The Altar

1 See Matilda Coxe Stevenson: "The Sia," in *Eleventh Annual Report of the Bureau of Ethnology to the Secretary of the Smithsonian Institution. 1889-1890*, Washington DC 1894, pp. 3–157.
2 See ibid., plate XXII, after p. 98; also a depiction of the altar during the "Rain Ceremonial", plate XXIII, after p. 100.
3 Ibid., p. 107.
4 See ibid., p. 105.
5 For more on the term *pûr'-tu-wish-ta*, see ibid., pp. 123 ff.

The Letter

1 See Edward S. Curtis: *The North American Indian*, vol. 17 (The Tewa, The Zuni), Norwood 1926, pp. 55–56; Gertrude Prokosch Kurath: "Game Animal Dances of the Rio Grande Pueblos," in *Southwestern Journal of Anthropology* 14-4/1958, pp. 438–448.
2 See anonymous: "Saturday Salad [column]," in *Santa Fé Daily New Mexican*, No. 283, January 25, 1896.
3 Warburg 2018b, p. 57; see idem 2018, pp. 167–172 (figs. W 15–20); see the illustrations of the chapter "The Transformation" in this publication.

4 See Luke Lyon: "History of Prohibition of Photography of Southwestern Indian Ceremonies," in *Reflections. Papers on Southwestern Cultural History in Honor of Charles H. Lange*, Santa Fe 1988 (The Archaeological Society of New Mexico, vol. 14), pp. 238–272; Patrick Perez: "'No picture! no picture!' Les conflits autour de la photographie chez les Hopi (Arizona, États-Unis)," in *Journal des anthropologues* 80–81/2000, pp. 283–296.
5 Warburg 2018b, p. 57; see idem 2018c, pp. 74 ff.

The Transformation

1 "Round About Town [column]," in *Santa Fé Daily New Mexican*, No. 281, January 23, 1896.
2 "Saturday Salad [column]," in ibid., No. 283, January 25, 1896.
3 Ibid.
4 See Uwe Fleckner: "'Almost No Picture Is Free of Errors ...'. Distance and Its Loss in Aby Warburg's Photographic Practice, in *Lightning Symbol and Snake Dance. Aby Warburg and Pueblo Art* (Christine Chávez and Uwe Fleckner, eds.), exhibition catalogue, Museum am Rothenbaum – Kulturen und Künste der Welt, Hamburg 2022–2023, pp. 140–145 (with additional literature).
5 George Wharton James: "The Snake Dance of the Hopis," in *Camera Craft. A Photographic Monthly* 1/1902, pp. 3–10, p. 10.
6 Warburg 2018c, p. 74; for more on Bullis's letter, see the chapter "The Letter" in this publication.
7 Warburg probably received prints of his photographs on February 1, 1896; see letter from Aby Warburg to Charlotte and Moritz Warburg, January 31, 1896, London, WIA, GC.
8 Aby Warburg, notes on the Buffalo Deer Dance in San Ildefonso Pueblo, 1896, London, WIA, ZK 040/020868–881, sheet 3a. For more on Sisneros, see Marilyn Norcini: "The Political Process of Factionalism and Self-Governance at Santa Clara Pueblo, New Mexico," in *Proceedings of the American Philosophical Society* 149/2005, pp. 544–590, pp. 567 ff.; see also some photographs that show Sisneros, in Santa Fe, New Mexico History Museum, Palace of the Governors, Photo Archives, inventory nos. 030764, 047474–75 and 050827 (under the name Victorion Sisneros); Barbara Freire-Marreco: *Victoriano Sisneros and other members of the local executive body of Santa Clara Pueblo*, 1911, Oxford, Pitt Rivers Museum, inventory no. 1998.95.1.
9 Warburg 1896, sheets 1–2; for more on this dance, see also Gertrude Prokosch Kurath: "Game Animal Dances of the Rio Grande Pueblos," in *Southwestern Journal of Anthropology* 14/1958, pp. 438–448; Jill D. Sweet: *Dances of the Tewa Pueblo Indians. Expressions of New Life*, Santa Fe 1985.
10 Warburg 1896, sheets 3a and 4.
11 Warburg 2018b, p. 57.
12 Warburg 2018c, p. 75.

The Hotel

1 Letter from Aby Warburg to Charlotte and Moritz Warburg, January 31, 1896, London, WIA, GC.
2 See Warburg 2018, pp. 173 ff. (figs. W 21–24).
3 See "Coronado Notes [column]," in *The San Diego Union*, February 18, 1896, p. 2 ("Dr. A. M. Warburg is here from Hamburg").
4 See www.hoteldel.com/history/ (retrieved on May 3, 2021).
5 Quoted from Benedetta Cestelli Guidi and Nicholas Mann (eds.): *Photographs at the Frontier. Aby Warburg in America 1895–1896*, London 1998, p. 153.
6 See guest book and account book, Hotel del Coronado, archives (entries dated February 17–22, 1896). My thanks to Gina Petrone, Hotel del Coronado, for her kind information.

7 Quoted from Guidi and Mann 1998, p. 153.
8 Letter from Aby Warburg to Mary Hertz, March 3, 1896, London, WIA, GC.
9 Aby Warburg: "Symbolismus als Umfangsbestimmung [1896–1901]," in idem: *Fragmente zur Ausdruckskunde* (Ulrich Pfisterer and Hans Christian Hönes, eds.), Berlin and Boston 2015, pp. 295–320, p. 295.
10 Ibid., p. 302.
11 Ibid., pp. 297–298, p. 302 and p. 314.

The Hunter

1 See Warburg 2018, pp. 207 ff. (figs. W 55–64). In the 2018 edition some of the people shown could only be provisionally identified; however, a new archive source (the Hotel del Coronado guest book) reveals that they were Mrs C. B. Knapp (fig. W 58), W. B. Snyder from Newark, and Ezra P. Mills from New York (fig. W 61), as well as Mills and his son Harold P. Mills (fig. W 62). My thanks to Gina Petrone, Hotel del Coronado, for her kind information.
2 Quoted from Benedetta Cestelli Guidi and Nicholas Mann (eds.): *Photographs at the Frontier. Aby Warburg in America 1895–1896*, London 1998, p. 153.
3 My thanks to Claudia Wedepohl, Warburg Institute, for her help in deciphering and interpreting this dedication.
4 See Aby Warburg: *Bilderreihen und Ausstellungen* (Uwe Fleckner and Isabella Woldt, eds.), Berlin 2012 (Gesammelte Schriften. Studienausgabe, vol. II.2), pp. 73–97 and pp. 303–365.

The Chinese

1 Letter from Aby Warburg to Mary Hertz, March 3, 1896, London, WIA, GC.
2 Ibid. Before deciding to abandon his travel plans and return to the American Southwest, Warburg had evidently booked a passage to Japan for March 14, 1896; see letter from Aby Warburg to Charlotte and Moritz Warburg, February 26, 1896, London, WIA, GC.
3 Warburg 2018b, p. 62; see also p. 64 (commentary).
4 See Lixin Sun: *Das Chinabild der deutschen protestantischen Missionare des 19. Jahrhunderts. Eine Fallstudie zum Problem interkultureller Begegnung und Wahrnehmung*, Marburg 2002.
5 See this publication, p. 149.

The Dance Evening

1 "Personal [column]," in *Santa Fé Daily New Mexican*, No. 269, January 9, 1896.
2 See anonymous: "Albuquerque Libraries: It's a Grand Old History," www.abcreads.blogspot.com/2011/07/albuquerque-libraries-its-grand-old.html (retrieved on December 14, 2020).
3 See letter from Aby Warburg to Felix Warburg, April 8, 1896; letter from Aby Warburg to Charlotte Warburg, April 21, 1896; letter from Aby Warburg to George Gibson Huntt, April 19, 1896, London, WIA, GC.
4 See concert program, Second Cavalry Band, Fort Wingate, December 27, 1896, London, WIA, GC.
5 Letter from Aby Warburg to Nina Warburg, April 10, 1896, London, WIA, GC (original English words). For more on Brainard's tragically famous expedition, see David L. Brainard: *The Outpost of the Lost. An Arctic Adventure*, Indianapolis 1929; Bessie Rowland James (ed.): *Six Came Back. The Arctic Adventure of David L. Brainard*, Indianapolis 1940.

6 For more on Bryan, see Warburg 2018a, p. 52 (commentary) and pp. 233 ff. (figs. W 81, W 83, and W 85–87).
7 See Uwe Fleckner: "Dancer in a laboratory of images: Aby Warburg's performative didactics," in *Philosophy of Photography* 1-2/2017, pp. 17–33.

The Sorcerer

1 See also the chapter "The Letter" in this publication.
2 See Edward S. Curtis: *The North American Indian. The Tewa. The Zuni*, vol. 17, Norwood 1926, p. 111. The now verified identification of "Zuñi Nick" as Warburg's "Nick the interpreter" in Zuni Pueblo still struck me as too speculative when publishing the documents on Warburg's journey to America; see Warburg 2018a, p. 33 and p. 52 (commentary).
3 See Patricia Janis Broder: *Shadows on Glass. The Indian World of Ben Wittick*, Savage 1990, pp. 170–171 and p. 169 (fig. 177, Ben Wittick: *Nick Dumaka, Victim of the Order of the Bow*, 1897 [incorrectly dated as 1885]); Will Roscoe: *The Zuni Man-Woman*, Albuquerque 1991, p. 91 (fig. 22, Adam Clark Vroman: *Porträt Douglas D. Graham und Nick Dumaka*, undated [around 1897]; print in Los Angeles, National History Museum, Seaver Center for Western History Research, inventory no. SCWHR-P-001-V1056; also a second picture in the company of a woman, inventory no. SCWHR-P-001-V1057) and pp. 100 ff.
4 See Curtis 1926, p. 111. Curtis added a footnote to this description: "As a matter of fact the informant, Zuñi Nick, was punished because he boasted that he was a sorcerer, that he was a Mexican, not a Zuñi; and the troops came from Fort Wingate in response to the plea of a missionary resident at Zuñi ..." (ibid.).
5 George Wharton James: "Indian Witchcraft," in *The Nebraska Advertiser*, No. 31, January 27, 1899, p. 5 (with a portrait drawing); identical versions of the article can be found in *Kinsley Graphic*, No. 12, February 3, 1899, p. 6, and—with different pictures—in *Waterbury Evening Democrat*, No. 40, January 20, 1899, p. 6, and *Worthington Advance*, No. 25, January 26, 1899, p. 3; a partly differing description of the events can be found in idem: *New Mexico. The Land of the Delight Makers*, Boston 1920, pp. 86 ff. (with a portrait photograph). A print of the photograph, which also served as the basis for the drawing, can be found in New York; see George Wharton James: *Nick the Witch at Zuni*, 1898, New York Public Library, The Miriam and Ira D. Wallach Division of Arts, Prints and Photographs, inventory no. 807375.
6 See Triloki Nath Pandey: *Factionalism in a Southwestern Pueblo*, PhD dissertation (unpublished), University of Chicago 1967, pp. 101 ff. and pp. 141 ff.; idem: "Anthropologists at Zuni," in *Proceedings of the American Philosophical Society* 116-4/1972, pp. 321–337, pp. 331 ff.; David M. Fawcett and Teri McLuhan: *Ruth Leah Bunzel*, in Ute Gacs et al. (eds.): *Women Anthropologists. Selected Biographies*, Urbana and Chicago 1989, pp. 29-36, pp. 30 ff.
7 Ruth Benedict: *Zuni Mythology*, New York 1935 (Columbia University Contributions to Anthropology, vol. 21), 2 vols., vol. 1, p. XXXIX; see Elsie Clews Parsons: *Pueblo Indian Religion*, Chicago 1939, 2 vols., vol. 1, p. XX and p. 64 ("the outstanding intellectual").

The Girl

1 Letter from Aby Warburg to Charlotte Warburg, April 21–22, 1896, London, WIA, GC.
2 Warburg 2018a, p. 33.
3 For more on Warburg's photography in the United States, see Uwe Fleckner: "'Almost No Picture Is Free of Errors ...'. Distance and Its Loss in Aby Warburg's Photographic Practice," in *Lightning Symbol and Snake Dance* 2022–2023, pp. 140–145.
4 Warburg 2018a, p. 33.

Notes

The Bullroarers

1 Uwe Fleckner: "Aby Warburgs Schenkungen an das Hamburger Museum für Völkerkunde, 1899–1902," in Warburg 2018, pp. 355–455, p. 447 (cat. no. 126).
2 See *Handbook of American Indians North of Mexico* (Frederick Webb Hodge, ed.), Washington DC, 4th edition 1912 (Smithsonian Institution, Bureau of American Ethnology, Bulletin, vol. 30), 2 vols., vol. 1, pp. 170–171, under "Bullroarer" (Walter Hough).
3 John G. Bourke: *The Medicine-men of the Apache*, in *Ninth Annual Report of the Bureau of Ethnology to the Secretary of the Smithsonian Institution*, 1887–1888, Washington DC 1892, pp. 443–603, pp. 476–477.
4 See Kenneth C. Hill et al. (eds.): *Hopi Dictionary / Hopìikwa Lavàytutuveni. A Hopi-English Dictionary of the Third Mesa Dialect*, Tucson 1998, p. 104, under "hotsikve('at)" and "hotsitve('at)".
5 Aby Warburg: *Inventar der Sammlung aus Neu-Mexiko und Arizona*, undated, London, WIA, 46.2.2.1 (cat. no. 107); see Fleckner 2018, p. 355.
6 See correspondence between Aby Warburg and the Royal Museum of Ethnology, December 1896, Berlin, Ethnologisches Museum, archives.
7 Karl von den Steinen, note for the files, December 7, 1896, Berlin, Ethnologisches Museum, archives; see letter from Albert Grünwedel to Aby Warburg, December 8, 1896, London, WIA, GC.

The Rock

1 See Cora Bender, Thomas Hensel, and Erhard Schüttpelz (eds.): *Schlangenritual. Der Transfer der Wissensformen vom Tsu'ti'kive der Hopi bis zu Warburgs Kreuzlinger Vortrag*, Berlin 2007 (Wissenskultur und gesellschaftlicher Wandel, vol. 16).
2 Jesse Walter Fewkes: *The Snake Ceremonials at Walpi*, in *A Journal of American Ethnology and Archaeology* 4/1894, pp. 1–126, p. 124.
3 For more on the history of photojournalism in Walpi, see Sharyn R. Udall: "The Irresistible Other. Hopi Ritual Drama and Euro-American Audiences," in *The Drama Review* 36/1992, pp. 23–43.
4 See Luke Lyon: "History of Prohibition of Photography of Southwestern Indian Ceremonies," in *Reflections. Papers on Southwestern Cultural History in Honor of Charles H. Lange*, Santa Fe 1988 (The Archaeological Society of New Mexico, vol. 14), pp. 238–272; Patrick Perez: "'No picture! no picture!' Les conflits autour de la photographie chez les Hopi (Arizona, États-Unis)," in *Journal des anthropologues* 80–81/2000, pp. 283–296.
5 Warburg 2018c, p. 84. *Pahos* was the name given to the Pueblos' traditional prayer sticks or prayer intermediaries. Usually painted and decorated with feathers and parts of plants, these ritual implements with their multifaceted coding serve as vehicles for religious ideas and various petitions, and are, for example, stuck into the earth near fields or wells or deposited as gifts in order to draw the deities' or spirit beings' attention to such places.

The Fleeing Woman

1 Warburg 2018a, p. 26 and p. 31; see also Warburg 2018d, p. 115 ("*Abbildungsscheu*").
2 See Leslie Marmon Silko: *Yellow Woman and a Beauty of the Spirit. Essays on Native American Life Today*, New York 1996, p. 175. For more on the causes of iconophobic rejection of photography outside Europe, see Thomas Theye: "Einführung," in *Der geraubte Schatten. Eine Weltreise im Spiegel der ethnographischen Photographie*, exhibition catalogue, Münchner Stadtmuseum 1989, pp. 8–59, pp. 42 ff.

3 Quoted from William Webb and Robert A. Weinstein: *Dwellers at the source. Southwestern Indian Photographs of A. C. Vroman, 1895–1904*, Albuquerque 1973, p. 32; see Hans-Ulrich Sanner: "Karl von den Steinen in Oraibi, 1898. A collection of Hopi Indian photographs in perspective," in *Baessler-Archiv* 44/1996, pp. 243–293, pp. 248–249.
4 The photographs Warburg took during his journey to America were not fully published with precise dates and locations and identification of their subjects until 2018; see Warburg 2018, pp. 151–348.
5 See Thomas Theye: "'Wir wollen nicht glauben, sondern schauen.' Zur Geschichte der ethnographischen Fotografie im deutschsprachigen Raum im 19. Jahrhundert," in *Der geraubte Schatten. Eine Weltreise im Spiegel der ethnographischen Photographie*, exhibition catalogue, Münchner Stadtmuseum 1989, pp. 60–119.
6 Warburg 2018c, p. 74.
7 See Sanner 1996, pp. 272 ff.

The Trader

1 Warburg 2018a, p. 33; see idem 2018c, p. 77; idem 2018d, p. 115.
2 See letter from Jesse Walter Fewkes to Aby Warburg, March 21, 1896; letter from James Mooney to Aby Warburg, March 30, 1896, London, WIA, GC; for more on Keam, see Lynn R. Bailey: *Thomas Varker Keam: Tusayan Trader*, in *Arizoniana* 4/1961, pp. 15–19; Laura Graves: *Thomas Varker Keam, Indian Trader*, Norman 1998.
3 Aby Warburg: *Ricordi*, London, WIA, III.10.1, folio 56v (entry dated April 22, 1896); for more on the photographs, see Warburg 2018, pp. 256 ff. (figs. W 104–115).
4 See the chapters "The Schoolchildren" and "The Chief" in this publication.
5 See anonymous [the editors and Thomas Varker Keam]: "An Indian Snake-Dance," in *Chambers's Journal of Popular Literature, Science, and Arts* 993/1883, pp. 14–16.
6 See Edwin L. Wade and Lea S. McChesney (eds.): *Historic Hopi Ceramics. The Thomas V. Keam Collection of the Peabody Museum of Archaeology and Ethnology, Harvard University*, Cambridge, MA, 1981; Richard O. Clemmer: "Museum Collections and the Search for 'Authentic Historical Consciousness' in the Age of Nationalist Imperialism," in *Anthropos* 106/2011, pp. 69–85, pp. 75 ff.
7 See Peter Bolz and Hans-Ulrich Sanner: *Indianer Nordamerikas. Die Sammlungen des Ethnologischen Museums Berlin*, Berlin 1999, p. 122; Clemmer 2011, p. 75.
8 Thomas Varker Keam, waybill for the works acquired by Aby Warburg, June 17, 1896, London, WIA (handwritten addition by Aby Warburg).
9 Aby Warburg: *Ricordi*, London, WIA, III.10.1, folio 56v (entry dated April 22, 1896); for more on the items acquired from Keam, see London, WIA, III 46.2.2.1; see also Uwe Fleckner: "Aby Warburgs Schenkungen an das Hamburger Museum für Völkerkunde, 1899–1902," in Warburg 2018, pp. 355–455, pp. 371–373 (cat. nos. 16–19), p. 375 (cat. no. 22), pp. 389–396 (cat. nos. 42–52), pp. 398–400 (cat. nos. 56–60), p. 402 (cat. no. 63), p. 409 (cat. no. 74), p. 416 (cat. no. 85), p. 418 (cat. no. 87) and pp. 421–424 (cat. nos. 90–94).
10 Warburg 2018a, p. 36.

The Navajo

1 See Warburg 2018, pp. 270 ff. (figs. W 118–124) and pp. 314 ff. (figs. W 162–180).
2 For more on the "filmic" sequences in Warburg's photographs and their implications for the "scientific" neutrality of such photographic practices, see Karl Sierek: "Warburgs Beitrag zur Zähmung der Leidenschaften in der Fotografie," in Katharina Sykora,

Ludger Derenthal, and Esther Ruelfs (eds.): *Fotografische Leidenschaften*, Marburg 2006, pp. 73–86, pp. 75 ff.; idem: *Foto, Kino und Computer. Aby Warburg als Medientheoretiker*, Hamburg 2007, pp. 53 ff.; Uwe Fleckner: "Aby Warburgs amerikanische Reise. Vom 'illustrierten Tagebuch' zur kulturpsychologischen (Selbst)Betrachtung," in Warburg 2018, pp. 1–23, pp. 5 ff.

3 See anonymous: "Edison's Vitascope Cheered. 'Projecting Kinetoscope' Exhibited for First Time at Koster and Bial's," in *The New York Times*, April 24, 1896, p. 5.

The Schoolchildren

1 See Warburg 2018a, p. 52 (commentary).

2 See Darlis A. Miller: *Matilda Coxe Stevenson. Pioneering Anthropologist*, Norman 2007, p. 82; Richard O. Clemmer: "Museum Collections and the Search for 'Authentic Historical Consciousness,' in the Age of Nationalist Imperialism," in *Anthropos* 106/2011, pp. 69–85, pp. 78–79.

3 See Justin B. Richland: "Aby Warburg's Travel to Hopiland. Lines and Limits to Knowledge," in *Lightning Symbol and Snake Dance. Aby Warburg and Pueblo Art* (Christine Chávez and Uwe Fleckner, eds.), exhibition catalogue, Museum am Rothenbaum - Kulturen und Künste der Welt, Hamburg 2022–2023, pp. 162–167, p. 164.

4 See Peter M. Whiteley: *Deliberate Acts. Changing Hopi Culture Through the Oraibi Split*, Tucson 1988.

5 See ibid., pp. 74 ff.; David Wallace Adams: *Education for Extinction. American Indians and the Boarding School Experience, 1875–1928*, Lawrence 1995; Margaret D. Jacobs: "A Battle for the Children. American Indian Child Removal in Arizona in the Era of Assimilation," in *The Journal of Arizona History* 45/2004, pp. 31–62; Clifford E. Trafzer: Jean A. Keller and Lorene Sisquoc (eds.): *Boarding School Blues. Revisiting American Indian Educational Experiences*, Lincoln 2006; Matthew Sakiestewa Gilbert: *Education beyond the Mesas. Hopi Students at Sherman Institute, 1902–1929*, Lincoln 2010.

6 Francis M. Neel: *Report of Superintendent of Navajo School*, in *Commissioner of Indian Affairs Annual Report*, vol. 1, Washington DC 1899, p. 160; for more on Neel, see Warburg 2018a, p. 55 (commentary).

7 Warburg 2018c, p. 93.

8 Quoted from Benedetta Cestelli Guidi and Nicholas Mann (eds.): *Photographs at the Frontier. Aby Warburg in America 1895–1896*, London 1998, p. 155.

9 For more on the drawings, see Uwe Fleckner, *Aby Warburgs Schenkungen an das Hamburger Museum für Völkerkunde, 1899–1902*, in Warburg 2018, pp. 355–455, pp. 453–454 (cat. nos. 134–145).

10 See Warburg's photographs published in Warburg 2018, pp. 279 ff. (figs. W 127–133).

The Lightning

1 See Earl Barnes: *A Study on Children's Drawings*, in *Pedagogical Seminary* 2/1892, pp. 455–463.

2 Warburg 2018c, p. 93 (the thunderstorm mentioned here was only added by Warburg); see Michael P. Steinberg: "Aby Warburg's Kreuzlingen Lecture: A Reading," in Aby Warburg: *Images from the Region of the Pueblo Indians in North America*, Ithaca and London 1995, pp. 59–114, pp. 64–65; Barbara Wittmann: "Johnny-Head-in-the-Air in America. Aby Warburg' Experiment with Children's Drawings," in Barbara Baert, Ann-Sophie Lehmann and Jenke Van den Akkerveken (eds.): *New Perspectives in Iconology. Visual Studies and Anthropology*, Brussels 2011, pp. 120–142.

3 Warburg 2018c, p. 93.

4 For more on the complicated history of the loss of the drawings, see Uwe Fleckner: "Aby Warburgs Schenkungen an das Hamburger Museum für Völkerkunde, 1899–1902," in Warburg 2018, pp. 355–455, pp. 358–359; for more on the actual drawings, see ibid., pp. 453–454 (cat. nos. 134–145).
5 *Das Kind als Künstler. Ausstellung von freien Kinderzeichnungen in der Kunsthalle zu Hamburg*, exhibition catalogue, Hamburg 1898, p. 17.
6 Quoted from Benedetta Cestelli Guidi and Nicholas Mann (eds.): *Photographs at the Frontier. Aby Warburg in America 1895–1896*, London 1998, p. 155. The reproduction was published in 1939; see Warburg 2018e, p. 146.
7 The signature "Howato" on the drawing was first mentioned in Benedetta Cestelli Guidi: "'Trattate con cura i miei libri e le mie rarità.' Aby Warburg collezionista," in Claudia Cieri Via and Pietro Montani (eds.): *Lo sguardo di Giano. Aby Warburg fra tempo e memoria*, Turin 2004, pp. 523–568, pp. 559–560; see Wittmann 2011, p. 122. For more on my identification of the boy, see Warburg 2018e, p. 150 (commentary).
8 See Cestelli Guidi 2004, p. 560.
9 Quoted from *Das Kind als Künstler* 1898, p. 32; a precise description of the experiment can be found in a letter from Francis M. Neel to Aby Warburg, November 4, 1896, London, WIA, GC.
10 For more on the fragmentation of the drawing through reproduction, see Wittmann 2011, p. 122.
11 Warburg 2018c, p. 71.
12 Ibid.

The Missionary

1 See Henry R. Voth's diary, North Newton, Bethel College, Mennonite Library and Archives (entries dated April 28 to May 1, 1896). In this publication the place name Oraibi introduced in Warburg research is used instead of the Hopi name Orayvi.
2 Ibid. (entry dated April 29, 1896).
3 Quoted from Benedetta Cestelli Guidi and Nicholas Mann (eds.): *Photographs at the Frontier. Aby Warburg in America 1895–1896*, London 1998, p. 155.
4 Quoted from ibid.; see Henry R. Voth's diary (entry dated April 30, 1896). For more on the items acquired from Voth, see Uwe Fleckner, "Aby Warburgs Schenkungen an das Hamburger Museum für Völkerkunde, 1899–1902," in Warburg 2018, pp. 355–455, p. 405 (cat. no. 66), pp. 407–408 (cat. nos. 71–72), p. 410 (cat. no. 76), p. 414 (cat. no. 80), p. 427 (cat. no. 99), and pp. 439–440 (cat. nos. 116–124).
5 See Cathy Ann Trotta: *Crossing Cultural Boundaries: Heinrich and Martha Moser Voth in the Hopi Pueblos, 1893–1806*, PhD dissertation, Northern Arizona University, Flagstaff 1997.
6 See Henry R. Voth: *The Oraibi Summer Snake Ceremony*, Chicago 1903 (Field Columbian Museum Publication, vol. 83 / Anthropological Series, vol. III–4).
7 See Fred Eggan: "H. R. Voth, Ethnologist," in Barton Wright: *Hopi Material Culture. Artifacts Gathered by H. R. Voth in the Fred Harvey Collection*, Flagstaff 1979, pp. 1–7, p. 6.
8 See letter from Henry R. Voth to Aby Warburg, May 14, 1896; letter from Henry R. Voth to Aby Warburg, September 14, 1896, London, WIA, GC (copies in the Heinrich R. Voth Collection, Bethel College, Mennonite Library and Archives).
9 For more on Voth's collection, see George A. Dorsey: "The Voth Collection," in *American Anthropologist* 1/1899, pp. 394–395; *The Henry R. Voth Hopi Indian Collection at Grand Canyon, Arizona*, Phoenix 1967; Barton Wright (ed.): *Hopi Material Culture. Artifacts Gathered by H. R. Voth in the Fred Harvey Collection*, Flagstaff 1979.
10 Don C. Talayesva: *Sun Chief. The Autobiography of a Hopi Indian* [1942] (Leo W. Simmons, ed.), New Haven and London 1970, p. 252; see Michael F. Brown: *Who Owns Native Culture?*, Cambridge, Massachusetts, and London 2003, pp. 11 ff.
11 Martha Voth's diary, North Newton, Bethel College, Mennonite Library and Archives

(entry dated November 2, 1893). In all likelihood, although the wording is not altogether clear, even Martha Voth had an opportunity to visit a kiva, something only men were normally allowed to do: “At ten o'clock Kwatschequa's son-in-law brought me a note from Heinrich saying that I should also come at once, for the Indians had asked after me and were in the kiva. I went at once, and when I arrived they had just eaten the bread we had baked for them, and were painting and dressing themselves to go back out and dance,” ibid. (entry dated November 3, 1893).

12 Henry R. Voth's diary (entry dated February 17, 1895).

13 Ibid. (entry dated December 28, 1895); detailed theological debates are described by Voth in, for example, ibid. (entries dated November 14, 1895 and January 19, 1898).

14 Quoted from Peter M. Whiteley: *Deliberate Acts. Changing Hopi Culture Through the Oraibi Split*, Tucson 1988, p. 84; see ibid., pp. 83 ff.

The Cane

1 Aby Warburg: Book of sketches, undated, London, WIA, ZK 040/020435, folio 57.

2 Aby Warburg: Sheet with drawings and notes, undated, London, WIA, ZK 040/020775.

3 For more on Voth's *paho* (older spelling: *baho*) collection, see George A Dorsey: “The Voth Collection,” in *American Anthropologist* 1/1899, pp. 394-395.

4 See John Fulbright: “Hopi and Zuni Prayer-sticks: Magic, Symbolic Texts, Barter, or Self-sacrifice?,” in *Religion* 22/1992, pp. 221-234; Lotsee Patterson and Mary Ellen Snodgrass: *Terms of the Americas*, Englewood, CO, 1994, pp. 16, under “Baho”.

5 Aby Warburg: *Inventar der Sammlung aus Neu-Mexiko und Arizona*, undated, London, WIA, 46.2.2.1 (cat. no. 106); see Uwe Fleckner: “Aby Warburgs Schenkungen an das Hamburger Museum für Völkerkunde, 1899-1902,” in Warburg 2018, pp. 355-455, p. 445 (cat. no. 122).

6 Gertrud Bing: “Vorwort [1932],” in Aby Warburg: *Die Erneuerung der heidnischen Antike. Kulturwissenschaftliche Beiträge zur Geschichte der europäischen Renaissance* (Horst Bredekamp and Michael Diers, eds.), Berlin 1998 (Gesammelte Schriften. Studienausgabe, vol. I.1-2), 2 vols., vol. I.1, pp. XI-XIX, p. XIV.

7 See Barton Wright: *Hopi Material Culture. Artifacts Gathered by H. R. Voth in the Fred Harvey Collection*, Flagstaff 1979, pp. 93-94, under “Ngölöshoya”; Kenneth C. Hill et al. (eds.): *Hopi Dictionary / Hopìikwa Lavàytutuveni. A Hopi-English Dictionary of the Third Mesa Dialect*, Tucson 1998, p. 319, under “ngölöshoya”.

8 Alexander M. Stephen: *Hopi Journal* (Elsie Clews Parsons, ed.), New York 1936, 2 vols., vol. 1, pp. 216-217.

9 I am grateful to Nancy J. Parezo, Tucson, for the reference to the provenance of the item; for more on Kuwanwikvaya (under the name “Wickwaya”), see Henry R. Voth: *The Oraibi Marau Ceremony*, Chicago 1912 (Field Museum of Natural History. Anthropological Series, vol. XI-1), pp. 1-88 (passim). Maraw (older spelling: Marau), named after a kind of dragonfly known to the Hopi as *maraw*, is a female religious society.

10 Henry R. Voth's diary, North Newton, Bethel College, Mennonite Library and Archives (entry dated July 7, 1895); see Martha Voth's diary, ibid. (entry dated November 25, 1893); for more on the conversion of the priest, see letter from Horton H. Miller, superintendent of the Hopi Agency in Keams Canyon, to the Commissioner of Indian Affairs in Washington DC, November 12, 1909, in Peter Whiteley: *The Oraibi Split. A Hopi Transformation. Part II: The Documentary Record*, New York 2008 (Anthropological Papers of the American Museum of Natural History, vol. 87), pp. 1087 ff.; this also includes some excerpts from Voth's diary in which the priest is mentioned, pp. 901 ff.; see also Voth 1912, p. 11; in a concluding report on his missionary work Voth explicitly states that “none came to a full decision for Christ”, quoted from Fred Eggan: “H. R. Voth, Ethnologist,” in Barton Wright: *Hopi Material Culture. Artifacts Gathered by H. R. Voth in the Fred Harvey Collection*, Flagstaff 1979, pp. 1-7, p. 2.

The Chief

1 Warburg 2018a, p. 41. The name is spelled in many different ways in the source literature.
2 See Peter M. Whiteley: *Deliberate Acts. Changing Hopi Culture Through the Oraibi Split*, Tucson 1988; idem: *The Oraibi Split. A Hopi Transformation*, New York 2008, 2 vols. (Anthropological Papers of the American Museum of Natural History, vol. 87); Richard O. Clemmer: *Roads in the Sky. The Hopi Indians in a Century of Change* [1995], New York and London 2018, pp. 84 ff.
3 For more on his support for the school, see Louise Udall: *Me and Mine. The Life Story of Helen Sekaquaptewa*, Tucson 1969, pp. 63-64; Scott Rushforth and Steadman Upham: *A Hopi Social History*, Austin 1992, pp. 123 ff.
4 Quoted from Whiteley 1988, p. 76.
5 Warburg 2018c, p. 80; for more on the *nakwakoci*, see Jesse Walter Fewkes: "The Butterfly in Hopi Myth and Ritual," in *American Anthropologist* 12/1910, pp. 576-594, p. 588.
6 Ibid.; see Warburg 2018c, pp. 80 ff.

The Ritual

1 See Barton Wright: "Hopi Kachinas: A Life Force," in Edna Glenn et al. (eds.): *Hopi Nation. Essays on Indigenous Art, Culture, History, and Law*, Lincoln 2008, pp. 111-121.
2 Warburg 2018a, p. 40.
3 Warburg 2018c, p. 77. This quote is from the 1923 text, which describes the events in far more detail than Warburg's first recording of them in 1897; see Henry R. Voth's diary, North Newton, Bethel College, Mennonite Library and Archives (entries dated April 28-29, 1896); Aby Warburg: *Ricordi*, London, WIA, III.10.1, folio 58r (entry dated April 30, 1896).
4 Henry R. Voth's diary (entry dated April 29, 1896).
5 For more on the accusations, see Don C. Talayesva: *Sun Chief. The Autobiography of a Hopi Indian* [1942] (Leo W. Simmons, ed.), New Haven and London 1970, p. 252.
6 Henry R. Voth's diary (entry dated August 22, 1898); see ibid. (entry dated August 15, 1898); see anonymous [Paul Ehrenreich]: "Dr. Paul Ehrenreichs Reise in Nordamerika," in *Globus* 74/1898, pp. 214-215.
7 See Justin B. Richland: "Aby Warburg's Travel to Hopiland. Lines and Limits to Knowledge," in *Lightning Symbol and Snake Dance. Aby Warburg and Pueblo Art* (Christine Chávez and Uwe Fleckner, eds.), exhibition catalogue, Museum am Rothenbaum - Kulturen und Künste der Welt, Hamburg 2022-2023, pp. 162-167, pp. 163-164; I am grateful to Justin B. Richland, Irvine, and Christine Chávez, Hamburg, for the discussion of this problem, which was long overlooked by researchers.
8 See Warburg 2018, pp. 314 ff. (figs. W 162-183).
9 Warburg 2018c, p. 83.
10 Aby Warburg: *Ricordi*, London, WIA, III.10.1, folio 58v (entry dated May 1, 1896); see Henry R. Voth's diary (entry dated May 1, 1896). The complaint about the "obscenity" of some parts of the ritual is a regular theme in the diary, and the missionary sought in vain to suppress the dancers' nudity; see ibid. (entries dated May 7, 1895; January 30, 1897; April 12, 1897; September 27, 1897; January 11, 1898; and May 21, 1898).
11 Warburg 2018c, pp. 79-80.
12 Ibid.
13 For more on Warburg's ethnological activities at this time, see Horst Bredekamp: *Aby Warburg, der Indianer. Berliner Erkundungen einer liberalen Ethnologie*, Berlin 2019.
14 Letter from Henry R. Voth to Aby Warburg, October 2, 1896; see also Henry R. Voth's reply to Aby Warburg, December 3, 1896, London, WIA, GC.
15 Warburg 2018c, p. 74.
16 Ibid., p. 83.

The Grasping Man

1 Warburg 2018c, p. 80.
2 See Claire Farago: "Silent Moves. On excluding the ethnographic subject from the discourse of art history," in Elizabeth Mansfield (ed.): *Art History and its Institutions. Foundations of a discipline*, London and New York 2002, pp. 191–214, pp. 196–197, and pp. 208–209.
3 See for example Aby Warburg: *Images from the Region of the Pueblo Indians of North America* (Michael P. Steinberg, ed.), Ithaca and London 1995 (cover); Benedetta Cestelli Guidi and Nicholas Mann (eds.): *Photographs at the Frontier. Aby Warburg in America 1895–1896*, London 1998 (cover); German edition: *Grenzerweiterungen. Aby Warburg in Amerika 1895–1896*, Hamburg and Munich 1999 (cover); Uwe Fleckner: *Photography with Obstacles. Aby Warburg's Pictures of his American Journey*, lecture, Peking University, Center for Visual Studies, March 13, 2018 (poster).
4 Warburg 2018a, S. 40; for more on this symbol, see Ekkehart Malotki: "Enculturating the Landscape. The Shrine of Salt Woman along the Ancient Hopi Salt Trail to the Grand Canyon, Arizona," in Harald Zapf and Klaus Lösch (eds.): *Cultural Encounters in the New World. Literatur- und kulturwissenschaftliche Beiträge zu kulturellen Begegnungen in der Neuen Welt*, Tübingen 2003, pp. 263–279, p. 266.
5 Letter from Aby Warburg to Franz Boll, October 21, 1918, London, WIA, GC; for more on Warburg's study of astrology, see Aby Warburg: "Bildersammlung zur Geschichte von Sternglaube und Sternkunde," in idem: *Bilderreihen und Ausstellungen* (Uwe Fleckner and Isabella Woldt, eds.), Berlin 2012 (Gesammelte Schriften. Studienausgabe, vol. II.2), pp. 389–460.
6 For more on Warburg's illness, see Ludwig Binswanger and Aby Warburg: *Die unendliche Heilung. Aby Warburgs Krankengeschichte* (Chantal Marazia and Davide Stimilli, eds.), Zurich and Berlin 2007.
7 Warburg 2018c, p. 74.

The Mask

1 See David Freedberg: "Warburg's Mask: A Study in Idolatry," in Mariët Westerman (ed.): *Anthropologies of Art*, Williamstown 2005, pp. 3–25; idem: *Las máscaras de Aby Warburg*, Vitoria-Gasteiz and Buenos Aires 2013, pp. 91 ff.; Doris McGonagill: "Memory and Mask: Aby Warburg on the American Geographical West, the European Ideological West, and the Ontogenesis of Images," in *Connections. European Studies Annual Review* 10/2014, pp. 43–54.
2 See, for example, *Warburg und die Natur*, conference at the "Naturbilder / Images of Nature" research center, Hamburg, Warburg-Haus, May 7–8, 2015 (poster); Horst Bredekamp: *Aby Warburg, der Indianer. Berliner Erkundungen einer liberalen Ethnologie*, Berlin 2019 (cover). The motif of Warburg wearing a mask has even made it onto an Argentinian art historian's thigh in the form of a tattoo; see Uwe Fleckner and Elena Tolstichin (eds.): *Das verirrte Kunstwerk. Bedeutung, Funktion und Manipulation von "Bilderfahrzeugen" in der Diaspora*, Berlin and Boston 2020 (Studien aus dem Warburg-Haus, vol. 20), pp. 3–4 (fig. 3).
3 For more on the use of Warburg's photographs in his lectures, see Warburg 2018, pp. 349–354 (concordance).
4 See Noël Dumarest: *Notes on Cochiti, New Mexico*, Lancaster 1919 (Memoirs of the American Anthropological Association, vol. 6.3), pp. 174–175; quoted in this publication on pp. 65–66.
5 See Luke Lyon: "History of Prohibition of Photography of Southwestern Indian Ceremonies," in *Reflections. Papers on Southwestern Cultural History in Honor of Charles H. Lange*, Santa Fe 1988 (The Archaeological Society of New Mexico, vol. 14), pp. 238–271; Chip Colwell-Chanthaphonh: *Sketching knowledge. Quandaries in the mimetic reproduction of Pueblo ritual*, in *American Ethnologist* 38/2011, pp. 451–467.

The Lecture

1 See Ludwig Binswanger and Aby Warburg: *Die unendliche Heilung. Aby Warburgs Krankengeschichte* (Chantal Marazia and Davide Stimilli, eds.), Zurich and Berlin 2007; Uwe Fleckner: "Aby Warburgs amerikanische Reise. Vom "illustrierten Tagebuch" zur kulturpsychologischen (Selbst)Betrachtung," in Warburg 2018, pp. 1–23, pp. 12 ff. (with additional literature).
2 See Ernst Cassirer: *Die Begriffsform im mythischen Denken*, Leipzig and Berlin 1922 (Studien der Bibliothek Warburg, vol. 1). Cassirer's source was Frank Hamilton Cushing: "Outlines of Zuñi Creation Myths," in *Thirteenth Annual Report of the Bureau of Ethnology to the Secretary of the Smithsonian Institution. 1891–1892*, Washington DC 1896, pp. 321–447.
3 Letter from Aby Warburg to Mary Warburg, March 23, 1923, quoted from Dorothea McEwan: "Zur Entstehung des Vortrages über das Schlangenritual: Motiv und Motivation / Heilung durch Erinnerung," in Cora Bender, Thomas Hensel, and Erhard Schüttpelz (eds.): *Schlangenritual. Der Transfer der Wissensformen vom Tsu'ti'kive der Hopi bis zu Warburgs Kreuzlinger Vortrag*, Berlin 2007 (Wissenskultur und gesellschaftlicher Wandel, vol. 16), pp. 267–281, p. 274; for more on Warburg's resumption of scientific activity, see ibid., pp. 271 ff.
4 Warburg 2018c, p. 65.
5 Ibid., pp. 69–70.
6 For this photograph, see in this publication p. 19 (fig. X), p. 158 and p. 160 (fig. 96).
7 Warburg 2018c, pp. 86–87.
8 Ibid., p. 94.
9 Warburg 2018d, p. 105.
10 Ibid., see Uwe Fleckner: "Aby Warburgs amerikanische Reise. Vom 'illustrierten Tagebuch' zur kulturpsychologischen (Selbst)Betrachtung," in Warburg 2018, pp. 1–23, pp. 19–20.
11 Letter from Aby Warburg to the directors of the Bellevue clinic, July 16, 1921, in Binswanger and Warburg 2007, pp. 98–100, p. 100; letter from Aby Warburg to Mary Warburg, Max M. Warburg and Heinrich Embden, April, 1924, ibid., pp. 108–110, p. 109; letter from Aby Warburg to Max M. Warburg, April, 1924, ibid., pp. 114–115, p. 114.

The Snake

1 See Cora Bender, Thomas Hensel, and Erhard Schüttpelz (eds.): *Schlangenritual. Der Transfer der Wissensformen vom Tsu'ti'kive der Hopi bis zu Warburgs Kreuzlinger Vortrag*, Berlin 2007 (Wissenskultur und gesellschaftlicher Wandel, vol. 16).
2 See, for example, John G. Bourke: *The Snake-Dance of the Moquis of Arizona*, London 1884; Jesse Walter Fewkes: "The Snake Ceremonials at Walpi," in *A Journal of American Ethnology and Archaeology* 4/1894, pp. 1–126; idem: *Tusayan Snake Ceremonies*, in *Sixteenth Annual Report of the Bureau of Ethnology to the Secretary of the Smithsonian Institution. 1894–1895*, Washington DC 1897, pp. 267–312; Henry R. Voth: *The Oraibi Summer Snake Ceremony*, Chicago 1903 (Field Columbian Museum Publication, vol. 83 / Anthropological Series, vol. III–4).
3 Warburg 2018c, p. 71 and p. 84.
4 Ibid., p. 84.
5 Ibid., p. 84 and p. 85. The term *tsu'tikive* only describes the last day of the ceremonies, and is made up of the terms *tsuu'a* (rattlesnake) and *tiikive* (on the day of the ceremony); see Kenneth C. Hill et al. (eds.): *Hopi Dictionary / Hopìikwa Lavàytutuveni. A Hopi-English Dictionary of the Third Mesa Dialect*, Tucson 1998, p. 650 (under "tsu'tikive"), p. 654 (under "tsuu'a"), and p. 592 (under "tiikive").
6 Warburg 2018c, p. 85.

7 Ibid., p. 86.
8 Ibid., p. 91.
9 Ibid., pp. 93–94.
10 See letter from Aby Warburg to Charlotte Warburg, March, 1896, London, WIA, GC.

The Telegraph Pole

1 Warburg 2018a, p. 46.
2 Warburg 2018b, p. 62.
3 Warburg 2018c, p. 94.
4 Ibid.
5 See Thomas Hensel: "Kupferschlangen, unendliche Wellen und telegraphierte Bilder. Aby Warburg und das technische Bild," in Cora Bender, Thomas Hensel, and Erhard Schüttpelz (eds.): *Schlangenritual. Der Transfer der Wissensformen vom Tsu'ti'kive der Hopi bis zu Warburgs Kreuzlinger Vortrag*, Berlin 2007 (Wissenskultur und gesellschaftlicher Wandel, vol. 16), pp. 297–360.

Abbreviated Titles

Warburg 2018

Aby Warburg, *Bilder aus dem Gebiet der Pueblo-Indianer in Nord-Amerika. Vorträge und Fotografien* (Uwe Fleckner, ed.), Berlin and Boston 2018 (Gesammelte Schriften. Studienausgabe, Vol. III.2).

Warburg 2018a

Aby Warburg, "Eine Reise durch das Gebiet der Pueblo-Indianer in New Mexico und Arizona, 1897," in Warburg 2018, pp. 25–55.

Warburg 2018b

Aby Warburg, "Entwurf zu 'Eine Reise durch das Gebiet der Pueblo-Indianer in New Mexico und Arizona, 1897'," in Warburg 2018, pp. 57–64.

Warburg 2018c

Aby Warburg, "Bilder aus dem Gebiet der Pueblo-Indianer in Nord-Amerika, 1923," in Warburg 2018, pp. 65–104.

Warburg 2018d

Aby Warburg, "Reise-Erinnerungen aus dem Gebiet der Pueblo-Indianer in Nordamerika, 1923," in Warburg 2018, pp. 105–127.

Warburg 2018e

Aby Warburg, "A Lecture on Serpent Ritual, 1939," in Warburg 2018, pp. 129–150.

Illustration Credits

© Billy Wilder, *Some Like It Hot* © 1959 Metro-Goldwyn-Mayer Studios Inc. All Rights Reserved. Courtesy of MGM Media Licensing: 49 / © bpk - Ethnologisches Museum, SMB, photo: Claudia Obrocki: 61 / © bpk - Ethnologisches Museum, SMB - Karl von den Steinen: 66 / Gabinetto Fotografico delle Gallerie degli Uffizi - Foto Roberto Palermo: 86 / Hamburg, Universität, Kunstgeschichtliches Seminar: 5, 16, 37, 51, 77, 78 / Hamburg, Warburg-Haus, Bilddatenbank: IV, V, 31, 32, 34–36 / © London, Warburg Institute Archive: I, VI–VIII, XI, 1–4, 6–15, 17, 19–21, 23–26, 38–48, 50, 52–60, 62, 63, 65, 67, 71–76, 79, 80, 83, 92, 95, 97 / Hamburg, Museum am Rothenbaum (MARKK): II, III, 70, 93 / Hamburg, Museum am Rothenbaum (MARKK), photo: Brigitte Saal: 18 / Hamburg, Museum am Rothenbaum (MARKK), photo: Paul Schimweg: 28, 69, 94 / Leiden, Collection Nationaal Museum van Wereldculturen, Nr. RV-1313-5: 27 / © Santa Fe, New Mexico History Museum, Photo Archives (NMHM/DCA), Nr. 000781: 29 / © The Trustees of the British Museum: 68 / Warburg 2018: IX, X, 30, 33, 64, 81, 82, 84–91, 96 / Washington, Library of Congress: 22.

?

An den beiden [verschwundenen] Wänden der K. m. d
fortlaufende Ornamentketten, z

himmlische
Wolken!

blitz(?)

Wandmalerei

The Snake and the Lightning. Aby Warburg's American Journey by Uwe Fleckner was published by Hatje Cantz Verlag 2023.

Translated into English by Kevin Cook and copy-edited by Burke Barrett.

Thomas Lemaître supervised the overall production.

Printing and binding was done at Livonia Print, Riga.

Munken Lynx 100g/m² was used as the content paper.

Printed in Latvia
ISBN 978-3-7757-5160-5

Hatje Cantz Verlag GmbH
Mommsenstraße 27
10629 Berlin
Germany
www.hatjecantz.com

A Ganske Publishing Group Company

Cover
Unknown photographer (probably Frank Allen, taken with Aby Warburg's camera): *Aby Warburg in front of his coach horses in a sandstorm between Bitahochee and Keams Canyon*, 1896

Front endpapers
Aby Warburg: *Map of the Hopi Villages on the First, Second, and Third Mesas*, 1895–1896

Back endpapers
Aby Warburg: *Ornaments from the murals at the San José mission church in Laguna*, 1895